Circles of Grace

A Trilogy on Disciple Making

Book One:

Ascending Grace

by David Oliver Kueker

disciplewalk.com

Caseyville, Illinois
www.disciplewalk.com

ASCENDING GRACE
Book 1, Circles of Grace Trilogy

First Edition 2009

Table of Contents

PREFACE

Several hundred years ago a mathematics professor wrote a novel where a little girl - Alice - fell down a rabbit hole and into an imaginary world where she had many adventures.

I'd like to invite you to take a tour of my imaginary world. If you find you don't care for it, there's no harm done - simply close the book and return to a real world that is more to your liking. It is, after all, only an imaginary world.

As an imaginary world, it's pretty quiet. There are no gunshots, drug deals, felonies, office politics, corrupt politicians, vampires, corporate conspiracies, dissolving marriages or any of the other drama that makes television exciting. It's pretty much just people sitting around talking about the New Testament meaning of discipleship, usually over plenty of coffee.

Of course, if you find that exciting, this imaginary world is probably to your liking. If so, I invite you to wander around this world for a while and imagine for yourself the adventures you might have as a disciple of Jesus Christ. Those who are familiar with Eliyahu Goldratt's novel, *The Goal*, will understand my purpose in using fiction to explain complex concepts and also the joy of being the "Jonah" in the story.

This book is dedicated to the people of Caseyville United Methodist Church, where I learned about unconditional love, differentiation and the freedom to be the person God made me to be. Thank you for those wonderful lessons!

David Oliver Kueker
Caseyville, Illinois, USA
October, 2009

CHAPTER ONE: The Problem
       Thursday, January 29

       "How exactly does one make disciples?"
       The question seemingly hung in the air in front of
me, Pastor John Wesley Adams, like a banner across the
front of the sanctuary of my church.
       As a *One Minute Minister*, I was practicing my
spiritual disciplines of time management on a Monday
morning, sitting in the church sanctuary praying over my
calendar and the plan of my activities of the day. The
basic principle was to act in harmony with Jesus as my
partner, and this meant prayer. Over time, this spiritual
discipline had come to be the most precious to me; I
would begin the day in prayer and the rest of the day I
would just follow the path I had planned out. It made for
less stress and anxiety. The point of these disciplines,
after all, was to help prevent burn out and keep me more
emotionally healthy - and they worked, at least for me.
And the first discipline was the work of prayer, or
prayerwork, as we called it.
       I also used the time for my morning devotions,
which consisted of reading a chapter of scripture a day.
My congregation was reading through the New Testament
one chapter per day, and they had started with Matthew 1
on January 2nd. I hoped they were reading it, but I had
no idea. As a pastor, we can recommend spiritual
disciplines, but we have no real idea whether anyone is
actually following them.
       Today was January 29, so I and whoever else was
reading had reached the end of Matthew. I normally read
my chapter twice, in the morning and again at bedtime.
At the end of the day, I'd read it to my wife Ruth and we'd
talk about it. Sometimes just a little, sometimes for a
while.
       I had gotten stuck, however, in that question.
"How exactly does one make disciples?"
       *Matthew 28:16-20 Now the eleven disciples went
to Galilee, to the mountain to which Jesus had directed
them. And when they saw him they worshiped him; but*

some doubted. And Jesus came and said to them, "All authority in heaven and on earth has been given to me. Go therefore and make disciples of all nations, baptizing them in the name of the Father and of the Son and of the Holy Spirit, teaching them to observe all that I have commanded you; and lo, I am with you always, to the close of the age."

In the context, going had something to do with it and probably preceded it. Jesus spoke as if he had the confidence that the disciples would understand exactly what he meant them to do. But what sort of going? Was going all that was necessary?

Where did someone go to make disciples? I looked around the sanctuary of my church and thought about Sunday mornings. The church wasn't full; there was plenty of room for all the new disciples I could make. If I could fill all these empty pews with lost people, then I could make disciples without ever leaving the sanctuary. That would be less work and more comfortable than some places that *going* might take me. But what exactly would I do to make a disciple? If it was sermons, mine weren't working that well.

Baptism followed going and making, for a convert at least. My denomination practiced baptism once, and we believed that the baptism was effective when it was administered - that God changed the baptized person's life in that moment. It's not that God responds to a person's faith, but that God keeps the promises made in scripture. And so we baptized children. If they later became disciples, we believed it wasn't necessary to baptize them again; God had already been there the first time. Not everyone agreed with that belief, but that was ours.

And after all these tasks in verse 19, three of them, came a single task in verse 20: *teaching them to observe all that I have commanded you.* So, teaching them did not make them disciples; teaching came after baptism. So what did come before? And how interesting - what we were to teach was not theology or doctrine, but "observation" - obedience, I assume that means. Obedience to *all that I have commanded you.* Coming at the end of the gospel of Matthew, did that mean teaching the commands in Matthew? Rather than teaching the doctrines of Matthew?

I tried to think of some of the commands I'd read in the past month and came up blank. I'd have to read the book again and pay attention to the commands. Is that what Jesus had meant, for the disciples to review his life with them and then repeat it with and for the benefit of others? If so, then the entire book of Matthew was a manual for disciple making. It was intended to be that and to be used for that. This would change the interpretation of everything and differentiate it from the other three gospels. If I read it again, this time I'd better make a list of those commands I was supposed to be teaching. And add to them commands from the other gospels as well.

But how exactly does one make disciples?

I began to go over my prayer list, identifying the people I would contact today as I prayed for each one of them, adding people to my list, subtracting others whose prayers had been answered. That's the second spiritual discipline of the *One Minute Minister*: *peoplework*; people are important, so people are the primary activity after prayer. And since people are important, they are scheduled - as visits, as phone calls, as emails, as in little notes on cards I'd had prepared: *I said a prayer for you today.* If I spent the day in touch with my people and did nothing else, it was the best use of my time. Prayerwork came first, peoplework came second and paperwork comes last, as it should. Paperwork wasn't exactly paperwork; it meant closure, finishing tasks completely.

How exactly does one make disciples? I made a note to send out an email later this morning to the pastors in my colleague group. I could copy the email to my district superintendent and also to my friend Mark, who headed up the Office of Congregational Development. Then I could think over the answers I received back. Perhaps one of those answers might lead to an answer from God. Or perhaps, from time in prayer, I'd find my own answer from God.

"How exactly does one make disciples?" I asked aloud and listened in the following silence for an answer. There would be an answer, obviously, because this was a question for which God intended us to know an answer. Jesus assumed we would know the answer. But while the silence was a comfortable, supporting silence, there was no answer yet. There would be one, because I knew that God is a God of closure.

I sent an email out to the pastors group I met with each week. Maybe Ian, Earl, Mitch, Louis or Larry would have the answer.

Hey - during devotions this morning I got stuck on a basic question I'd like to raise for discussion. It's one I feel I should understand but I found that I didn't have a clue if I took it literally. I was reading over the Great Commission in Matthew 28.

Here's the question: how exactly does one make disciples?

Any suggestions? You can email me or hold your answer for the group meeting at lunch on Tuesday.

John Wesley Adams

The answers were waiting for me later that afternoon.

Dear John: We're adapting the Alpha course for our church. It originated in a charismatic Episcopalian church in England; over there it meets in homes where people gather for dinner and participants go on a three day retreat. Videos do the teaching. In our version, we're going to run it as a large group each week at the church fellowship hall, with a potluck, and skip the retreat. We can project the videos on the wall and have popcorn - just like the movies! No one else is doing it the way we are, but I believe it will be very successful. It's made a lot of disciples in other church settings and it's about time someone tried it in our area. Ian

Dear John: We're subscribing to a service that gives us the names of people who are new residents in our area. It's not cheap, but that way we can do direct mail with them. We've also purchased a series of very colorful mailing materials that key into sermon series - five weeks of messages on stress preceded by a graphic of a man suffering with what looks like the world's worst cluster headache. Then seven weeks on how to make your marriage happier; the graphic on that is a bride and groom statue, like you would find on a wedding cake, only arguing. The bride is furious, arms crossed and everything, the groom's embarrassed and holding his hands out like he's helpless. Lot of dysfunctional families out there. We're guaranteed that these mailings will increase our attendance for us or we get 50% of the money back. I'll bring samples to our group meeting next week. Earl

John: Things are running smoothly right now, but I'm always open to new ideas. Keep me posted on what you're thinking. Mitch

John: I'm not sure about making disciples, but we are decorating the sanctuary in bright colors for Epiphany. The season after Christmas shouldn't be a let down; we've got to keep the excitement and the positive emotions up from the Christmas season until we get to Lent, or we'll have some drop off. Louis

Dear John: I'm a little concerned about your email on making disciples. Don't forget: God is our focus, worship is our priority. **Don't let yourself get distracted!** *If we follow the lectionary, keep the liturgy pure and focus on worship, the presence of God will purify the devotion of the faithful. Don't neglect what is important to go chasing off after people for whom attending church isn't even a priority. If you don't take care of your sheep, they'll wander off and you'll have fewer and fewer. I'm*

I thought about my January in the light of the emails from my friends. My people seemed to be glad of a light schedule after all the busy activities of Christmas. Maybe Ian was right and people would like to begin a class on discipleship in the month of New Year's resolutions. Apparently a lot of people had benefitted from the Alpha course, although I had never heard of it. Why did it work so well for some - was it the quality of the videos? Would it be a mistake for Ian to move the course out of homes and into the fellowship hall with everyone watching the videos in a large group? Would our kind of people allow a small group to meet in their home for 3 months, or would that feel to them like a violation of privacy? And the question, I mused, was "how exactly does one make disciples?" Wouldn't the participants in this class already be church goers, based on how Ian was planning to use it? Perhaps my request that my church people read a chapter of the Bible a day wasn't enough; perhaps I should push them to take a class like the one Ian was pushing.

Earl's email mentioned direct mail, which was focused on non-attenders rather than church goers. Mail would "go" out into the world. But how many of those receiving a piece of direct mail already attended another church? How many were affiliated with a church but didn't attend for one reason or another? Was direct mail the way to make disciples? The topics for the messages would be attractive to people stressed by those problems, but would they hold the interest of believing church members who did not have those problems? Would the people brought in by the series on stress stay for the following series on marital problems or would they drift away? And once someone got to worship, were they now a disciple? Were people who attended worship disciples?

Louis' email was likewise disquieting. Surely disciple making was more than redecorating the temple. I knew there were people in my church who would love the chance to express their creativity and love of color on redecorating the sanctuary for the season; perhaps I should work out a way for my members to have more self expression in the liturgy. It would boost excitement and ownership in the congregation, but how would it draw in people who were not disciples? Would my people be so proud of the way the place looked that their excitement would convince others to attend worship?

I didn't understand Larry's response at all. I knew he didn't like contemporary worship and other changes my other friends had made in their churches. His congregation was the most conservative and traditional of all the ones in our group. But if the lectionary wasn't working previously, how would staying more religiously with it help? Larry was negative, but I shouldn't discount what he was saying because of that. His church was the second largest of all of ours anyway; perhaps he did know something we didn't. There were plenty of people apparently who did not want change when they came to church.

Mark sent me an email which didn't make a lot of sense; he'd forwarded my email question to a consultant named David Oliver, saying that this was the sort of question that Oliver liked to answer. Mark would think about his answer to my question; I was happy about that as I didn't think snap answers would be very helpful to me.

Oliver's question when it came was brief:

I'm in between planes. I have two questions for you: What does the dictionary say a disciple is? What does Jesus say a disciple is? Email me your answer.

I love the next to last thing I do each night. The last thing, as I roll onto my back and close my eyes, is that thank God for everything good that I enjoy in my life. I just keep being thankful until I fall asleep. It usually doesn't take long.

The next to last thing I do before I fall asleep is to talk with my wife about everything good in life. We have some pretty deep discussions, sometimes with the light on, sometimes with the light off, and sometimes just lit by

9

the moon shining in through the bedroom window.

Being a good delegator, I had asked her to do the dictionary work for me. She had papers spread across my side of the bed while she read a romance novel. One of the little rules we have is books only in the bedroom. There was a television once, but we found that we stayed up way too late. It wasn't that anything interesting was on; it was more like we were watching and waiting for something interesting. Faith expresses itself in unusual ways sometimes, including faith that there will be something worth watching on television. So we took out the TV in the bedroom and made a commitment: no TV, no news of disasters, no gun shots or serial killer murders solved in 60 minutes. Just her and I and the quiet of a book. We talked more and relaxed sooner and fell into a more restful sleep.

"What did you find out?" I asked her.

"You can wait until I have your full attention," she said, turning back to her book. It's an old routine we have; she won't talk until I'm there beside her, either in bed or in the chair next to her. I divested myself of keys, change, wallet, cell phone and all the other detritus that accumulates in a man's pockets throughout the day. In a few minutes I was sitting in the chair at her side.

"Good," she said, picking up the first page of printout from an online dictionary. "Cambridge Advanced Learner's Dictionary. Definition #1: disciple - noun: *a person who believes in the ideas and principles of someone famous and tries to live the way they do or did.*"

"What do you think about that one?" I asked.

"Cerebral" she said thoughtfully. "Random House Unabridged Dictionary. Definition #2: *any follower of Christ.*

"What do you think about that one?" I asked.

"Simplistic," she said simply. "The American Heritage Dictionary of the English Language, Fourth Edition. Definition #3: *One who embraces and assists in spreading the teachings of another. An active adherent, as of a movement or philosophy.*"

"What do you think about that one?" I asked.

"Vanilla," she said blandly. "Webster's Revised Unabridged Dictionary. Definition #4: *One who receives instruction from another; a scholar; a learner; especially, a follower who has learned to believe in the truth of the doctrine of his teacher; an adherent in doctrine; as, the disciples of Plato; the disciples of our Savior.*"

"What do you think about that one?" I asked.

"What do you think?" she asked me.

"I like the second one."

"It's vague enough to mean anything."

"That's why I like it. The second assignment will be harder," I said.

"Why would that be?" she asked. "Can't you just do a search on your computer and print up every mention of the word 'disciple' in the four gospels? Then you can check out each context where Jesus uses the term."

"That won't be hard at all," I said.

"If Jesus is going to talk about discipleship, he's going to use the word. That's basic."

"We'll go over them together?"

"Of course," she said, smiling.

"I'm glad you are a part of this with me," I told her, not for the first time.

"How could it be otherwise?" she said, not for the first time.

I quietly read the chapter for the day - Matthew 28 - out loud to her while she curled up by my side.

"There's four parts," she said.

"Right. *Go - make - baptize - teach.*"

"When are you done?" she asked. "I don't think there is an endpoint."

"Teaching goes on forever?" I asked.

She bit her lip and thought for a bit. "No, not like that. There's something about that - teaching forever - that doesn't seem right."

"Like housework goes on forever?"

"Things get dirty after they are cleaned, yes, but all the dictionary definitions speak of a disciple as a pupil. Someone who learns something correctly shouldn't have to repeat it endlessly."

"Some kinds of learning and teaching are repeated endlessly," I said.

"Like what," she demanded.

"Music. Scales. Mozart concertos."

"True enough," she said. "But that's a skill, not a concept."

"What does *teaching* refer to? It could be skills. Teaching doesn't automatically have to be ideas and concepts. Even though the dictionary definitions all infer that they are."

"I think you've got something there, honey," she said. "We just automatically assume that what Jesus wants us to learn are the concepts - the theology, the doctrine, the correct beliefs."

"I wonder if we are tempted to go there in order to avoid something else more important."

"What do you mean?" she asked.

"Isn't faith easier if we keep it all up in our head with big words and concepts? We can use logic and argue all day and never need to actually DO anything."

We thought about it in silence for a moment. "There is plenty of that sort of avoidance," I conceded. "It's gone on for centuries."

"Fills up a lot of libraries."

"Of the making of books there is no end."

"Where is that?" she asked.

"Solomon, I think. Canticles."

"Ah, your basic song of songs. That is Solomon's." Her eyes grew dreamy. "But you are missing something big here."

"What?"

"What does the verse say? It identifies the type of teaching, doesn't it?"

I read verse 20 aloud: "*teaching them to observe all that I have commanded you.*"

"It's not concepts," she said. "It is actions, the result of commands that are obeyed. Not doctrine."

"Not doctrine," I agreed.

"I like the word *observe* with that. You should be

able to see, observe, behavioral learning. They tell us to use the camera test - what a camera would see."

"I don't understand what you mean."

"If it's behavior, a camera can see it and record it. What a camera can't see isn't behavior - it's a concept."

"Can you give me an example?"

"Agreement is a concept - how would a camera observe true agreement? The answer to that questions would give you specific handles to shape behavior. It's the same to wealth, peace, and true love. They are concepts until you identify the behavior that underlies the concept."

"So Jesus was teaching behavior rather than doctrine?"

"Can you contradict that statement?" she asked.

"We're reading a chapter of the gospels a day for the next two months. If there's a contradiction, we'll find it." I thought for a minute. "The church over the centuries has drawn abstract thinkers who have built an astonishingly complex logical structure we call systematic theology. A structure that takes people - at least those who can follow it - farther and farther away from the simple experience of God. When you think of such an elaborate construct, it makes you wonder if it is for protection, for defense. What is the church protecting itself from with its theology?"

"Or what is it avoiding?"

"I'm not sure. After all, I went to seminary, I took the classes to get the graduate school degree, and I like the abstract stuff. I'm not the best one to ask."

"The original disciples were fishermen, small business owners, in other words."

"One tax collector."

"Pretty direct people. Jesus could have chosen academics as disciples, but he did not."

"I have a feeling that some of us wish he had." I thought for another minute. "Jesus was pretty direct. Perhaps over history the church has over intellectualized his directness."

"Perhaps." She yawned. "We'd better summarize while I can still think."

"Discipleship is learning - that's all the dictionary definitions. But learning what?"

"What is to be learned is about behavior - behaving as Jesus instructed them to behave."

"Ethics leads us into another intellectual maze," I said. "So it's something more direct than simply right and wrong."

"It's not so hard for ethics to be what a camera sees, even if it can be intellectualized."

"At the simplest, the learning identified in verse 20 is to learn to obey the commands of Jesus. As perfection is a distant possibility, that's learning that never stops."

"I know there is something that we are missing," she said. "But that's all we have right now."

"Being a disciple is learning how to obey Jesus - which goes on forever," I summarized. "The Great Commission teaches this: You go, you make disciples (however it is that you do that) of all nations, baptize them, and then enroll them in a never ending class on learning how to obey all that Jesus commands."

She yawned again. "I wonder if Peter's wife had trouble getting him to shut up and come to bed."

"I'll try to do better," I promised as I moved from the chair to my side of the bed. And then we talked about other things, no less important, until her breathing was soft and rhythmic. I turned on my back and began to consider all that I was thankful for, beginning with the person on my right. It had been an unusual Thursday and there was a lot to be thankful for.

Friday, January 30

In the sanctuary on Friday morning, one of those Jesus commands jumped up out of the text of Mark 1 and demanded my attention.

Mark 1:14: Now after John was arrested, Jesus came into Galilee, preaching the gospel of God, and saying, "The time is fulfilled, and the kingdom of God is at hand; repent, and believe in the gospel." The words sounded familiar, so I checked the beginning of the gospel

14

of Matthew, and there it was: *Matthew 4:17 From that time Jesus began to preach, saying, "Repent, for the kingdom of heaven is at hand."* The implication in Matthew is slightly different - not just what Jesus was saying at the time, but what Jesus *began* to preach. This implied an ongoing preaching of repentance - and if disciples were to do as Jesus commanded, perhaps ongoing forever. Matthew's use of the phrase is almost as a summary of Jesus' preaching. Repentance, for imperfect human people, would be never ending learning. One of Ruth's collection of refrigerator magnets expressed it this way: *Be patient with me, because God's not finished with me yet.*

When would we be finished repenting? I thought. Ruth's probable answer came immediately to mind: when we lost interest in obeying Jesus.

The idea of repentance didn't bother me because I knew it was much more than feeling guilty or being self critical. To repent meant to *turn from sin* and *turn toward God.* A person who is totally focused on sin has not turned away from it; he or she is just facing it. When we realize that our direction is toward something that is not God's will - the best definition of sin that I know - we need to turn and find out in which direction God is - that's turning toward God. Then we need to move in that direction.

Perhaps that's part of the problem - our understanding of God. We perceive God as all knowing, all powerful and always present. God is everywhere. Therefore, how can we turn toward God? When God is everywhere, God is as much here as there. If that is true, how can we move toward God? Jesus, however, was incarnated to live as a person in history. He was in one place, and people could identify his position clearly in terms of two factors: *Which way to Jesus? How far is Jesus?*

This reminded me of another verse and after a bit of difficulty I found it just after one I knew by heart:

John 3:16-21 For God so loved the world that he gave his

only Son, that whoever believes in him should not perish but have eternal life. For God sent the Son into the world, not to condemn the world, but that the world might be saved through him. He who believes in him is not condemned; he who does not believe is condemned already, because he has not believed in the name of the only Son of God. And this is the judgment, that the light has come into the world, and men loved darkness rather than light, because their deeds were evil. For every one who does evil hates the light, and does not come to the light, lest his deeds should be exposed. But he who does what is true comes to the light, that it may be clearly seen that his deeds have been wrought in God.

Jesus was the light of the world. When he appeared, there were suddenly two directions: toward the light and away from the light. And people chose the direction they desired.

When I walked into the office after prayers, I sent the following email to David Oliver, the consultant that Mark had recommended.

Dear David:

    The dictionaries all say, in one form or another, that a disciple is a pupil, a student. Thinking on Matthew 28:20, this learning is about obedience rather than doctrine or theology. Because we are far from perfect, learning to obey Jesus would continue forever.

    Is this what you want?

                               John Wesley Adams

Dear John:

    So making disciples would be like enrolling someone in a school that goes on forever? That's not going to be very popular; no wonder people avoid it. Sounds like you have a good handle on ascending grace.

    I'm connected with a group of people who are attempting to organize a new church in your area. One of them will contact you and arrange a meeting. I'm pretty sure that Sam can answer the questions you have

at this stage.
        David Oliver

        "At this stage," I wondered out loud. What stage
was that? And what was ascending grace?

CHAPTER TWO: Follow Me
    Saturday, January 31

    Saturday morning I was up earlier than normal; it was my day to sleep in, but not this time. My phone call from Sam Franklin yesterday evening had been short and to the point.
    "Can you meet me in your front yard at 7:30 tomorrow morning?"
    "Yes, but why?"
    "Because that's when I want to meet with you."
    "Can't we work out a more convenient time?"
    "Why do you think that discipleship is about what is convenient for you?"
    The comment stung a little bit. "Can you explain why you want to meet so early instead of discussing another time?"
    "Why do you think discipleship is about adjusting to your schedule?" The man on the phone laughed. "Let me save you some time. Discipleship is not win-win. Discipleship is not flexible. Discipleship is not negotiable. Discipleship is not convenient. Either you are ready to meet me at 7:30 tomorrow morning or you are not. Decide."
    "What if I have a conflict? What if I have another obligation?"
    "Then you will have a decision to make. If you decide not to meet, I'll call you again next week, or maybe the week after that, and you'll have a decision to make."
    "Why are you so strict about this?" I asked, feeling bewildered.
    "It's just a part of the process," Sam explained. "You are either ready or you are not ready. If you want to wait another week or two to understand something about discipleship, that's your decision. Believe me, I understand what you are feeling," Sam said, and I could feel the warmth in his voice. "But this is something essential about discipleship. What's your decision?"
    I didn't want to wait a week to learn more about discipleship, but a part of me wished I was learning from a

book that I could pick up and put down on my schedule.

As I read the chapter for the day to Ruth last night after we talked about the phone call, she indicated what might be the point of it all:

Mark 1:16-20 And passing along by the Sea of Galilee, he saw Simon and Andrew the brother of Simon casting a net in the sea; for they were fishermen. And Jesus said to them, "Follow me and I will make you become fishers of men." And immediately they left their nets and followed him. And going on a little farther, he saw James the son of Zebedee and John his brother, who were in their boat mending the nets. And immediately he called them; and they left their father Zebedee in the boat with the hired servants, and followed him.

Was it convenient for those four to just leave everything in that moment? I knew from John's gospel that they were no strangers to Jesus; they were acquainted with him and his teaching. So this invitation came, like mine from Sam, at a time that was not of their choosing. They didn't produce date books and try to work out a more convenient time that would allow them to wind down their business and then follow. The invitation came and they could either follow or not follow. The invitation might come again, or it might not.

Ruth pointed out another factor that I had missed. Jesus was not waiting on the beach for them to decide. *Follow Me* implies that he kept moving and every minute they dithered, they were falling behind. Perhaps the concept in *Follow Me* was another way of expressing the concept that underlay repentance: *turn from sin and turn toward God and move toward God.* As I gave thanks that night, I was troubled by the thought of Christ on the move and my being left behind, minute by minute farther behind, if I wasn't concentrating on following him. If there was someway to stop Jesus from moving, then I wouldn't have to work so hard to keep up. As I dropped off, I wondered if the church in history had done just that. Could we have turned a living, moving Jesus who said

"Follow me" into a statue Jesus around whom we could gather and rest?

It was cold; that was my first thought when the doorbell rang Saturday morning at 7:30 a.m. I came to the door and no one was there, but I saw a man standing by a car parked on the street. He was hatless and his white hair shone in the morning light.

"Would you like to come in?" I called from the front door.

He shook his head and smiled. "Would you like to come out?"

"Frankly, no. It's cold."

"It is cold. Would you come out anyway?"

I got my coat. I don't know what it had to do with disciple making, but it was apparent that I was not going to have much choice in the matter.

"I'm John Adams," I said when I reached the older man on the street. He was tall and conveyed an impression of quiet strength and dignity.

"I'm Samuel Franklin. Most people call me Sam. I'm sure you have a lot of questions."

"I do," I said. "My first one is this: why can't we go inside where it's warm and let me ask my questions over a cup of coffee?"

"It may sound a bit mysterious, but the reason is that inside, where it's warm and comfortable, is not where you will find answers to your questions about discipleship."

"You got something against coffee, Sam?"

He laughed. "I love coffee. But I love Jesus more, and he's out here with us."

"Are you going to be my teacher, then?"

"Actually, you're going to be teaching yourself. But I'll be one of those helping. Are you normally a decisive man?" he asked.

"I don't know how to answer that question. I suppose so, although I like to think big decisions over and pray about them. I pray about the little ones too."

"Here's one of your teachers then." Sam slipped

the glove off his right hand and pulled out a handful of change. "Pick one."

I picked out a penny. "Is this one the lucky one?"

"They all work just fine, John. Now flip it and tell me what you get."

I flipped his penny high in the air and missed it on the way down. The brown penny dropped into the grass and out of sight.

"Better take a quarter this time," Sam advised. "They are a little bigger and shinier."

I flipped the quarter and caught it. "Heads." Sam turned to the right and started walking. "Follow me," he called back over his shoulder.

I hurried to catch up. "And the point of that was?"

His answer was cryptic. "When you are young, you go where you want. You don't know where you are going, but what does that matter with all that energy and curiosity? When you are older, others will gird you and take you where you do not want to go. That's the difference with maturity."

"Are you paraphrasing scripture?" I asked. Part of what he said sounded familiar.

He laughed. "I do that a lot; I'm glad you got the reference. Do you know where it's from?"

"No - not right now. Where is it from?"

"When I was a child, my mother would answer a question like that with the same phrase: look it up. Looking things up got me through college."

"Your mother must know my mother," I said.

"They might at that."

"What's the lesson of the quarter then?"

"The quarter teaches you about following, and specifically about following orders. You ever serve in the military?"

"Why?"

"The primary purpose of basic training in the military is to develop the ability to obey, instantly and without questions. We don't mind questions and we don't mind people thinking things over, but the ability to obey in our society is deplorable and deficient, whether it is

21

Jesus Christ or a sergeant giving the orders."

"I volunteered the year we got married but flunked the eye test; so I went to seminary instead."

"That's a course correction. How did you feel about it at the time?"

"I was very disappointed."

"And now?"

I shrugged. "It all worked out. I would have wound up in Seminary anyway, and this way I finished six years sooner."

"Following is about decisions," Sam explained. "When you are the leader, you make the decisions. When you are the follower someone else makes decisions."

I needed to think about that a bit. "And this means what?"

"Your dictionary definitions said that a disciple was someone who followed Jesus, right?"

"That was one definition."

"Here's what that means: followers don't make decisions. They obey."

"Oh." It made sense. "So Jesus makes the decisions, and I follow them. Is that right?"

"That's right. And if you are the leader, you make the decisions. In our movement, we have a sign for that sort of decisive leadership." Sam made the sign of an L at his forehead, forefinger and thumb extended at right angles.

I laughed out loud. I couldn't help myself. "Sam," I said, "I'm no teenager but even I know that's the sign the kids use for a Loser."

"In our understanding, John, leaders are losers. In our movement, there are no leaders; there are only followers."

"Only followers. I get that."

"Good. That's your first lesson. You are not the leader; Jesus is, if your intent is to follow Jesus."

"But, Sam, I'm following you; that makes you the leader." I made the L sign at him.

"Ah," he said, "but I'm not the leader; I'm just another follower. You're following another follower. When you are able to sense which direction Jesus is headed, you won't need to follow me; you'll find your own direction. But until then, you can follow me while I follow Jesus. That's your first lesson."

"What's the point of the quarter, then?"

"The problem with discipleship is not one of belief; most people believe in something they call God. Nor is it false doctrine that leads people astray; most people are ignorant, but what they do know is surprisingly orthodox. The problem is that when Jesus comes walking down the beach and calls you to follow him, you will find that you lack the ability to do it."

"Disciple, discipline," I said.

Sam nodded. "What you learn in discipleship is discipline. To set aside what you want to do and, instead, do what Jesus wants you to do, is the essence of discipleship."

"What if you don't know?"

"How would you learn if you don't know?"

I floundered for a moment, searching for the answer.

"Where would you go to find out what Jesus wants?" Sam prodded.

"The Gospels," I said. "Of course."

"So you read the gospels. Over and over, until you know them like a path you can walk in complete darkness."

"And what if the gospels don't apply?"

"All spiritual answers ultimately rely upon the guidance of the Holy Spirit. But that's also a learned skill. For this moment, you can just relax because you are walking the path with someone rather than attempting to learn it all by yourself." Sam pointed to his heart. "I'm experienced on this path; I know it." Sam tapped me on my chest. "You're new to this path; you don't know it, but you'll learn it if you walk it with me. I'll follow Jesus; you follow me until you know the difference."

"That's pretty simple," I said.

"It's simple until the path goes somewhere you don't want to go."

23

"Like out into the cold," I admitted.

"Exactly. The biggest hurdle in discipleship is really a very small one: it's not going to be convenient all the time or comfortable all the time. The plans of the God of heaven are not organized for your pleasure; sometimes other priorities are more important."

I nodded. I got it now.

"And that's when being prepared to follow makes a difference. That we can teach ourselves. What's something you don't like doing and would prefer to avoid?"

"Balancing my checkbook."

"When you get home this morning, do that first. If you keep that up, when you are called to follow, you will be able to obey without hesitation."

"What about the quarter?" I asked.

"You can use it for exercise," Sam laughed. "Whenever you are faced with a decision that is unimportant, instead of doing what you want, flip a coin and act accordingly."

"How about an example?"

"During Lent we sometimes use a coin for fasting. Before sitting down to a meal or preparing one, we flip the coin. If it comes up tails, we eat; if it comes up heads, we fast. You won't starve, and you might eat more at your next meal, but nothing will show you faster who is in charge of you, your mind or your hungers."

I had a feeling that I knew what was in charge in my case.

"Remember," Sam continued, "don't use the coin to avoid obligations or keeping promises; that's a lesson in discipline itself. The coin makes unimportant decisions a training tool. Did it matter which direction we started walking?"

I shrugged. "I guess not."

"So it was an opportunity to surrender our decision making power to an outside influence, in this case a coin. As you work this lesson, you will gain strength at surrendering your willpower to the influence of Jesus Christ."

"Why are we walking, Sam? You still haven't

24

explained to me why we can't have this conversation inside a warm house over coffee."

"There's a whole list of reasons. The first one is that when Jesus said 'Follow me' he meant it literally. He didn't wait around - the call to follow came and then he left. He had places to go, people to help and work to do. It was up to you to keep up."

"And the point of that?"

"Jesus is in motion; Jesus has a goal. In theology, I believe, the correct word for that is teleology. Following Jesus is teleological; he has a purpose and always acts toward the fulfillment of a future purpose. What's the opposite of teleological?"

"Ontological?"

"Correct. Excellent. Ontological - being. A steady state ... ever heard the cliche: *stop behaving like a human do-er and just be - a human be-ing*? The church for centuries has acted as a giant entropy trap ... holding back people who want to do something until the focus was on sitting around talking about ideas."

"Concepts. Theology. Ideas. Doctrine."

"Exactly. The church has cultivated stillness until they have approached absolute zero - the state of being where nothing moves and nothing changes."

"I'm familiar with that inertia."

"I used to teach physics, John. It's not inertia, which is the tendency of a body to remain in the state it is in. It's systems. Jesus is a reinforcing process of change; the church is a balancing process of managing things so that everything runs smoothly, and as a result often prevents change. That's the temple system in the New Testament as well."

"They killed Jesus."

"They did. Disciple making threatens everything in the status quo of what churches are."

"Please say more about that."

"Can I postpone that for another day? I've got another teacher I'd like to introduce you to."

"All right; I'll just follow along."

"Excellent." Sam reached into his pocket and

pulled out a large black plastic garbage bag. "Here you go."

I took it in good humor and shook it open, looking inside as if I expected to find something. "Sam, there appears to be nothing here."

"Nothing but an opportunity." He came to a halt in front of a house about two blocks from mine. "What can you tell me about these people, John?"

I looked over the yard; a few children's toys were scattered about. "They have children," I said.

"You know anything more?"

"No."

"Names?"

"No."

"Occupation?"

"No."

"Race? Married or living together? Two parents or a single parent? Education? Age? Wealth?"

"Not much at all," I said, looking at the house. It needed some work.

"Why don't you know these things?" Sam asked gently.

"Because I don't care?" I tried not to sound defensive.

"No," Sam said decisively. "There is no possibility that it is because you don't care. You do. The reason you don't know these things is simply because you don't notice. You are not paying attention, or more properly, you are paying attention to other things. One important factor in discipleship is to notice people; people are important."

"I've heard that before," I muttered.

"I'm sorry," Sam said.

"It's part of the *One Minute Minister* stuff."

"Tell me about it ... but another time. The garbage bag is your teacher; time to let it teach you a lesson."

I didn't understand what he meant; I looked in the bag again. And then I saw it ... there was a cigarette butt on the ground by my feet. I looked at it and I looked at Sam. "This?"

"That?"

"What exactly do you want me to do?"

"What do you think you should do with a garbage bag in your hand, Pastor John?"

I bent over and picked up the cigarette butt and flipped it into the bag. "Discipleship, I think you are about to tell me, isn't very sanitary."

Sam smiled and pulled a pair of medical latex gloves from his coat pocket. "I use these for small dead animals. The rest of it is a matter of prejudice rather than actual germs."

Dead bird discipleship? Did I really want to do this?

Sam's smile, if possible, grew even wider. "So if Jesus wants you to pick up a dead bird, would you follow him or just go home muttering about it all?"

"Dead bird," I said.

"Get to work," he said. Suddenly I looked around me and the world was full of litter and trash. I had never noticed it before. It was all over the place, on either side of the street.

As I began to pick up the garbage and stuff it in the sack, Sam began to sing.

I have decided to follow Jesus
I have decided to follow Jesus
I have decided to follow Jesus
No turning back, no turning back.

Though I may wonder, I still will follow;
Though I may wonder, I still will follow;
Though I may wonder, I still will follow;
No turning back, no turning back.

The world behind me, the cross before me;
The world behind me, the cross before me;
The world behind me, the cross before me;
No turning back, no turning back.

Though none go with me, still I will follow;

Though none go with me, still I will follow;
Though none go with me, still I will follow;
No turning back, no turning back.

Will you come with me and follow Jesus?
Will you come with me and follow Jesus?
Will you come with me and follow Jesus?
No turning back, no turning back

We sang the song back to my house while I picked up garbage. "Why do you think we did this, John?"

"I don't know, but you're going to tell me." I knew that he had a point to make.

Sam smiled. "Discipleship is about noticing people, and especially noticing your neighbors. It's not a bad thing, is it, to benefit your neighbors, even in a small way?"

"No, it's not."

"Figure out what Jesus said about your neighbors and we'll talk about the next step on Tuesday."

"Why not Monday?" I asked.

"I'm busy," he smiled, shrugging his shoulders.

I shook hands with him and he left me there, standing in my yard holding a half full garbage bag, staring with wonderment at the homes of my neighbors as if I was a blind man suddenly granted the gift of sight.

By that evening I had balanced the checkbook. It wasn't unpleasant once I'd gotten started, and knowing what was in the bank did give me a sense of security. I thought a lot about what Sam had said about my neighbors; there wasn't a great deal in the gospels about them, but what was there was pretty specific. My neighbors were my concern.

"You are just focused on the church, John," Ruth told me as we discussed the commandment to *love your neighbor as you love yourself.* "You've been focused on the neighborhood around the church building for so long that you don't even think about the neighbors around your home."

Ruth had pointed out the flaw. Our denominational theme had been for decades that we should focus on the neighborhood around the church building, around the institution. Those who obeyed that directive would shift their focus from the neighbors around the Christian to the neighbors around the institutional building. They were already strangers in the church neighborhood and now could justify being strangers in their own.

"And who is my neighbor," I whispered. The question asked by the lawyer of Jesus, attempting to avoid the commandment. Which led to the story of the good Samaritan, which starts with the man in the ditch. Two church leaders pass him by on the way to the temple; if they stop to help him, they might not be able to fulfill their temple duties because of temple regulations about contact with dead bodies. The temple had a priority over the man in the ditch, because they were serving God. *Who is my neighbor?* To those two men, their neighbors were the people assembled in the temple for worship; they were the only people who mattered.

"What did you say, honey?" Ruth asked.

"And who is my neighbor?"

"It's a commandment, John, right?"

"Yes," I said.

"If you don't know, then you better find out."

I found it a little hard to be thankful that night. *Who is my neighbor?* I really didn't know, and it was important to Jesus that I did.

Tuesday Morning, February 3

I was a bit more ready for the cold this morning and walked out as Sam pulled up. "Ready for discipleship training?" he asked with a laugh.

"Ready as I'll ever be," I smiled.

"Got your quarter?" I showed it to him in my hand and he made the motion to flip it.

It was heads, the same as yesterday. "Follow me," Sam said dramatically and headed off in the opposite direction. Clearly, disciple making was not going to be logical. As I followed him he handed me the garbage bag and I began to be a benefit to my neighbors.

Noticing the litter, I also noticed more around me. Sam smiled at cars that drove past us as people went in to work. He even waved. I stooped; he waved. When we walked past one house as the man was coming out to his car he said a cheery good morning and got one in return.

"You see what is happening?" he asked.

"Now that I am noticing my neighbors, my neighbors are noticing me."

"That's right."

"What's the topic for today?"

"Today we will leave the practical and go where educated people love to camp out - the realm of the abstract ideas about disciple making."

"I'm all for that. Will we ever add coffee to it?"

"We could, but the walking's good for you. What kind of metaphor for 'follow me' is it when you sit around a table eating doughnuts? That's not following; it's consuming."

"I liked the point you made yesterday. Jesus said 'follow me' and then he left. He didn't wait around; he had things to do."

"Yes."

"There were times he stopped to teach."

"True, but then he was on the move again. It's a very simple test of interest and commitment. Think about what it was to live in Palestine in those days. Jesus is headed in your direction, slowly. As he gets closer, you think about walking out to where he is; it's a long walk, so you put it off. The next day he's closer; not as much trouble, so you go. The next day, he's right in your town; you go because it costs you nothing. The next day, he's a bit down the road; seeing him reminded you of how special he is, so you make the effort. The next day, he's farther away and there's some sacrifice involved. Simply by moving, Jesus could easily measure the commitment level of people following him by the simple test of whether they show up or not."

"We've organized things a little differently," I said. "We have a place where people gather each week."

"And we're not as able to identify commitment in the people. By making it easier, we've lost the ability to identify those who want more of God as opposed to those who simply want more for themselves."

"I think you understand my question. When will we get to the sit down teaching part?"

"In our discipleship system, we call this a *speed bump*. It's a little difficulty that we leave in place. We don't make things harder for people, we just don't remove every impediment. Are they willing to make the effort, small as it is, to step up and over the barrier in order to follow Jesus? If they are unwilling, the speed bump functions like a fence - or a play pen - to keep the person in the place where the challenges match their level of commitment."

"What happens if you take out the speed bumps and make everything easy?"

"You tell me," Sam said.

"You are swamped with people who aren't really interested but who all make demands on your time."

"Is that a familiar circumstance for you?"

"Yes."

"Jesus taught out in the wilderness, miles from even a place where people could buy food. Everyone who followed him there was serious about being with him and learning what he had to say. He did not make it easy for them; he made it difficult and challenging."

"That runs counter to what our experts tell us about how to do evangelism."

"I know. What does that tell you?"

"I'm not sure what you mean."

"Think on it, John. You are part of a vast cultural system, a denomination of over eight million people in the United States of America and millions more in other countries. Systems resist change; change interferes with keeping the status quo running smoothly. Nothing disrupts the status quo like new people who don't understand how to behave in church and who have needs

31

that distract us from the churchy things we love to do. What sort of methods of evangelism will be recommended by the leadership of a system committed to running smoothly and keeping everything the same?"

"Methods that don't work."

Sam laughed. "Methods that sound good, look good, worked somewhere else, but that won't change anything. And if we don't change anything, then we just get more of what we have now. And if that system inertia is one of losing members and running downhill, so be it - as long as we decline in a way that keeps everything running smoothly downhill with a minimum of fuss and conflict."

"I'm afraid that's what we have."

"And that's normal, John. There's nothing unusual about that. Ever heard of Ernst Troeltsch?"

"No."

"German church historian who applied the Hegelian dialectic to discern patterns of church history. I'll email you the link to Elmer Town's book, *Is the Day of the Denomination Dead?* The whole book is online."

"Let's back up. What is the Hegelian dialectic?"

"The Hegelian dialectic is a pattern of change over time, or more accurately, the pattern by which systems respond to pressure to change over time. There are three phases: *thesis, antithesis* and *synthesis. Thesis* is the current established order or status quo, which is challenged by an *antithesis.* After a period of interaction where they influence one another, a new *synthesis* develops out of that interaction which becomes the *thesis* for the next cycle. Sometimes the *antithesis* takes over and becomes the new *thesis,* sometimes the *thesis* rejects the *antithesis* absolutely, but more often functional aspects of the *antithesis* are adopted into the *thesis,* altering the system so that it functions more effectively."

"I think I understand."

"What Troeltsh found is that an institutional, bureaucratic church functions like a *thesis*; because this church does not meet the needs of all the people, a small, highly disciplined, devoted group of believers develops which Troeltsch called a 'sect' that functions as the *antithesis*. A sect has a clear mission, high energy, close relationships, fervent faith and is unburdened with hypocrisy and history. It focuses on its mission, which usually involves conversion; the sect will attempt to reform the denomination or will simply reject it as hopelessly dysfunctional. Frequently the denomination will respond to the criticism of reform with persecution or rejection, thereby hardening the resolve of the sect to fulfill their mission."

"Sounds like a revival."

"Exactly. The resulting hard work, strong faith and clear focus results in growth in membership, influence, property and wealth. What Troeltsch identified, however, was that over two hundred years the sect gradually and irreversibly drifted from its mission until it, too, became a denomination with all of the faults and problems that it initially had condemned. Likewise, it will develop within itself an *antithesis* which attempts to reform it and which becomes a new sect."

"Sounds pretty hopeless. My denomination began as exactly that sort of a reform movement within another denomination. In our case it only took about eighty years for new sects to form and split off for the very same reasons the original movement began."

"The question, unless you are a historian, is what is happening not over centuries but right now. And not over a denomination of eight million diverse members, but within the church you serve now."

"You are implying that the same forces are at work in my church?"

"Absolutely. Within your congregation today you have both *thesis* and *antithesis*, institutional church and impending revival."

"By revival, you mean the *antithesis*?"

"Yes. All the characteristics of the sect are embodied in the system within the larger institutional church system; the *antithesis* pushes for revival, commitment, dedication, fervent prayer, strong faith, Bible reading, conversion, evangelism and all the other factors of what Troeltsch called a sect. The *thesis* wants to keep everything running smoothly as before, in never ending cycles. The key point for us is that it is the *antithesis* that wants to make disciples - not the *thesis*."

I forgot about picking up litter for a moment; standing still, I felt the cold wind in a way that I hadn't noticed while I was moving. "That's a provocative statement."

"Imagine your church as a Hegelian system. There can be more than one distinct *antithesis* challenging the *thesis*, but to keep the illustration simple we will keep the description to two interacting elements. We have a *thesis* which we can call the church system; it's goal is to keep everything comfortable, in balance, running smoothly and with a minimum of negativity, problems or conflict. In our movement we like to call this the "Temple System" since we find all the basic institutional structures within the temple. Challenging the *thesis* is the *antithesis* we call the discipleship system." Sam pulled a piece of paper from his pocket and gave it to me. "Read this," he requested. "Out loud."

I unfolded the paper and read aloud: *"The primary evangelistic strategy of the 21st century is the establishment of new faith communities . . . A faith community is created when a worship experience is tied to a discipleship system. A worshiping group without a discipleship system is not a faith community; it is simply a place to worship God. A faith community intentionally creates settings that link worship to discipleship and spiritual formation."* A footnote identified the source as Craig Kennet Miller, *NextChurch.Now: Creating New Faith Communities*, page 6.

Sam began walking again. "We've blended a variety of systems insights to this original quote to form our understanding. We understand a healthy faith community to be made up of two system components which function cooperatively. First, a temple system functioning as *thesis*, which exists to provide worship and all that worship requires: building, sanctuary, choirs, liturgy, lectionary, staff, finances, and plenty of parking.

Second, a discipleship system functioning as *antithesis*, which exists to make disciples from among the unchurched - evangelism - and fully mature them in the faith. The two systems function very differently, but can function together harmoniously. The temple system functions in repeating cycles; the discipleship system is teleological as disciples move from one stage of maturity to another."

I'd been thinking so hard I hadn't realized that we'd again come full circle and were less than a block from my house. "I think I can understand this. Everything in my church is in cycles, like you said. The Christian year, the lectionary, the fall women's bazaar, the spring salad luncheon, church board every first Thursday."

"That's the way the temple system works, in cycles that smoothly manage the activities of the church."

"I work in and for a temple system then."

"You do. One of the defining characteristics of a temple system is organizing to accomplish spiritual work through paid, professional staff."

"Does that prevent me from making disciples?"

"It doesn't have to prevent disciple making. It's more like the temple work is your day job. If you ignore your duties in the temple, you won't get paid. That's the penalty for being a professional Christian."

My laugh at the term was immediate. "So I've turned pro?"

"If you are good enough, you can get paid for doing what other people can only do for love. That's what amateur means - did you know that? One who does something only for the love of it."

"I have trouble seeing how I can do both - make disciples and satisfy the temple. They are practically opposites."

"You can. Do you find that you have trouble because you have two arms - a right hand and a left hand? Do you have trouble walking because you have two legs instead of only one?"

"No, I don't."

"Just the opposite, right? The trick is to let them

35

work together. Don't think too hard about it, because they will work together naturally. They are made that way, although you wouldn't know it when you look at all the problems in the churches."

I came to a stop in front of my house and tied the drawstrings on my garbage bag.

"Are you up to meet tomorrow?"

"Sure," I said. "I want to know more about this."

"Can I give you some homework then?" Sam asked.

I nodded.

"Take a piece of paper and fold it vertically into two columns. Label the left column as the discipleship system and the right column as the temple system. Make a list of everything that happens in your church - committees and events - but only put an item in one column. Does it make disciples in graduated stages? Or does it keep the church running smoothly in repeating cycles?"

"I can do that."

"Bring it with you tomorrow. We'll go out for coffee this time."

"So I won't be following you?"

"No, you'll just be following me to a place where we can have coffee. We don't want to get into a rut now, do we?"

"Or an endlessly repeating cycle," I said and he laughed.

I brought the problem that Sam had given me to the weekly Tuesday lunch I had with my minister friends. It's professional and it's for fun. The professional piece is called a covenant group meeting where it is intended that we encourage each other, hold each other accountable and keep us honest about what is happening in our churches. Anyone can raise any topic for discussion. As a result, sometimes the discussion has nothing to do with church and everything to do with our personal lives.

So I brought my homework from Sam to the meeting. We met at Olive Garden after the lunch rush got out; that way we didn't have to wait long for a table. Artfully folding a piece of paper in half and getting out a pen, I began to jot down the various events and groups that happened in my church. It was too hard to figure out whether they belonged in the left hand discipleship system column or the right hand temple system column, so I just tried to get the totality down on paper. Later I could divide them.

The guys ignored me as they wandered in and placed their orders with Anna, our waitress for the day, joking about little things the way a group of guys will. The custom is to wait until everyone has been served, have a prayer and then do group talk while we eat. The first person served by the waitress has to say the prayer, otherwise food gets cold.

"Thank you, God," intoned Ian, "for all things interesting in this life. And for good food. Amen." He spread out his napkin in his lap, stirred his iced tea and focused his attention on me. "All right, John, we're all ears. What are you working on there? Is it a formula for disciple making?" A wave of guy laughter wafted over the table.

"Could be," I offered. "Want to help?"

"Sure." Ian was extraverted; nothing bothered him more than a minute of silence. He was the associate pastor for "weird things," as he called it, at a larger suburban church; he was in charge of drama, mission trips, their "edgy" contemporary worship service and recruiting the rock musicians that made it possible. He was dressed up today; he wore a tie with his jeans.

"The challenge is to list everything that happens in my church, whether it's a small group, a committee or an event. Then I have to decide whether it belongs in one category or another."

"What are the categories?" asked Earl. Earl was the pastor of the largest church among us. They did some edgy things, but it seemed to me that they mostly waited for others to experiment with a new idea, and then took it up when the basic problems were worked out. So sleek, so chic, but not dangerous. No risks.

"I've been spending some time talking about disciple making with a retired principal by the name of Sam Franklin," I said.

"I know him," Louis said. "He's well respected in our town. He ran the high school for 20 years."

"He talked this morning about change in systems. There is a thing called the Hegelian dialectic..."

"What did you say?" Larry interrupted. He doesn't have the best people skills and usually looks like he's angry about something.

"Hegelian dialectic," I repeated.

"Gesundheit," Ian offered.

"There's a sequence of three phases - *Thesis, Antithesis* and *Synthesis*. Hegel applied them to history; someone named Ernst Troeltsch applied them to church history."

"And, so" Earl said, trying to speed up the conversation.

"Basically, the traditional church is the *Thesis*, the way things are, and is focused on keeping everything running smoothly."

"That's the goal," Mitch said.

"The *Thesis* doesn't like change and prefers to keep things as they are."

"Works for me," Louie said with Larry nodding away in agreement.

"The *antithesis* is always challenging the *thesis* with ideas for change. Sometimes they are incorporated into a new *synthesis*; sometimes they are rejected."

"An idea is a terrible thing to waste," Earl said.

"Franklin's contention is that the *Thesis* system is cyclical, maintains homeostasis and corresponds to the traditional church, or what he calls the 'temple system.'"

"And it's resistant to change," Ian said. "I've had a lot of experience with that sort of system."

"Not all change is good, Ian," Louis reminded us. "Traditions solidify because they work; they get results."

"Change is good if it leads to results," Earl said. "We don't have resources to waste on producing another Edsel."

"My mother had an Edsel and liked it just fine," Larry objected. "Have you ever actually seen one? Or are you just passing judgement?"

"We want mini-vans, not Edsels," Earl countered. "We want what people will buy."

"I want a Jaguar convertible. I'm not a soccer mom," Ian said.

"What's the other system, John?" Mitch asked.

I pushed in before my friends could begin another debate that would take up our whole lunch time and resolve nothing. "Disciple making, he says, is an *antithesis* that pushes for change. Nothing challenges a system to change like new people. There is within each church a discipleship system that combines evangelism and Christian education, bringing people into the church from the outside and maturing them spiritually through successive stages. The temple system is a balancing process and the discipleship system is a reinforcing process, whatever that means."

"That's Peter Senge," Mitch said. "Interesting."

"Who's that?" Earl asked.

"Peter Senge, *The Fifth Discipline,* published in the '90s. Over a million copies sold. MIT business school. Applying systems theory to corporate management, with the end results that organizations learn from their experiences and therefore improve."

"Learning organizations? Is that an oxymoron?" Ian asked.

"Organizations can learn, but most learn slowly," Earl said.

"Like paint drying," Ian said. "Thrilling."

"Like oak trees growing," Louis said. "Dependable."

I shrugged. "It's still over my head, but I've got homework to do and I want your help on it before you all go back to your office. On this paper I've listed all the various events and components of my church."

"And what's the assignment, should you choose to accept it?" intoned Ian dramatically.

"Each item belongs in one system or another. It

either makes disciples or it maintains the status quo."

After discussing methodology, we agreed to vote with head gestures as I read off each item and discuss any that seemed interesting. That way everyone could keep eating.

"It was a fiasco," I told Ruth that night. "They thought everything was in the discipleship system."

"Everything?" she asked.

"Almost everything. The Board, the finance committee, the personnel committee, the annual finance campaign were allowed to be in the temple system. But everything else - every activity or program - they saw in some way or another as making disciples. And they would argue endlessly to make their point and I didn't quite know how to dispute it."

"How about the flea market on the parking lot sponsored by the women's organization?" Ruth asked.

"That! That!" I exclaimed, exasperated. "It has to be disciple making because of its visibility. They saw billboards and church signs as disciple making. Even plenty of parking was essential to disciple making."

Ruth giggled. "You're kidding."

"I wish I was, Ruth. This is insane."

She hugged me tight. "You'll make sense of it. You know you don't have to agree with them even if their churches are larger than ours."

"I know I don't have to agree with them. I'm just astonished at how much I disagree with them."

"How do you mean, honey?"

"Their list has almost everything in the discipleship system column. My list is just the opposite; everything is in the temple system column."

"It is the traditional church system, honey, so that makes sense to me."

"Then why isn't it just as obvious to them?"

"What did you put in the discipleship system column from our church, honey?"

I looked off into the distance. "Only one thing. The confirmation class. It's the only thing that fits the definition Sam gave me."

"How so?"

"Sam said that the temple system cycles, while the discipleship system is a process of stages that do not repeat, like a ladder. Everything else in our church cycles; discipleship moves forward in stages, the way that fourth grade follows third grade. If something cycles in the discipleship system, it's like repeating third grade - not good. Confirmation is the only thing we do that does not repeat endlessly. You do it once and you are done. And there is nothing that we do that has a prerequisite, where you have to complete the first step before you can do the second step."

When I rolled over in bed that night to be thankful, I did a lot of thinking before I was thankful.

Wednesday, February 4

I met Sam Franklin that Wednesday morning at the restaurant of his choice; it was another example of "follow me." He was already there. As I walked through the crowded chain restaurant, I noticed that his table was set so that he could see the whole room but had a modicum of privacy.

"John, this is Bill Clark," Sam introduced me to the man at his table, who stood to shake hands. "John is the pastor I told you about," he said to Bill.

"Good to meet you, Pastor John," Bill said. "I wish I could stay and get to know you, but I have to go to work."

"Perhaps some other time," I said.

"I'll probably see you at the Gathering in a few weeks, if not before. Thanks again, Sam," Bill said, and left.

"What's the Gathering?" I asked Sam.

"People in the area who practice this system of disciple making get together once a month on the second Saturday; we call it the Gathering. Bill will be there, and you're welcome to come also if you like."

41

"I think I would."

"Do you have your homework?"

I laid it on the table. A waitress appeared and began to clear off Bill's breakfast dishes.

"Denise, this is Pastor John," Sam said.

Denise smiled at me and continued to police the area. "Would you like coffee? A menu?" she asked.

"Both," I said. Coffee and the menu appeared in moments; Sam got very good service.

Sam didn't bother to pick up the homework. "What did you learn about the two systems yesterday?"

I took a deep breath. "If what you said about the temple system cycling is true, then we have virtually no discipleship system functioning at my church. If a discipleship system consists of a linear progression of stages that a person does not repeat, we have only one thing that qualifies."

"And that would be?"

"Confirmation class; once you've gone through it, you don't repeat it."

"How about baptism? You meet with parents before a child is baptized, don't you? And likewise with an adult convert?"

"Then that would be the second thing. We don't have a discipleship system."

Sam took a sip of coffee and I put cream and sweetener into mine. "John, what you've described is not at all unusual. The other item that some churches have that is linear is a new member class. And that's it. That's the way it is."

"So we don't really have a discipleship system."

He laughed. "Your body is made up of interacting systems. The creation," he waved at the world of nature outside the windows of the restaurant, "is constructed out of interlocking systems." He leaned forward to look at me intently. "Your church is the body of Christ, and it is made out of systems." He shrugged. "You have a discipleship system."

"How could we?"

"I taught physics rather than biology, John, but I

know the body normally comes with all its parts. It's there, it's just invisible to you. What does that tell you?"

"That it's not a priority at my church?"

Sam nodded.

I thought for a minute. "That it's present, then, but not performing very well? Otherwise we'd see more disciples."

Sam nodded.

"That it's not receiving much energy or investment? If it was in the budget, you could track it."

Sam nodded. "You're forgetting two things that are very important."

I thought for a minute and took a sip of coffee. "What?"

He held up a finger. "People."

I thought about it for a minute; in the *One Minute Minister* system, people were very important. "So there are people who are working in the discipleship system."

"There are. And?" He held up a second finger.

"The people who are working together aren't organized?"

"That's right; there is no organization, which means the task is out of focus and happening in what might seem to be a haphazard manner. Peter Wagner says that 5-10% of worship attenders in the typical church have the gift of evangelism. In your church, do they know that they have this gift? How are they using that gift? Do they cooperate and help each other in this work? Do they receive training or supervision in order to get the best results from their efforts? That's the benefit of organization."

I took another sip and thought about it.

"So, your average attendance is?" Sam asked.

"About a hundred."

"So you have from five to ten people with this gift of evangelism. Do you know who they are?"

"No."

"Think about it for a minute."

I did. "No one comes to mind."

"That's because you are using them in other

capacities, which is like walking on your hands; you can do it, but it's not as effective. Do you want to know who they are?"

"Sure I do!"

"Ask your new members who influenced them to become a part of your church. Someone who is gifted will be surrounded by the results of their gift, even if they are untrained and underutilized. You will find that a handful of people are the cause that underlies most of your new members joining the church."

"The Pareto Principle suggests that it would be 20%," I said.

"I could wish. Given the lack of focus, organization and investment, it's probably close to that 5%."

"What do I do when I find them?"

"You let the gifted people use their gifts to organize your discipleship system."

"That makes sense. I'll bet you have some suggestions as well."

"Of course," he smiled. "But that's not the first thing, or even close to the second."

"What am I missing?"

"The other people to involve are the people who have the gift of maturing disciples. Discipleship is a process of grace. Evangelistically gifted people minister in cooperation with God in prevenient grace; maturation gifted people minister in cooperation with God in sanctifying grace."

"You're going to explain how you define those terms to me, right?"

"Of course. And my definitions won't be quite like those you learned in seminary."

"Of course," I chuckled.

"What we have here is the answer to an age old riddle, which really should be no riddle at all: what comes first, the chicken or the egg?"

"And what does come first?"

"The chicken - logically and biblically. In the creation story in Genesis, Adam and Eve are created as fully grown individuals - chickens - although not very

44

mature in terms of obedience. In nature, a baby - an egg - can't survive without parenting. That's the key, essential point that solves the whole mess. Chickens come first, and if they are taught correctly, they'll begin to produce eggs that produce chickens that produce eggs."

"Sounds like a cycle to me; you said that the discipleship system was a linear progression."

"It is linear when you consider the position of a person within that system; one step follows another. But the goal is multiple generations of *disciples making disciples making disciples,* which is a cycle."

"That makes sense with chickens and even with people. It doesn't square with what is happening in my church."

"And what is happening in your church?" Sam asked as he picked up the list of activities. "Nothing that unusual," he said as he looked it over. "A typical temple system with a few unusual features - every church has their own unique characteristics. These things are good," he said, setting the list down again. "They just don't make disciples."

"That's not what my colleagues say."

He chuckled dryly. "I'm not surprised. What did they say?"

"Our covenant group meets on a weekly basis, Tuesdays at lunch. I involved them in the homework and they helped me to put each item into the discipleship system column or the temple system column."

"And they came up with this list with only one item in the discipleship system?"

"No, they did not. They saw practically everything as making disciples. Everything except a few administrative committees."

"And this was hard for you to accept?"

"They logically defended each item; they could connect it in some way to disciple making, so it was a part of the discipleship system for them."

"What's an example of what you found hardest to swallow?"

"Parking."

"Ah," he said, smiling. "And their argument?"

"It's classic. *'When people in America come to worship, they like to bring their cars.'* So the key element in disciple making is to have plenty of parking."

"It's true. Do you see the problem?"

"We have plenty of parking, both in front of and behind our church, and across the street in the bank parking lot. Since the bank is closed on Sunday, we can use all their spaces."

"And those spaces are full on Sunday and your church is overflowing?"

"No."

"So it's not parking that makes the difference. It can hinder disciple making, but not cause it."

"My colleagues said that worship visitors found it offensive to have to park across the street from the church. Twenty years ago on the advice of a consultant our church bought the houses behind the building, leveled them and put in more parking."

"And those spaces are full on Sunday and your church is overflowing?"

"No. And their excuse for that is that the spaces are behind the church on a residential street."

"And what we learn from this is that there are plenty of reasons why something doesn't work as intended. But there's something even simpler at work here."

"What is that?"

"How did you say it? *'When people in America come to worship, they like to bring their cars.'* Remember, we call it a *temple system* but Craig Miller called it just *worship*, or the *worship system*. In the temple system, everything revolves around worship and the goal of every activity is to support and improve the results that come from worship. And the end result of that is the temple where the people worship."

"I understand that."

"There was a temple in Jerusalem. Do you think it was crowded?"

"Yes. On religious holidays and festivals the

population of Jerusalem could quadruple because of out of town visitors."

"So the temple had plenty of parking, right?"

"Right." I laughed at the absurdity.

"Or the temple had whatever it needed to have that worship that drew in all those people, and of course the flow of funds that came in through the temple. If they had needed parking to make money, believe me, there would have been parking."

"Larry had a slogan for it that he said he put on the church sign: *God is our focus and worship is our priority.*"

"Nothing changes, John. It's the same temple now as it was when Jesus attended it. You agree that Jesus was in the temple, right?"

"Of course. Jesus taught in the temple all the time."

"And everyone who attended the temple was a disciple of Jesus?"

"No, of course not."

"But they were there to worship God, which is a good thing?"

"Yes."

"So attending the temple is not the same thing as being a disciple of Jesus?"

"Obviously not. There might have been thousands listening in the temple but only a dozen disciples of Jesus."

"Then coming to the temple for worship and following Jesus are two separate things?"

"Obviously. Jesus did most of his ministry outside the temple."

"So when the Great Commission says that we are to *make disciples*, why do we assume that this is equivalent to *getting people to come to worship*?"

"That's why my friends put everything into the discipleship system; if it contributed in any way to people coming to worship, they saw it as making disciples."

"That's what they are," Sam said, "professionals, highly trained, highly educated, focused on building

47

bigger and better temples by getting more and more people to come to worship. Everything in their concept of God's will revolves around worship. That's why we call it a temple system."

"I can't fault that description."

"In our movement, we call this a *two step* action. *Two step disciple making* means the first step is to get people into worship, and then in worship we will make them disciples. All the energy is invested into worship and into getting people into worship. That's pretty typical, right?"

"That's their position."

"And it's working, right? Churches are overflowing, aren't they?"

"Some are."

"Ah, the megachurch. And where did those worship attenders come from?"

"The research I've read says that they mostly come from other churches."

"That research is correct. So we have a transfer of disciples into what is called a receptor church. Sheep are wandering and looking for a better barn with a good floor show and gourmet hay."

I laughed. "I can't fault that description either. That seems to be what everyone is recommending."

"It's a good idea - if your goal is to increase the size of your worship service. And if your goal is to make disciples through the temple system rather than through a discipleship system, you have to get those people into your worship service. That's the two step philosophy of indirect disciple making."

"You've lost me again."

"Our theory is that disciple making happens because the discipleship system, however neglected or impoverished, is still at work within the church. What the temple system notices is that if non-believers attend worship long enough, sometimes they become disciples. The challenge from a temple viewpoint, then, is to get non-believers to attend worship regularly."

"That's a pretty difficult challenge."

48

"And changing worship to meet the needs of non-believers often causes it to fail to meet the needs of believers, so it's a difficult blend to achieve."

"And there is conflict."

Sam nodded. "On the other hand, if you make disciples through the discipleship system, they happily adjust to whatever worship is offered because that worship seems normal to them. If you use the worship system, the temple system, to make disciples, you have to make radical changes in worship to get unbelievers to regularly attend a worship service. If you use the discipleship system to make disciples, new born Christians imprint on the first worship they experience; as far as they are concerned, it's normal."

"So changing worship isn't necessary in order to grow?"

"It's essential that worship meets the needs of the people; it needs to be satisfying and indigenous. But it is not necessary to change worship in order to make disciples if you utilize the discipleship system."

"That's just so unusual."

"When I was teaching before I became a principal, this would be the time that I would pass out a handout. So here it is." Sam reached into his briefcase and pulled out a sheaf of papers, which he set on the table in front of me. "Today I feel like a teacher because I have handouts."

"Where do you get this information?"

"Most of it is from David Oliver's website."

"What website is that?"

"When he finished his dissertation for his doctor of ministry degree in church growth using discipleship systems, he put the whole thing online for anyone to use. Basically, it's three seminars supported by four chapters of heavily footnoted scholarly research. What I'm giving you are bits and pieces out of the seminars because I want you to be able to read the actual quotes online; they provide details that I believe you will find helpful, including footnotes so that you can read further. You can read over it and I'll answer any questions you might have."

"Thank you, Sam."

"This first reference is about the value of small churches as disciple making bodies. Have you ever heard of *Natural Church Development*?"

"I think so. Isn't that the study of what factors work for church growth everywhere, in every culture and type of church?

"Yes, it attempts to identify universal, or 'natural' factors for growth. I won't even ask you to guess what they discovered as the three most significant negative factors for growth.

"Growth preventers?"

Sam nodded. "The top two - they don't mention which one is first - are liberal theology and traditionalism. The third factor is the size of the church. The larger the church, the more difficulty it will have making disciples."

"That seems contrary to everything we are told today. The megachurches are constantly set before us as an example to follow." I picked up the handout and read it quickly.

G. Are small churches doomed? Institutions perceive smaller churches as near the end of their "life cycle" and too small to compete in the new reality of a changing marketplace. Small churches represent more than a third of church attenders in the Illinois Great Rivers Conference.

The results of the Natural Church Development (NCD) research, however, indicate that the third strongest negative factor to church growth is church size: "*The growth rate of churches decreased with increasing size. This fact in and of itself came as no great surprise, because in large churches the percentages represent many more people. But when we converted the percentages into raw numbers, we were dumbfounded. Churches in the smallest size category (under 100 in attendance) had won an average of 32 new people over the past five years; churches with 100-200 in worship also won 32; churches between 200-300 average 39 new individuals; churches between 300-400 won 25. So a 'small' church wins just as many people for Christ as a 'large' one, and what's more, two churches with 200 in worship on Sunday will win twice as many new people as one church with 400 in attendance.*"

Schwarz found that the average growth rate in smaller churches was 13% (over five years), whereas in larger churches it was a mere 3%. A small church in the NCD sample with an average attendance of fifty-one typically converted thirty-two persons in five years; megachurches in the NCD sample averaged 2,856 in attendance but converted only 112 new persons in five years. The same number of persons participating in fifty-six small churches averaging fifty-one in attendance would have produced 1,792 converts in five years. A small improvement in small church disciple making capability will have a huge growth outcome due to the number of small churches. (Source: Christian A. Schwarz, *Natural Church Development: A Guide to Eight Essential Qualities of Healthy Churches* , 46-48, 28-29)

"This handout," Sam said, "is about the tendency of larger churches to grow by drawing in Christians rather than making disciples out of the unchurched. This is growth by addition; people are being added, and there are many people who come into these churches. If these churches were actually maturing people to become disciple makers, however, there would be an explosion of growth *within* these churches rather than transferring *into* these churches. We believe that this is the primary difference between an American megachurch of 5000 and a third world cell church of 50,000."

"What's a cell church?"

"Cell churches are congregations organized around a network of small groups called cells. Each cell works a system of evangelism and maturation of new believers as their primary purpose. That's our definition of a discipleship system: evangelism and maturation. The world's largest cell church is Yoido Full Gospel Church in Seoul, Korea, with over 700,000 members. We believe that the techniques of evangelism they use can be used in any size church because their discipleship system focuses on what happens in a group of twelve people or less. They have 70,000 of these groups and each one functions as a decentralized, discipleship system."

"I think I've heard about this church."

"Their process is described in detail on David Oliver's website - it's chapter two in his dissertation."

"That would be interesting."

"We believe that every institutional church would benefit from starting a pilot group - a little church within the big church - which would practice these principles. At the very least, it would help organize the five to ten percent that have the gift of evangelism to use their gift within the church. We also believe that the lack of such a highly committed group is a primary reason why people leave small churches looking for something more - which is what draws them to the megachurch that offers a great diversity of programming and powers the whole receptor trend."

He then set another handout in front of me.

How then do large churches grow?

Carl George: *"In most cases, however, once a church passes four hundred, it tends to become a receptor church, with a high percentage of its newcomers being drawn from other smaller churches in the community. In other words, between 75 percent and 90 percent of the new members in the typical church of four hundred or more are transfers, not converts. There exists a widespread notion that North America's medium and large size churches are evangelistic centers. This view is in most cases, regrettably only a myth. Instead, these churches are by and large centers for reprocessing believers, new and old alike, that throng to them from smaller churches.*

This situation leads to one of the largest spiritual dilemmas of our time: The bigger a church becomes, the less evangelistically responsible it needs to be in order to grow. As a church grows, it inherits the other churches' evangelism efforts. Regrettably, very few churches larger than four hundred do their own soul winning or primary spiritual formation. Rather, they simply reap the benefits of other churches' perceived failures."

This is not church growth, but the accelerated decline of other churches to the benefit of the receptor church. The vast majority of the members of megachurches are converted elsewhere but come to the megachurch for its excitement, varied program activities and its perceived quality of discipleship teaching. (Source: Carl F. George, *The Coming Church Revolution: Empowering Leaders for the Future,* 37-38. Cf. Carl F. George, "New Realities for the 21st Century Church," *The Pastor's Update* 94, tape 7033 (Pasadena, CA: Fuller Theological Seminary.)

Receptor churches teach an attractive discipleship that

does not make disciples, or there would be an explosion of new Christians originating *within* these churches rather than transferring *into* these churches. *Receptor growth* is growth by addition; *disciples making disciples that make disciples* is growth by multiplying generations (2 Timothy 2:1-2).

The major difference between a megachurch of two thousand and a cell type church of twenty thousand or 700,000 is the role of the Discipleship System in making converts from non-Christians and then making disciple makers out of those new disciples. The highly organized, network based Discipleship Systems in large, third world cell churches allow rapid growth without disturbing the functional harmony of the church homeostasis, thereby overcoming a major cause of resistance to church growth.

"This next handout," Sam said, "is about the most effective disciple making system in the world, known as a 'church planting movement' or a 'church multiplication movement.' It uses lay leaders to start small, independent churches which rapidly multiply."

"What's the difference between that and a cell church?"

"The primary difference, we believe, is the way the groups are interconnected. From our viewpoint, Church Planting Movement or CPM churches support each other and link together in loose, informal networks. Each local church provides a strong discipleship system and a very simple temple system - often little more than the minimum necessary to be considered a 'church.' Because of the simplicity of the way they implement 'church' they are frequently called 'simple churches.' This allows most of their energy to be invested in the discipleship system. In the cell church, the cells *are* the discipleship system, but the functions of the temple system are provided by the mother church. A cell, for example, attends a worship service but does not carry the responsibility of planning, organizing or providing a worship service or any other churchy activity; the mother church provides it for them, so they can concentrate on implementing the tasks of the discipleship system, which is the making of disciples."

"What is the difference in connection that you mentioned?"

53

"The simple churches are largely independent and therefore can adapt rapidly to local conditions; generally this works very well in rural areas and under persecution because the simple churches can easily operate independently. Cell leaders in a cell church, however, are linked in a hierarchical network which provides extensive supervision, on the job training and ongoing support; this infrastructure manages the details, controls for high quality operations and provides for the spiritual needs of the cell leaders. Most cell churches are found in urban areas where people can also participate in the activities of the mother church." He gave me the handout.

Church Multiplication Movement Discipleship Systems

TAILS. The church multiplication movement strategy is rapidly planting indigenous churches under similar conditions in China without flashy public worship considered a requirement for growth in the United States. Southern Baptist Mission Executive, David Garrison: *In his initial survey, the strategy coordinator found three local house churches made up of about 85 Han Chinese Christians. The membership was primarily elderly and had been slowly declining for years with no vision or prospects for growth. Over the next four years, by God's grace, the strategy coordinator helped the gospel take fresh root among this people group and sweep rapidly across the Yanyin region.*

Aware of the enormous cultural and linguistic barriers that separated him from the people of Yanyin, the missionary began by mobilizing Chinese Christian co-laborers from across Asia. Then, partnering these ethnic Chinese church planters with a small team of local believers, the group planted six new churches in 1994. The following year, 17 more were begun. The next year, 50 more were started. By 1997, just three years after starting, the number of churches had risen to 195 and had spread throughout the region, taking root in each of the five people groups.

At this point the movement was spreading so rapidly that the strategy coordinator felt he could safely exit the work without diminishing its momentum. The next year, in his absence, the movement nearly tripled as the total number of churches grew to 550 with more than 55,000 believers. (Source: David Garrison, "Chapter 2: CPMs Up Close; A Region in China," in the booklet *Church Planting Movements*, available

"Does the discipleship system need the temple system at all?" I asked

Sam shrugged. "You are asking about what happens when persecution destroys or prevents the temple system of the institutional church from operating. In Ethiopia, persecution of the Mesere Kristos movement prevented public worship for nine years. During the nine years without any temple system, the discipleship system continued to function. When the government changed, the church could begin to worship again in public and function as a temple system. And, surprise, the church had grown tenfold - from 5000 to 50,000 - under persecution and without any public worship or the other aspects of the temple system. While some understand this as persecution purifying the church, we believe that a simpler explanation is that all of the energy went into the discipleship system, because it could continue to operate from person to person under persecution. This continuing growth when persecution prevents public preaching suggests that, with an effective discipleship system in place, the form worship takes is irrelevant to disciple making."

Sam gave me one more handout.

HOMEWORK: The Persecution Exercise.

An atheistic dictatorship has taken power in our country. All churches and religious groups are abolished and outlawed. Public worship is outlawed, all pastors are put in prison or executed, along with any lay leaders who protest this policy. All church committees are disbanded. All church funds and property is confiscated; church buildings are turned into museums, recreation halls or community centers where no religious activity is allowed. Any public gathering for religious purposes or public demonstration of faith is considered a threat to the ruling government and a crime punished by execution or imprisonment.

3.01 What will happen in your church in the following week?

3.02 What will you personally do? What will others in your church do?

55

"This last item is your homework assignment,
although I'd like to suggest a change in what we are
doing."

"I'm really enjoying this information, although it
seems overwhelming at times." I took a sip of coffee to
gather my thoughts. "What I mean is that all that I've
heard is obvious, simply and painfully obvious, after I
think about it. But it's almost like idea whiplash - my
understanding has shifted so much in the past week."

"You need some time to adjust to what we've been
talking about before you pour more information into your
brain. And that's the problem and the temptation - to
focus on playing around with ideas rather than obedience
and implementation. You need to move from thinking to
doing. " He took a sip of his coffee. "What you've learned
so far is probably more than you need as a foundation. We
don't really share this abstract church information with
new disciples; I've shared it with you because, as a
professional pastor, you need to be able to integrate these
ideas with your seminary training, your denominational
polity and what you do as a professional in the temple."

"Is there a conflict?"

"David Oliver likes to talk about the day he
realized that he was a bivocational church planter. He was
on his way back from a Michigan simple church planting
retreat when he realized that he was by nature a church
planter and that working in the discipleship system was
his calling in ministry. His day job was to be the pastor of
a local church operating the temple system and fulfilling
all the day to day expectations of pastoral work. He found
he needed the philosophical framework to understand
how to do both and keep sane."

"I do want to remain sane," I said. "My wife
expects it of me."

"So we cover this theory when we talk with
pastors; we find that pastor's need the theory to find
balance. Otherwise, they try to use the temple system to

56

accomplish the work of the discipleship system and their results are poor. "

"So blending the two doesn't really work?" I asked.

Sam shrugged. "Truly blending wouldn't be a problem. The problem lies in not respecting the function of each system. This takes two forms. They usually either try to force aspects of the temple system to do the work of the discipleship system or they try to push people called to work in the discipleship system to instead work in the institutional church temple system. The temple system perceives this pushing as an attack and reacts accordingly, with hostility and conflict, and the opportunity for change shuts down. The most common example is trying to change worship so that worship makes disciples."

"Trying to make worship take the place of the discipleship system?"

"Yes. Here is a final handout which details Jesus' conflict with the Temple system of his day. Jesus created a functioning, discipleship system within the Jewish religion of his day. The perceived threat to the status quo led directly to his death due to the plotting of the Temple leaders. We believe that the purpose of the gospels is to demonstrate and teach the disciple making methods of the discipleship system of Jesus which results in the church of the book of Acts. We believe that the path to a New Testament church of power and vitality, able to change the lives of individuals and societies, lies in following the pattern Jesus taught the original disciples."

The handout was a list of scriptures, which I set on the stack unread. "I'm overwhelmed again," I admitted.

"I know," Sam said. "But I wanted to leave you with these materials to digest over the next month - or months."

"Thank you," I said. "I've come to really appreciate our talks."

"You are very welcome. On the other hand, I'd like to shift gears from the abstract to the specific. You had a question about how one makes disciples. I'd like to introduce you to someone who will take you through the specific stages of our method of making disciples. Are you ready for something practical and specific rather than abstract and theoretical?"

"I think that would be refreshing," I said.

"I'm going to ask you to meet with Bill Clark. You met him when you arrived this morning. I've been working with him in the system for a while and he's ready for a new apprentice. I'll still be available to answer questions on theory, but starting fresh with Bill will give you a very clear experience of just how our system works without my theory getting in the way."

"He can call me and we'll set up a time."

"Great!" Sam said.

That night Ruth and I read through the list of scriptures Sam had given me about the conflict between Jesus and the temple system, taking a minute to discuss each one.

HANDOUT for John Wesley Adams
Jesus and the Temple System

John 2:13-22 The Passover of the Jews was at hand, and Jesus went up to Jerusalem. In the temple he found those who were selling oxen and sheep and pigeons, and the money-changers at their business. And making a whip of cords, he drove them all, with the sheep and oxen, out of the temple; and he poured out the coins of the money-changers and overturned their tables. And he told those who sold the pigeons, "Take these things away; you shall not make my Father's house a house of trade." His disciples remembered that it was written, "Zeal for thy house will consume me." The Jews then said to him, "What sign have you to show us for doing this?" Jesus answered them, "Destroy this temple, and in three days I will raise it up." The Jews then said, "It has taken forty-six years to build this temple, and will you raise it up in three days?" But he spoke of the temple of his body. When therefore he was raised from the dead, his disciples remembered that he had said this; and they believed the scripture and the word which Jesus had spoken.

John 11:47-53 So the chief priests and the Pharisees gathered the council, and said, "What are we to do? For this man performs many signs. If we let him go on thus, every one will believe in him, and the Romans will come and destroy both our holy place and our nation." But one of them, Caiaphas, who was high priest that year, said to them, "You know nothing at all; you do not understand that it is expedient for you that one man should die for the people, and that the whole nation should not perish." He did not say this of his own accord, but being high priest that year he prophesied that Jesus should die for the nation, and not for the nation only, but to gather into one the children of God who are scattered abroad. So from that day on they took counsel how to put him to death.

Mark 11:15-18 And they came to Jerusalem. And he entered the temple and began to drive out those who sold and those who bought in the temple, and he overturned the tables of the money-changers and the seats of those who sold pigeons; and he would not allow any one to carry anything through the temple. And he taught, and said to them, "Is it not written, 'My house shall be called a house of prayer for all the nations'? But you have made it a den of robbers." And the chief priests and the scribes heard it and sought a way to destroy him; for they feared him, because all the multitude was astonished at his teaching.

Luke 19:45-20:8 And he entered the temple and began to drive out those who sold, saying to them, "It is written, 'My house shall be a house of prayer'; but you have made it a den of robbers." And he was teaching daily in the temple. The chief priests and the scribes and the principal men of the people sought to destroy him; 48 but they did not find anything they could do, for all the people hung upon his words. One day, as he was teaching the people in the temple and preaching the gospel, the chief priests and the scribes with the elders came up and said to him, "Tell us by what authority you do these things, or who it is that gave you this authority." He answered them, "I also will ask you a question; now tell me, Was the baptism of John from heaven or from men?" And they discussed it with one another, saying, "If we say, 'From heaven,' he will say, 'Why did you not believe him?' But if we say, 'From men,' all the people will stone us; for they are convinced that John was a prophet." So they answered that they did not know whence it was. And Jesus said to them, "Neither will I tell you by what authority I do these things."

Mark 14:55-59 Now the chief priests and the whole council sought testimony against Jesus to put him to death; but they found none. For many bore false witness against him, and their witness did not agree. And some stood up and bore false witness against him, saying, "We heard him say, 'I will destroy this temple that is made with hands, and in three days I will build another, not made with hands.'" Yet not even so did their testimony agree.

"What do you think about all these handouts?" Ruth asked me after reading over them briefly.

I thought for a minute. "It feels to me like an iceberg. The part you can see above the waterline is going to be pretty simple. That's the practical aspect of what we are being called to do."

"How do you mean that?"

"The discipleship system that Jesus practiced had to be simple in order to be operated successfully by uneducated fishermen. Jesus could have taken over the temple, could have recruited the rabbis, could have utilized the religious establishment."

"He didn't choose to do that."

"So, just doing what Jesus did shouldn't be that complicated. But because it works, what Jesus did is connected by multiple threads to every sort of research - sociology, anthropology, psychology, etc. You can analyze what Jesus did from all kinds of perspectives. There's so much to understand." I thought for a minute. "It's like the difference between driving a car and getting under the hood, taking apart the engine and understanding how each part works. That's the part of the iceberg or the car that's under the surface. You don't need to know every detail on how the engine works in order to drive the car, but it's interesting."

"Is that what Sam meant when he said that they normally didn't show all these handouts to lay people and that he gave them to you as a pastor?"

"With my education, I've got questions that would distract me from just applying the methods. So now I can pursue answers to my questions, or I can set them aside temporarily and learn what to do in making disciples."

"Or you can do both."

"The theory will still be there. I'll ask better questions if I know the steps of the process first."

60

"So when will you meet with this Bill Clark?"

"I'm to call him tomorrow morning; he suggested lunch."

"What do you know about him?"

"Not much," I said with a shrug. "Sam's been working with him for several months. He's the assistant manager of a tire store."

"And he's going to mentor you," Ruth said with a smile. "I wonder what's going to happen to all your questions and theoretical debates, since he won't have your years of seminary education."

"It feels odd to me, but I can't imagine it was very different for Nicodemus to quiet himself in order to learn from a fisherman like Peter or a tax collector like Matthew."

"So this feels like a Jesus thing, then?"

"Yes. Everyone has something to teach us about following Jesus. And people like me with big egos who like to use big words and keep the discussion theoretical may just have to deal with the adjustment. Certainly education is helpful, but the educated church is far from perfect. Perhaps there is a good reason why Jesus chose specifically to work with and through common people."

She laid a hand on my shoulder. "I think a little humility looks very attractive on you, husband." Her smile led to other subjects that kept us busy until it was time to be thankful.

CHAPTER THREE: Justifying Grace
Saturday morning, February 7

I sat across the table from Bill Clark at the coffee shop we had chosen as a meeting place. On a late Saturday morning there were a scattering of families with children, sometimes single parents, and some couples enjoying coffee and conversation.

Bill pulled an index card out of a pocket full of them and smiled. "If I don't write things down, I never remember." I answered his questions as he wrote down the name of my wife, my contact information, the name of our son, his grade and where he went to school. I told him about our hobbies and what we liked to do for fun.

Then it was his turn. He told me about his wife Cindy, who ran a licensed day care in their home in Murphyville. They had been high school sweethearts, grown up in Murphyville and had never left. They had one daughter in 2nd grade who was learning to read, a son in Kindergarten and two little girls in Cindy's day care. Carla, Ethan, Ellen, Angela.

"Which denomination and church do you belong to?" I asked.

"We have a saying in our movement, John. The answer to that question is that *I am a follower of Jesus Christ; at the moment, I and my family attend the First United Methodist Church in Murphyville.*"

"And what's the significance of that?"

"Where we attend church can change; sometimes we are called out of one church and into another. What's important is following Christ where that path leads."

"I suppose you are right."

"Sometimes words have power and you have to be somewhat careful about keeping distinctions clear. I knew what you meant, but the way we learn to say it keeps it clear: I don't belong to a church, I belong to Jesus Christ."

"I understand that."

"You also attend church, I assume, at the one you pastor."

"Correct."

"But you don't belong to the church; sometimes your calling requires that you oppose the desires of your members, and one day your calling may require you to leave for another church."

"That's correct."

"We are following Jesus; while his path will not likely lead us away from participating in a church, it doesn't lead us so much to a church as through a church. Don't be too surprised if you see my family in your church this Sunday."

"We have a nursery," I said automatically.

"My wife will appreciate that," he said. "Not every church provides one for young parents."

"You would be welcome."

"Thank you. This thing that we are doing - following Jesus - happens at a higher level of quality when we share the journey with other people. Jesus himself said so: *For where two or three are gathered in my name, there am I in the midst of them* - Matthew 18:20. If you and I are going to be partners in disciple making, we are probably also going to share the same church, at least for a while. Normally, I'd ask you to share my church with me, but in this case I understand that I probably need to come to you."

"Partners in disciple making?"

"I'm getting ahead of myself." He took out another index card and drew a horizontal line across the bottom of it. In the center of the line he drew a heart. "We are taught that disciple making is a process of grace. It is something that God does. It was Jesus who said that HE would build HIS church. We are helpers; it's not something we do or as if it depended all upon us. In disciple making we cooperate with God working in three phases of grace."

He wrote the word 'justifying' underneath the heart. "We understand justifying grace to be that moment when our hearts are changed. Some people refer to that moment as 'Jesus coming into my heart' and others speak of being 'filled with the spirit.' In Romans Paul speaks of the witness of the spirit speaking to our heart that we are children of God."

"I think John Wesley spoke of his heart being strangely warmed."

"So we use a heart to indicate that moment of grace; the purpose of the heart is to indicate that this is an emotional experience. It's something we can feel. Make sense?"

"Yes. In some denominations, salvation comes at an earlier point or is non-emotional."

"We aren't necessarily speaking of the time when a person is saved; I grew up Baptist, so I'm familiar with the terminology and comfortable with it. I also know that some denominations believe that salvation begins at the time of baptism. Our movement doesn't wish to debate theology on the basis of what some call 'the dividing line of faith' before which one goes to hell and after which one goes to heaven. Our movement is concerned with the point where one has an experience of the spiritual which is life changing. We also speak of it in this manner because it is obvious from experience that a person can have multiple experiences of this type - where all things are made new and they begin fresh."

"In Acts there were multiple times when the believers prayed and were filled with the spirit," I said.

"Exactly. We call this moment justifying grace. It is a single point in time when we refer to it. Everything which precedes that moment is God working in our lives to bring us to a moment of reconciliation and justifying grace. We call grace that precedes prevenient grace." He wrote prevenient grace on the card underneath the arrow to the left of the heart. "We make disciples when we cooperate with God in prevenient grace and involve ourselves properly in the lives of people prior to their moment of justifying grace." He reached into his pocket and pulled out a tri-fold brochure and handed it to me.

"Please read over the front of the brochure."

Jump
Groups

A Simple System
for Making Disciples

"Go therefore and make disciples of all
nations, baptizing them in the name of
the Father and of the Son and of the Holy
Spirit, teaching them to observe all that
I have commanded you; and lo, I am with
you always, to the close of the age."
Matthew 28:19-20

"Why do you call me 'Lord, Lord,'
and not do what I tell you?" Luke 6:46

You then, my son, be strong
in the grace that is in Christ Jesus,
and what you have heard from me
before many witnesses
entrust to faithful men
who will be able to teach others also."
2 Timothy 2:1-2

JUMP = Jesus Understands My Problems

Bill Clark

Bill's contact information was printed under his
name. He set his finger on Matthew 28:19-20. "We believe
that these two verses represent the complete discipleship
system taught by Jesus. As the climax of the book of
Matthew, they summarize all that goes before them. We
also read the rest of the gospels in harmony with them."
He requested that I read v. 19 aloud for him.

"Go therefore and make disciples of all nations, baptizing them in the name of the Father, and of the Son and of the Holy Spirit," I said.

"This verse," Bill said, "refers to the action of prevenient grace that leads to a moment of justifying grace. Now please read verse 20. The directive to baptize indicates the gate or door into new life and another phase of grace."

"...teaching them to observe all that I have commanded you," I read.

"We believe that this verse summarizes the work of sanctifying grace. In the first half of sanctifying grace, we cooperate with God and become better Christians; in the second half of sanctifying grace, we cooperate with God and become disciple makers." Bill wrote on the card again. I looked at the finished diagram.

Prevenient   Sanctifying

Justifying

"This is something new to me," I said. "I've never really heard about two phases of sanctifying grace."

Bill shrugged. "From God's viewpoint there may be only one. We teach the two halves because we want to show respect to 2000 years of church history which led to a fatal error in disciple making."

"What are you talking about?"

"How would you define the concept of holiness?"

I had to think for a minute; how do you define a concept that is so simple? "Right and wrong, good and evil, holy and unholy. God honoring or not. Deeds and thoughts are either one or the other."

"That is the historic position. Our definition of holiness is more simple and specific: holiness is obeying Christ."

"Of course. That's what I said."

"No, there is a difference. We both understand that Jesus was sinless and perfectly holy. When you read the New Testament, there were numerous times when Jesus was accused of doing things that were wrong."

"According to the accuser's point of view."

"And upon what did they base their point of view?"

I groped for an answer. "On ethics. On logic. On tradition. On the commandments of the Jewish law."

"So Jesus differed from their understanding of what the law required. How are we to understand the difference today?"

"What do you mean?"

Bill tapped the table. "We also have our logic, our ethics, our traditions and our teachings on the commandments. It's obvious that our rules flex most of the time to let us do what we want and not feel too guilty about it - or flex the other way so that we always feel guilty and ashamed. That's the problem with human logic."

"I suppose that's a consistent reality, whether in the New Testament time or today."

"Our definition of holiness is simpler. Obey Jesus."

"I heard something like that in seminary. What was it? *When the Bible speaks, we speak; when the Bible is silent, we are silent.* Is that what you mean?"

Bill nodded. "Only simpler. Go down the list of the commands of Jesus. Are you obeying them? If so, that is holy."

"I don't have a list of those commands," I said.

"Why not?" Bill asked. "It's quite clearly a command that someone was supposed to teach them to you. Why didn't they give you a list?"

"No one taught me in that fashion," I admitted.

"No one taught you to observe all that Jesus commanded you?"

"They taught me a lot of things, but not that. Perhaps it was mixed in with all the rest, but that was not what I was taught."

"Then," Bill said, tapping the brochure for emphasis, "those who taught you were not obedient to the command of v. 20 of the Great Commission. Teaching the commands of Jesus is both simpler and profound; it is the means of sanctifying grace. Furthermore, you were probably taught concepts without much attention to helping you 'observe' them with your behavior. True?"

"True. But that's normal," I protested.

"It was normal," Bill said, "but it is not correct, nor is it holy. Our movement seeks to restore New Testament Christianity by restoring the teaching of behavioral obedience to Jesus' commands. That's the essence of sanctifying grace."

"What do you do with traditional spiritual disciplines?"

"Such as?"

"The means of grace: holy communion, prayer, fasting, lectio divina, etc."

"Do they help you to observe all the commands that Jesus taught?" Bill asked.

"Indirectly, I suppose."

"If they help, sanctifying grace flows through them. But as an activity, they are less than effective at teaching obedience to Jesus. Jesus didn't just say 'pray' he said 'pray like this' - how does this spiritual discipline help someone pray in that way? And incorporate into one's prayer life all of the other commands on prayer taught in the gospels?"

"Can you give me an example?"

"Jesus says, when you pray, go into your closet. Does that mean that you can only pray in a closet? What does it mean?"

"It means that prayers are to be communication with God, not a show of faith to impress others. At least, that's what it means to me."

"I think you are right ... but when will that be discussed?"

"Eventually - but I see what you mean. If the curriculum for the class on discipleship is first the commands of Jesus, it's going to come up sooner than it would otherwise."

"That's what we believe as well - that what Jesus

taught should come first and even be mastered. One of the primary problems of the church over the centuries is that it has taken people around and around in circles at the kindergarten level and never helped them to grow out of those very early elementary lessons of the faith."

"There's a verse on that."

"Actually, there are several in Paul and one in Hebrews."

"So, sanctifying grace focuses on learning how to obey the commands of Jesus?"

"Yes. It starts there and proceeds from there. All of the commands of Jesus are the topic of the first half, and one in particular is the focus on the second half."

"What exactly is this second half?"

"With very few exceptions in all the writings of the Christian church over the centuries, one command in particular has not been taught as required by the Great Commission."

"I don't follow you."

"Holiness has focused on all of the commands but one: the Great Commission itself. That's what's missing in spiritual kindergarten and what is the emphasis of the second half of sanctifying grace."

"Say more."

"This is not actually a straight arrow," he said, pointing at the arrow on the card over the three words - prevenient, justifying, sanctifying. "People at the beginning levels see sanctification as an arrow heading away from the world and heading up into heaven." He turned the card so the arrow was pointing upward at an angle. "The holier you are, the farther away you get from the things of the world." He then drew an arc connecting the line after sanctifying grace with the line just before prevenient grace. "Sanctification is actually a circle rather than a straight arrow. In sanctifying grace, you first learn all the commands of Jesus ... but if you learn to observe the Great Commission itself, you return to the beginning to work in prevenient grace in order to help someone else find a living faith."

"That makes sense." I tapped the heart. "Here I

become a disciple." I tapped the line over sanctifying grace. "Here I become a better disciple. If I remain obedient, I also obey the Great Commission and become a disciple maker." My finger traced the arc of the circle.

"And what comes next, after you make a disciple? You should know that this is the missing part in all of church history."

"Let me think." I stared at the card. "If I lead someone up to a moment of sanctifying grace - v. 19 - then I must obey v. 20 and teach them also to obey all the commands of Jesus, just as I was taught."

"Including?"

"Disciple making according to v. 19?"

"Exactly. And then they must?"

"Teach their disciples to obey?"

"It's a cycle. 2 Timothy 2:1-2: *You then, my son, be strong in the grace that is in Christ Jesus, and what you have heard from me before many witnesses entrust to faithful men who will be able to teach others also.*"

"You're right, this has not been taught. That I have a responsibility to make disciples, and teach my disciples not only to make disciples but how to raise them to make their own disciples."

"What's been taught in its place?"

"Nothing."

"Sometimes." Bill shrugged. "Or more frequently, that it is the church's task to train up the individual to be a better Christian, a better disciple. Or it is the clergy's task. Or worse, that it is your own job - to train yourself up to be a better disciple."

"I'm thinking of all those spiritual disciplines..."

"Exactly. Each one is a way for *you* to make *yourself* a better disciple. But the Great Commission does not emphasize a *self made disciple*. It emphasizes *a better disciple made by another disciple*." Bill looked at me with an intense focus. "Do you understand what this means?"

"What?"

"You are a Christian who has raised yourself or been raised by an institution. You are, by definition, an orphan. Can you imagine the difficulties an adult abandoned as a child has in learning how to raise up others to become something that he or she has never experienced?"

"I'm not an orphan, but I know that parenting skills are learned."

"The church has lost the concept of spiritual parenting and now raises all of its spiritual children in an institutional orphanage."

"That would not be pretty."

"Dr. Oliver has a parable on his website on this; I think I have a copy here." He rummaged around in his briefcase and withdrew a single sheet of paper. "Here it is. Do me a favor and read it out loud."

I took it and read it aloud:

D. Cell Parable: The Orphanage

The young couple looked with adoration upon their first child, a little boy.

"You are so beautiful," they cooed.

They looked up from their baby to the lifestyle to which they had become accustomed. Two high paying jobs and exciting, demanding careers. A very expensive home and two brand new Porsche sports cars. Vacations in Cancun, Broadway plays and season tickets to all the professional sports teams in their city. Workouts at the health club to stay slim and trim; dinners out at expensive restaurants.

"We have been blessed," they said. "God has been so good to us."

"God has answered all our prayers."

"Our baby is going to need our church's help to grow up in faith."

"I totally agree."

"I see a problem with our independent lifestyle and raising the baby," one said.

"I see the need for things to change now that we have a baby," the other said.

"Raising this baby would mean we would have to grow up, and give up our self-indulgent lifestyle."

"You're right. This baby needs mature parents who will love him with all their hearts."

"Raising this baby would mean that we would have to put a priority on parenting and let the other things be less important. We'd have to change and put the children first."

"That's the sort of parents our baby needs, honey. I totally agree."

"We're so active in our church ... leaders in so many important ministries."

"So much of God's work depends upon us."

"We would have to cut back on our church activities and put the baby first."

"But we gain so much enjoyment out of what we do for the Lord! How can we give any of it up?"

They looked at their calendars, and they were sad, for they were exceedingly busy.

"I know what we should do. We'll go see the pastor."

"Honey, I totally agree. Our pastor is so smart, so mature, and knows all about raising kids and being responsible."

"Exactly. Our pastor will be able to help us with this challenge."

They bundled up the baby and got in the Porsche. They looked with love upon the baby the whole trip to the church. "You are so beautiful," they cooed. They left the baby on the pastor's door step, rang the doorbell and sped away.

The pastor opened the door and saw the baby. "Another one!" the pastor thought, picking up the baby. "You are so beautiful!" the pastor told the baby, carrying him through the door into the church. Through the door one could hear all the other babies crying.

"The next paragraph is the conclusion to the parable," Bill said.

E. Generational disciple making is like making babies and raising them to full adulthood, which includes the learned ability to raise their own children to full adulthood. Children learn parenting from being parented. Four generations are described by Paul in 2 Timothy 2:1-2. Were you abandoned by your spiritual parents?

"Kind of a surprise ending, eh?" he asked.

"Yes," I said, swallowing. "*Through the door one could hear all the other babies crying.* There are days on my job when it feels exactly like that."

"The pastor in the parable does the right thing. But the parents have a role and the institutional church has taught them to avoid their responsibility to these spiritual

72

children."

"Perhaps that's why I felt so at home becoming a leader in the church and then a pastor; I could provide some of the spiritual nurture that had been lacking in my own life." I picked up the brochure. "Is this from Dr. Oliver also?"

"Yes. It's his discipleship system."

"What's the next lesson? Or are we done."

"It's up to you. "

"Let's go on."

"Open the brochure to the first column and take a moment to read it."

Here's what it said:

We are *convinced*

that a living relationship with Jesus Christ as Lord is the most powerful method of solving human problems and healing broken human lives.

"How do I become a Christian?"
"How do I rededicate my life to Christ?"

We become Christians when God answers a prayer like the following:

The Centering Prayer

Lord Jesus, today I am far less than the person I want to be or can be with your help. I ask today that you would be more and more the center of my life. Guide me to all that is good, cleanse me from all that is not. Teach me Your ways and form in me Your nature. Help me to serve you as I am gifted. Work through me to redeem my neighborhood. I am a sinner; please be my Shepherd, my Savior and my Lord. Amen.

This same prayer works whether we are asking for the first time to become a Christian or renewing our commitment to become a better Christian.

There is a powerful discipleship system for spiritual growth developed by Neil Cole called a **"Life Transformation Group"** (or "LTG" for short) in his book *Cultivating A Life For God*. An LTG uses three elements - Bible reading, Questions and Partnership - to help us jump up to a higher spiritual level and a higher quality of life. That's why we call it a **Jump Group.** The five parts of the discipleship system are listed in this brochure. I would like to invite you to try this system of spiritual growth as an experiment in growing your faith!

Bill's signature was under this text.

"What's the meaning of this being the same prayer for becoming a Christian as for rededicating your life?"

Bill shrugged. "They are both experiences of justifying grace. In essence they are the same thing. You don't go backward; you grow from the point you were at. Furthermore, it's hard for some people to identify 'the first time' so it's easier to have a prayer that works for 'every time' someone would wish to give his or her life to Christ."

"I've never heard of Neil Cole. Who is he?"

"Neil Cole is a church planter from Southern California. Oliver has adapted a lot of his church planting material for our use. The JUMP group is a simplified version of Cole's *Life Transformation Group.*"

"How is it simplified?"

"Dr. Oliver felt that in its original form, it was too intense and demanding for the typical mainline church person. So the revision is to allow people like us more time to get up to full speed. You'll see what I mean when we get to the sanctifying grace page of the brochure."

"This column is for justifying grace, then?"

"Yes. Let's go over the big picture," Bill suggested. "Our experience is that it is more helpful for pastors to be able to integrate our system if we do this."

"Meaning that others don't need it?" I asked.

Bill shrugged. "Most people just want to know what to do and it's enough to tell them the steps. But the question 'why' is a question pastors want to have answers to in our experience."

"I think that would also be true of me; what you and Sam have told me so far cooperates with most of my education and experience."

"Let's start with a joke - maybe you've heard it. There are two kinds of people in this world," Bill said.

"And?" I said.

74

"The two kinds of people: those who believe that there are only two kinds of people and those who do not."

"I have heard of it," I said.

"Who hasn't?" Bill said.

"And the point is?"

"What we believe to be the basic building blocks of church systems is based on this two part structure." Bill took a sheet of paper from his briefcase. "Here is our handout on this structure."

MODULE 1: SYSTEMIC APPROACHES TO CHANGE
Section 1: The Balancing Loop in Peter Senge's *Limits to Growth* Archetype

The image for a Reinforcing Loop is a snowball rolling downhill increasing in momentum and intensity. Happiness is an emerging trend.

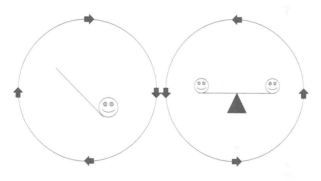

The image for a Balancing Loop is a teeter-totter.
Happiness is keeping everything in balance.

Reinforcing Loop   **Balancing Loop**

"Peter Senge uses these two components to describe the patterns into which systems form themselves. These patterns, which he calls archetypes, are built up out of two basic building blocks: reinforcing processes and balancing processes. This is the simplest system archetype and is made up of one of each."

I looked at the handout. "And the name of this archetype is *Limits to Growth*?"

"We think it is very interesting to apply this system

75

pattern to identify *limits to growth* in church growth situations."

"That would be interesting," I said.

"Senge draws these as two circles the same size. Happiness for a balancing loop is for everything to remain stable and comfortable. Balancing loops preserve homeostasis; they evolved and exist to control their environments and keep them running smoothly. Please look at the list of values in the Balancing Loop column."

Balancing Loop
Smooth Cycles
Preserves Stability
Comforting
Resisters
Management
Micro-managers
Details
Reactive
Responds to Anxiety
Institutional
Risk averse
Pragmatic majority - 84%
Church of Power (church)
Thesis and Synthesis
Inward focus
Maintenance
Resistance to Growth
Prevents Competency Limits
Under control
Thermostat correction

"Recognize any similarities with your local church?"

"Absolutely. The church board, the trustees, the finance committee and all of the traditional church members."

"The balancing process people are in tension with the people in the reinforcing process. Both loop or repeat endlessly, but the reinforcing loop is a process for change."

"A teleological process," I said.

76

"Yes, Sam loves that word. A process that attempts to persuade, sell, influence, manipulate or even intimidate the balancing process into change."

"An antithesis to the thesis," I said.

"Yes, Sam loves those terms as well," Bill said. "Can you see how these two systems can lead to church conflict if they can't learn how to cooperate?"

"Endless conflict," I said.

"And this conflict limits growth," Bill said.

"How?"

"Here's how Senge describes it: the reinforcing trend brings a change related to growth which puts pressure on the ability of the balancing system to cope. As the balancing system struggles to keep everything functioning smoothly, problems develop because the change is a bit beyond its current ability to cope. Usually these problems involve a delay, often in increasing the capacity of the system to deal with the additional work. These delays often cause problems with the reinforcing process, resulting in the growth going away."

"Can you give me an example?"

"The sales team is a reinforcing process, attempting to change the number of customers and orders. When they succeed, this puts stress on the ability of the balancing loop to fulfill those orders. This usually results in a delay due to the depletion of inventories, the need to expand manufacturing, a shortage of raw materials or some other problem in supplying the product. Sometimes the delay causes poor quality service or is related to a need to expand trained, quality staff. These problems cause customers to go elsewhere, thereby solving the 'problem' of growth beyond system capacity."

"Do you have a church example?"

"Double your current worship attendance; all those new people are the reinforcing loop demanding services from the balancing loop. What happens?"

"Income goes up. The need for more parking allows us to fulfill a long term plan to buy property next door."

"And that takes time?'

"Yes."

"Meanwhile, your new members park two blocks away on the streets and walk?"

"Or our committed members park two blocks away and walk."

Bill laughed out loud and after a while I joined him.

"You can see the problem with that, right John?"

"My long term members would call for reserved parking next to the door for themselves."

"Didn't they use to rent pews to raise money?"

"Renting parking ... perhaps parking meters ... there's a fund raiser," I said.

"There's conflict involved in adjusting to new people. Due to the conflict and the natural delay in expanding service to these new people, the discomfort in attending your church increases. If it increases enough, it outweighs the benefits of attending your church, and attendance recedes to the level where your church can cope smoothly with it."

"That's pretty pessimistic," I said.

"And pretty realistic," Bill said. "So what happens when problems develop that threaten the growth that the reinforcing people worked so hard to cause?"

"They get unhappy with the balancing process?"

"They get unhappy and they begin to exercise leadership."

I made the sign of the 'L' on my forehead. Bill nodded and said, "Look at the list of characteristics under the reinforcing loop."

Reinforcing Loop
Emerging Trend
Brings Change
Exciting
Conductors
Leadership
Big Picture
Vision
Proactive
Responds to Potential

Entrepreneurial
Ready to gamble
Visionary Minority - 16%
Church of Piety (sect)
Antithesis
External focus
Mission
Evangelism
Ignores Limits
Out of control
Pushes the trend

"These are all characteristics of leadership, right?"

"Yes," I said. "But they are good, aren't they?"

"Yes, they are good. But what is the result of the exercise in leadership in this type of case?"

"Resistance in the balancing loop. Passive aggressive and covert."

"Which makes the problems worse?"

"Yes," I said.

"Because the leaders don't have the cooperation of the followers?"

"Yes."

"And what happens if the pressure from leadership increases?"

"The resistance increases?"

"Yes. Over and over again. To what point?"

"I don't know," I said.

"To the point of violence and system collapse. There are two things we learn from this understanding of systems. First, because the Balancing Loop never gives in, leadership of this type never works. Pressure escalates until the balancing loop collapses. And what happens then?"

"Uninhibited change? A freely flowing system where no one can control others? Freedom?"

"Can you give me an example of this sort of freedom?"

"How about the teenage years?"

"And what would happen if teenagers ran the world after all the more mature people disappeared?"

"It wouldn't be pretty," I said "It would be self-indulgent and dysfunctional. It would lurch from one hypothesis to another, one crisis to another, one solution which wouldn't work to another."

"Why?"

I shrugged. I had no answer.

"Because when the balancing system collapses," Bill said, "the part of the system that keeps order disappears. The managers disappear, leaving the leaders in charge of the system."

"A system of leaders uninhibited by managers?"

"Yes."

"And this isn't good?" I asked.

"It's a total disaster. Remember, the balancing system keeps order and stability; that's a function of management. Leadership brings change and direction, but doesn't provide the production capacity to achieve any of those ambitious goals and plans. That's what management does."

"Do you have an example?"

"Absolutely. Israel destroyed the balancing system in Palestine. And the USA destroyed the balancing system in Iraq by taking out Saddam Hussein."

"Don't you believe that this was a good thing?"

"Successful change is not merely about the change; it's restoring stability and smoothing functioning after a change. That's the only way that a change lasts. What's the result of a non-functioning balancing system?"

I thought for a minute. "Chaos. Terrorism."

"When there is nothing but a reinforcing system, the reinforcing system attacks and destroys the developing balancing system, just as moderate leaders were killed off in Palestine and Iraq."

"Saddam Hussein did that prior to the war," I said.

"True, but the vacuum of stabilizing forces creates an ongoing nightmare. So an essential priority in change is not the change itself, but how to maintain the balancing system during the change. That's the main characteristic of effective, successful change."

"Could you explain that? I'm not sure I

understand."

"We call it *Senge's Solution*. For effective change it is important not to challenge or attack the balancing system; that results in a counter attack that prevents the change."

"What should be done instead?"

"If you can strengthen the capacity of the balancing system to maintain order and smooth functioning while incorporating the change, it will often do exactly that."

"So this is a shock; you are saying that effective management is more important for change than leadership."

"Exactly. Leadership without management is a pep talk to an army without ammunition, food or gasoline. The people who call for leadership as the solution for everything automatically assume that top notch management will be present to implement their ideas. But quality management is rare and poor management is the cause of practically every failure."

"So how do I do this in my church?"

"Recognize your managers and recognize your leaders; each group needs different leadership from you to be effective. Encourage each person to serve in the area of their greatest effectiveness. Second, shift your leaders more to innovation and entrepreneurial activity - new stuff - while your managers keep the routine machinery running. Third, guide your leaders into developing functional prototypes rather than grandiose plans."

"What do you mean by a grandiose plan?"

"Most impractical leadership plans begin with the destruction of the balancing system machinery. For example: tear down the existing building and build a new one. It is extremely rare for a management system to allow itself to be destroyed in order to create something new. If the new thing is created as a prototype - usually a small group - then it can usually be expanded and adopted by the balancing system without a problem."

"I understand resistance to tearing down a building, but I've never known a church to do that," I said.

"How about changes in worship? Do away with everything that people like now in order to hypothetically attract new people at some point in the future? In a retail store it would be suicidal to alienate your existing customers."

"But how would you do a prototype of a worship service? You would have to change the main service."

"Think about it for a minute," Bill said.

"You could experiment with new worship forms in a new worship service. But adding a new service on Sunday would be expensive. In order to be a real test, it would have to have the best time slot."

"Destroying the current reality ... you can do better." Bill told me.

"Sunday night then."

"One time, then once a month to start. Let it draw its own audience."

"Or a special service - Ash Wednesday."

"Or a small group. Or a small season - like Lent. Or a small time - the fifth Sunday of the month, four times a year. The balancing system doesn't mind experimentation as long as it is not an imposition. Start small."

"So don't replace, add something and go with what works?"

"Yes. We call it the Structural Principle: *The problem is not to change or replace structure but to utilize existing structures for disciple making.*"

"Does the reinforcing process ever destroy the balancing process by accident?"

"Never. We believe it is an error for Senge to draw the two as equal sized circles." Bill turned the piece of paper over and drew a large circle. "This is the balancing system circle." Then he drew a smaller circle about one fifth the size. "This is the reinforcing circle."

"That small?"

"That small ... or smaller."

"Can you justify that size?" I asked.

"Yes, and scientifically. Have you ever heard of the diffusion of innovations?"

"No."

82

"The diffusion of innovations is the scientific sociological study of change in cultures and organizations. It's findings are generally accepted as universal, applying to every nation and culture, primitive and modern."

"So there is a scientific study of change?"

"Yes," Bill said. "The basic book is Everett Rogers' *The Diffusion of Innovations*. And it blends very well with Senge's limits to growth systems archetype."

"So it's another two part structure."

"If you twist it a bit, as David Oliver has done, in applying it to churches."

Underneath the small circle Bill wrote the terms "reinforcing process" and "visionary minority." Under the larger circle he wrote the terms "balancing process" and "pragmatic majority."

"These bottom terms are Oliver's. The diffusion of innovations has actually calculated the percentages. The balancing process controls 84% of the people, votes and resources. What does that leave for the reinforcing process?"

"Only 16%," I said.

"This is why 90% of changes fail to be fully adopted. The majority prefer things to be kept as they are."

"But it would seem to me that the percentages would be reversed," I said.

"Where would you get that idea?" bill asked.

"From the popular culture. After all, everything is changing, isn't it?"

"Really? Please explain exactly how everything is changing."

"The pace of change is accelerating rapidly. Everyone knows that."

"John, when everyone knows something, it's no longer true. If things are changing. But point out a change to me."

"OK, fashion."

"What exactly changes, John?"

"All the styles change all the time."

"Of course they do, John, Here they do," he said,

tapping the 16% circle. "These people are constantly changing. Now, identify a change for the pragmatic majority."

I looked at the larger circle and thought about the fashion sense of the majority. Young people wore jeans now, 20 years ago in the '90's, forty years ago in the '70s, sixty years ago in the '50s. Tennis shoes had changed but were still basically shoes. High heeled shoes for women changed but were still basically the same. "Technology," I said. "Cell phones."

Bill shrugged. "Variations on a theme. What's the latest change with cell phones?"

"Texting?"

"Exactly. Texting follows email which follows telegrams which follows snail mail. It's the same basic thing only improved by technology."

"Computers?"

"Computers mimic things that were done before computers. Word processing follows type writers. Databases follow file cabinets. Ipods and MP3 players follow home stereos. Microwaves follow ovens."

"Is there a principle of familiarity here?"

"Exactly," Bill smiled. "If it's an improvement on an existing system, the balancing system can very easily incorporate the change into normal standard operating procedure. Elaborations on a familiar theme are easier to accept; discontinuous change is a lot harder."

"This is all very interesting," I said.

"Later when you meet with David Oliver he will discuss the implications of the diffusion of innovations for disciple making."

"High tech disciple making?" I asked.

"Not at all," Bill said, pulling a second piece of paper from his briefcase. "Take a look at this."

Change Within Systems

Creation is constantly changing, and change is a part of creation's intelligent design. Balance is maintained in nature by systems; systems pervade all of creation, including human behavior and culture. Spirituality is not a static reality but a

84

journey of growth; conversion is a change, evangelism is a change, and learning is a change. Grace, whether prevenient, justifying, or sanctifying, is a process of change; therefore, grace and the gospel are always extraordinary, entering systems as foreign influences contrary to the status quo. Change comes to a system first as new information, then as new decisions, and finally as new behaviors. Obedience to the Great Commission requires understanding systems and how to further change within systems of human culture; most planned change initiatives fail. Scientific, sociological study of systems, culture, and change, therefore, is a valuable resource in forming an ecclesiology which seeks to reproduce the discipleship system taught by Jesus in the New Testament. That discipleship system is designed with a dual function. It overcomes resistance to change as it makes disciples in the manner specified by the four requirements of the Great Commission.

The gospel enters human social networks in four basic ways. Traditional church growth theory advocates a "person of peace" approach along networks of family and friends; two other forms of kinship are shared interests and geographical proximity. A fourth approach, the diffusion of innovations, provides a scientific explanation for systemic change and explains how these social networking strategies function. The diffusion of innovations is concerned with "how to bring about change in a social structure and how to speed up the rate of adoption of that change." The goal of this project is to provide simple, effective tools for the majority of individuals in the majority of churches in the ministry context to experience Jesus as Lord, become disciples and spread that experience through their relational networks as disciple makers. This chapter assumes a familiarity with concepts and terminology explained and referenced in the rest of the project in order to concisely present an implementation strategy.

Systems preserve current homeostasis. Systemic resistance to change is a primary barrier to the spread of the gospel. Peter Senge's Limits to Growth systems archetype describes how systems limit church growth through the interaction of reinforcing and balancing processes. Systems, by their nature, can only accept, support and promote changes that seem to have no chance of altering homeostasis. As all that is commonly known to be true supports homeostasis, a new paradigm of successful systemic change will be paradoxical, contrarian, and fiercely resisted. A second goal of this project is to prepare disciple-making tools which can operate without

85

"The system will normally resist anything that has a realistic chance of changing it and disciple making is a significant change." Underneath the larger circle Bill wrote a new term: *church system.* "Your local church basically operates as a balancing system with all the goals listed in the column describing a balancing loop. It exists to keep everything running smoothly and comfortably."

"Wow. That is exactly the way it works," I said.

"And the greatest discontinuous change your church will face is incorporating and adopting to the desires and needs of new people, especially if they are different because they are a younger generation or another ethnic or socioeconomic group."

"That's true. We can't even hold onto our own children."

"Is that really honest John? Isn't it more true that church systems reject their own children? Reject their values and their needs?"

"That is more true. Unfortunately."

"Our intention is to change the target focus of the reinforcing loop from changing the temple to changing individual people. We want to divert the energy of new converts from trying to change the church system into something we feel is more rewarding: growing up within the nurture of the discipleship system. To us this means investing energy first into becoming disciples and then investing energy into fulfilling the Great Commission. Trying to change *the way we've always done it around here* usually frustrates and alienates everybody."

I was familiar with that sort of frustration.

Bill looked at his watch. "Are you and Ruth busy after church tomorrow afternoon?"

"I don't think so."

"How would you like to come over to our house for lunch? Burgers, hot dogs, basic stuff."

"I'll check with Ruth, but we usually go out for lunch. So I don't think we have any conflict that would keep us from doing that."

86

"That would be great!" Bill closed his briefcase and clicked the latches into place.

"I can show this to Ruth?"

"Of course. You want another copy?"

"No, this one's fine. And do I have homework?"

Bill smiled. "You're starting to figure us out now, aren't you?"

"With Sam, there was always homework."

"The assignment for this phase is to write your own version of the Centering Prayer. But you've got a few weeks to think about it before you do it. And I've got some samples of other prayers you can look at if you want."

"Great!" I said, with pleasure. This was fascinating stuff. "I'll see you tomorrow!"

Ruth reminded me how easy it was for me to get wrapped up in concepts and forget the practical. "Did you ask him what I could bring with us to lunch?"

"No."

"John, I have to bring something."

"He said burgers and hot dogs on the grill. You could make a salad or we could buy some chips."

"I'll think of something."

I took her through the brochure and showed her the Centering Prayer. We prayed it out loud together:

Lord Jesus, today I am far less than the person I want to be or can be with your help. I ask today that you would be more and more the center of my life. Guide me to all that is good, cleanse me from all that is not. Teach me Your ways and form in me Your nature. Help me to serve you as I am gifted. Work through me to redeem my neighborhood. I am a sinner; please be my Shepherd, my Savior and my Lord. Amen.

"John, do you understand the implication of what they are saying?"

"Which particular implication, Ruth?"

She rolled her eyes at me. "You are so conceptual. What is the practical application of what they are

87

teaching?"

"I am supposed to help someone else become a Christian?"

"And then?"

"Help raise them till they are fully grown?"

"And then?"

"And then they'll help someone else become Christian and help them to be fully grown. It's not rocket science, Ruth. It's pretty simple."

"John, you are not getting it. Maybe that seminary training has clogged up your ears or you really are the administrator of a spiritual orphanage."

"Maybe I am running an institution. It doesn't have to be like an orphanage."

"John, you can cram 50 or a 100 kids into an orphanage; you hire a staff to take care of them. Even in the church, you want to hire staff to do the work you can't get to. You are still thinking institutionally."

"I'm good with groups of people."

She rolled her eyes at me with exasperation. "John, I want to have another baby."

I froze. "Honey, if you want another baby, we'll have another baby. But we ought to think about it and pray about. Little John takes a lot of work, and it feels like we are finally getting caught up. I don't want to neglect him if we have another child."

"John, I want to have twins!"

Something is wrong here.

"Triplets, John," she shouts. "No - quints!"

"Honey, you'd have to quit your job if we had quintuplets."

"No, John, you'd have to quit your job too! Don't you get it ... what they are talking about is you taking total responsibility for another person, just like a parent. An orphanage graduates kids and they go off on their own. They go away! But if you have a child, that responsibility is forever, and then you are responsible for grandchildren, and so on and so on forever!"

"Oh, no. You are right." I thought of all the demands made upon parent of infants. "I think running the orphanage would be easier than parenting baby Christians."

"John, you have to take this seriously. The kind of involvement that Bill is talking about is a lot more than you have now with any of your church members. Are you willing to invest that much of yourself personally?"

"I hadn't thought about it like that, Ruth. I honestly hadn't."

"I think I know why this died out over 2000 years of church history," Ruth said. "People chickened out and left it up to the church to raise their spiritual children. It was easier."

It was rather disquieting to hold her that night, and harder than normal to be thankful. If this was what God wanted in order to make disciples, my life was going to get a lot more complicated. That night I dreamed of baby Christians in diapers, all crying to be changed. It was not an easy night.

CHAPTER FOUR: Be One
(Sunday, February 8)

I got a surprise Sunday morning; Bill and his
family, all six of them, almost filled one of our empty
pews. I introduced Ruth; she immediately sat down with
Cindy and they started talking about kids. I kept an eye on
them as I made my way around the sanctuary doing my
normal routine of greeting everyone and catching up on
the details of their life. In a smaller church, relationships
are important because people are important. Bill seemed
entirely at ease visiting with his two year old while Ruth
was holding their baby. As the service started I went into
my normal zone of tending to business. During joys and
concerns I brought Bill a wireless microphone and
introduced him as my guest; he introduced his family.
After the children's time, Ruth walked them down to the
nursery so that the kids could spend time with Nell, the
woman who had worked in our nursery for years. It was as
much her ministry as mine was to preach. It was a good
Sunday, and it seemed like Bill and Cindy were enjoying
the service and the sermon.

After the service was over, Ruth and Cindy left
together while Bill waited for me. The women would take
the children over to Cindy's house and Bill and I would
follow later. Bill ran his fingers over the books in my office
and pulled out one to look over. "I'll be fine," he told me,
"I know you need to lock up and take care of things." He
put that book back and pulled out another while settling
himself in one of my guest chairs. Twenty minutes later
we were on the way to the store to pick up some chips and
soda pop for the picnic.
Bill's house was a small ranch in a working class
neighborhood of Murphyville. A little sign in the front
yard indicated that Cindy's Day Care happened here; as
we pulled up I could hear the kids yelling with joy in the
backyard.
"They love the equipment," Bill said. "We've got
lots of toys and on Sundays they don't have to share with

anyone. When they get cold from being outside we'll send them down into the basement."

I helped Bill carry things into their little house and set them on the kitchen counter top. Ruth and Cindy were sitting at the kitchen table visiting while watching the kids play on the miniature playground Cindy had set up in the back yard for her daycare.

Bill kissed his wife and I kissed mine. He opened the second refrigerator in the kitchen and we put the soda pop we had bought in where it would get cold. "See something you like?" he asked, and I got a can of my favorite.

"Fire started, hon?" he asked Cindy.

"Ready for you, Maestro," she replied.

Bill opened the other refrigerator and pulled out a foil covered plate of meat ready to grill. We walked out into the back yard, enjoying the sunny day. St. Louis doesn't get that cold in the winter anyway, but it was an unseasonably warm week on top of that. So it wasn't at all unpleasant to stand up near the grill, absorbing the radiating heat. Bill began to unload the meat onto the grill.

"Are we going to eat all of that?" I asked. It seemed like enough food to feed an army.

"No," Bill grinned. "We use the grill about once a week and always cook extra." He indicated the preformed quarter pound hamburger patties. "If you cook these on the grill and freeze them, they taste right off the grill when you warm them up in the microwave."

"That's true," I said.

"With four kids, you learn how to economize in money and time. On the evenings when I work, Cindy pulls out the hot dogs. The kids call it a picnic and they love it."

"Sounds like a great idea. How did you like church?"

Bill smiled at my impatience for feedback. "It was good; I liked it. You showed a respect for the scripture that I appreciate."

"I'm pleased."

91

"You may be seeing more of us. That wouldn't be a problem, I assume."

"Oh, not at all," I said. "But I thought you were members at Murphyville Church. Did I misunderstand?"

"No, we are. But remember - we are followers of Jesus Christ who only attend a church. We don't belong to the church; we belong to the Lord."

"Still, aren't you members?"

"We are. Murphyville is Cindy's home church. But if Jesus calls, we follow him."

"You'd be welcome at my church."

"I'd be welcome in both places. Churches have learned a lot about welcoming people to worship. But that's not really the reason why we will be with you."

"Then what is?"

"You and I are partners. There's a greater efficiency if we attend the same church that isn't there when we are divided. Plus, we'll run into each other at the church and that will allow our partnership itself to grow and develop."

I opened the can of soda pop and saluted him with it. "To the best of all possible futures," I said.

"To the King and the kingdom," Bill replied. "There's another reason for us to take a break and visit your church. Our movement is getting ready to plant a new church in the Murphyville area; it's a tough time for the mother church and the pastor."

"Why would that be?"

"Well, there is usually some resistance to change at a time like this. Misunderstandings develop, anxiety increases. And there is little in the way of a problem to keep people cooperating in a consistent manner. There's too much of a temptation for a church to slip into the old pattern of finding unity through identifying an enemy."

"What do you mean by that?"

"The easiest way a system can prevent change is to allow a counter movement. Energy is invested in the opponents of a change so that their opposition counterbalances the forces for change. And all change has to stop until the conflict resolves. If the force for change increases, the system allots more energy to the opposition to keep things in balance."

I was familiar with that pattern. "You keep referring to a 'movement' - what exactly do you mean?"

"Five years ago Dick French was the pastor at Murphyville. They had asked for someone who could make the church grow and so the bishop sent Dick to the church as the new pastor. Our previous pastor had stayed almost 20 years and was retiring to Florida. Dick believed what they had requested and brought in a bunch of new ideas. A crowd responded and within six months the church had grown 18% in attendance."

"That's pretty awesome," I said.

"Not as much as you would think," he said. "The balancing process clamped down and for the next four years the church only grew 6% a year."

"That's still pretty good."

"Dick brought in David Oliver early on as a consultant and that helped keep the church growing and the conflict low."

"What happened?"

"Oliver's approach is low key and non-confrontative. There were some of the new folks who wanted to exercise power in the church and they began to work more effectively with the existing church people."

"Were there problems?"

"A few, but not that many. It's basically an example of the classic problem of new folks and old timers. The new folks have a consistent understanding of what it means to be church in our world today and a focus on making disciples. The old timers, honestly, want the church to remain the way it was back in their younger years."

"That's not unusual."

"The person of Dick French became the battleground for these two pushing, pulling entities. A year ago he was transferred to another church on the other side of the state."

"Which side got the new pastor?"

"Dick was able to clearly explain the dynamics of

what was happening to the personnel committee. Sam Franklin was chair at the time and had worked pretty closely with David Oliver. They were able to keep the system calm and we were able to broker a solution which made almost everyone happy." He looked at me expectantly. "Can you guess what it was?"

"I might." I thought for a moment; Sam had explained quite a bit to me. "Tell me again: who got the new pastor?"

"Our new pastor is very warm, personable, a good preacher who really enjoys visiting people in the hospital and in their homes."

"In other words, the classic pastor of the last century."

"Exactly."

"So the old timers - your word, not mine - were cared for in the appointment of a new pastor."

"Yes."

"Why was there not more conflict? Aren't the new people unhappy?"

"The potential was there for conflict. But, no, we aren't unhappy."

"Why?"

"What is conflict about anyway?"

I thought for a minute. "The power to make decisions; the distribution of scarce resources."

"There you go - no conflict."

"Now I'm really confused."

Bill smiled. "It's really simple; we are two very different kinds of people. We are so different, there isn't any conflict. Does that give you a clue?"

"How can that be so?"

"Pick an area of conflict and I'll explain."

"Worship wars, for a start. Aren't you fighting over what is going to happen in worship?"

"You met with Sam for over a week. What do you think?"

"Give me a hint."

"Two sets of people that are very different. One cares a lot about worship."

94

"The old timers."

"Why do you think we care about worship at all?"

"Oh." I thought about it a bit more. "The old timers are the worship system. Exactly."

"And if we tried to take over the worship system and control it for our benefit, there would be war, right?"

"Exactly."

"But we don't care about worship."

"But ..." I was speechless; once again, my customary professional position had misled me. "You don't care about worship?"

"Yes," Bill said, smiling and nodding. "Why would we not care?"

"The old timers are the worship system."

"Always," Bill said.

"And the way you came into the church... you are the discipleship system."

"Yes. Exactly that."

"So there aren't any real conflicts about worship because ..."

"We don't care about worship. Nothing needs to be changed to please us. Nothing needs to be done to cater to us. We're happy with the worship that is offered because we don't care."

"Why not?"

"If you breathe to stay alive, you have to have oxygen. The old timers get their oxygen from the worship service; it meets their needs for spiritual life. If you deprive someone of their oxygen, of what they consider the source for life, you are going to have a fight on your hands."

"I still don't understand why it isn't important to you."

"Spoken like a professional worship planner. In fact, you get paid for organizing and presenting quality worship. Of course it matters to you, John. As far as old timers go, you are one of them and paid by them."

"OK, I'll grant you that. I am a part of the worship system."

"We don't care about worship because we get our

oxygen from something else. We aren't really in the worship system here; we could have been if the situation had been different, but it isn't. We get our oxygen from the discipleship system, so we don't have to contend for control over worship."

"What about other conflicts?"

"What else is there in the worship system to fight over?"

I thought for a minute. "Programs - how they will be run, what will be offered, who will be in charge."

"We don't care about programs; none of us found Jesus Christ through a program. We are workers in the programs of the temple system, but we usually don't allow them to make us leaders."

"Why not?"

"If you are willing to work, they will let you contribute your energy. And serving is a part of obeying Christ. But if you are willing to let them put you in charge, then they try to control how you run your own program. So we volunteer but we don't usually allow ourselves to be talked into chairing anything in the worship system. It just leads to a power struggle. And besides, a ministry in the temple system should be led by a person called to that ministry; as we feel we are called to focus on disciple making, we have no difficulty yielding temple ministry leadership positions to those in the temple system called to lead them."

Worship, program, leadership - what was left to fight over. "Money? How about funding for your priorities?"

"In the discipleship system, what's important to us is free."

"What about staff?"

"What about it? Staff are involved in worship ... in program ... in maintenance of the temple. In the discipleship system we are all volunteers. Everything we want is free and freely given; like love or sex, the last thing you would want to do is pay for it."

I was bewildered and I guess it showed on my face.

"John," Bill said patiently, "you work for the

temple system. What a discipleship system does is something entirely different. If I needed money for something having to do with the Lord's work, I could make a few phone calls and have thousands of dollars at my disposal. But in the discipleship system, what's really important to us does not cost money."

"I'm sorry, but you are right. This is so new to me. But how would you get that money - just like that?" I snapped my fingers.

"Easy." Bill snapped his fingers back at me. "In the discipleship system, we are tithers. Jesus said that where your treasure is, there your heart is."

"Are you saying that people would reallocate money out of their giving to help you pay for your project."

"Yes," Bill smiled. "I can see you have a problem with that."

"But what will that do to the church budget?"

"John, this is all new to you but once you can see it from both sides it will be very simple. People in the discipleship system are tithers, so they are a big source of revenue for the temple system. Is that what you are saying?"

"Yes, I'm sure that the budget of the church is allocated on the expectation of that income."

"And what does the budget pay for, John?"

"Salaries. Repairs and debt service on the building. Insurance. Utilities. Office supplies. Program..." My voice trailed off.

"Exactly. The budget pays the bills of the temple system."

"And you are the discipleship system."

"Exactly. We have no bills to pay."

"The temple system, however, has grown dependent on your giving."

"No doubt. But you are missing something far more significant and simple."

"What?"

"As a disciple, I don't give to the temple. I don't give to the budget."

"Do you pledge in a church stewardship campaign?"

"No. My giving does not belong to the church. I give to the Lord Jesus Christ, who gave himself for me. I can't be bound by a promise of a pledge - which, in essence, is a contract. What I give belongs to the Lord; it's not my decision to pledge or not pledge."

"This could lead to all kinds of financial instability."

"Yes - in the temple system. But I'm not a part of the temple system. And if they tithed, people in the worship system would have plenty of money to solve any shortfall. As it is, their point of view is about how much it costs to keep the temple running. I'm not concerned about that at all because I'm not in the temple system."

"But you benefit from it."

Bill laughed out loud with delight. "Not that much; I don't get my oxygen from there, remember? But because I tithe and most of my tithe goes to unrestricted purposes, I give on average three times as much as a temple system person. So I've more than paid for whatever benefit I've received. But remember, I give to the Lord, not the temple. It's just that the Lord doesn't mind it going to the temple."

"Do the old timers understand their fiscal vulnerability?"

"Yes. But while the potential is there for them to take it for granted, they don't and we wouldn't let them. They are pretty responsible and respectful of us."

"This is really quite new."

"It's a paradigm shift, John. A change in perspective changes everything."

"My perspective is resisting this change."

"You are, as Sam likes to call it, a professional Christian."

"Why do I feel sort of guilty when you say that?"

Bill laughed heartily. "No criticism is implied at all. I have my own profession and you don't want to get me started arguing about the advantages and disadvantages of different kinds of tires. When something is your work, your bread and butter, it influences how you think about it in major ways."

"I can see that. But can a professional Christian be a disciple?"

"Of course. But if discipleship causes a conflict with your day job, you are going to have a struggle until you decide where your treasure is going to lie. You can be a professional Christian and an amateur disciple."

"Sam said that the meaning of amateur is doing it out of love."

"Exactly. And what you do out of love for Jesus Christ is a very different set of actions than what you do as a professional employee in the temple system."

"I think I like doing both."

"It's your calling, John. I, on the other hand, am incredibly passionate about well balanced radial tires." Bill gave me a moment to think and asked me a question. "Can you see the conflict now experienced by the high priest of the temple?"

"Remind me."

"The verse is from John 2." He got out a small New Testament and read: "John 2:13-22. *The Passover of the Jews was at hand, and Jesus went up to Jerusalem. In the temple he found those who were selling oxen and sheep and pigeons, and the money-changers at their business. And making a whip of cords, he drove them all, with the sheep and oxen, out of the temple; and he poured out the coins of the money-changers and overturned their tables. And he told those who sold the pigeons, 'Take these things away; you shall not make my Father's house a house of trade.' His disciples remembered that it was written, 'Zeal for thy house will consume me.' The Jews then said to him, 'What sign have you to show us for doing this?' Jesus answered them, 'Destroy this temple, and in three days I will raise it up.' The Jews then said, 'It has taken forty-six years to build this temple, and will you raise it up in three days?' But he spoke of the temple of his body. When therefore he was raised from the dead, his disciples remembered that he had said this; and they believed the scripture and the word which Jesus had*

99

spoken."

Bill closed his New Testament and replaced it in his pocket. "Jesus was perceived as destroying the temple and with it an entire religious way of life. In so doing, he was believed to be destroying the political power of the priests as well as destroying their profession. When God does miracles through a carpenter from Nazareth, the status quo is threatened. And, worse, when God does miracles through the hands of an untutored fisherman like Peter and John, who needs a temple or a priest? When the Passover with all its expensive tourist revenue is replaced by a loaf of broken bread and a single cup of wine, what happens to the temple? John 2 says that Jesus will replace the temple system with his body - the body of Christ - the discipleship system."

"That's too big a stretch for me."

"Let this simple idea settle in: the body of Christ replaces the temple. I'm a part of the body of Christ. I love the worship, I love a good sermon, I love helping with the Vacation Bible School, I love sorting through cans for the church food pantry. The body of Christ is at home in the temple; it's just that my allegiance is to the Lord Jesus Christ who died for me and rose so that I could walk in newness of life. My allegiance is not to a temple, any temple. A temple is just a means to an end."

"And what is that end for you, Bill?"

"I exist to do the will of my Lord and Savior Jesus Christ."

"Isn't that a conflict for you at times?"

"Not when I'm surrendered. The Lord wants me to love my wife, love my kids, pay my bills, tell the truth and live simply. That's not a conflict; it's simply a way to live."

"I'm going to need you to explain the discipleship system to me before I can understand it better."

"Let's do that after lunch. If I know my wife at all, by now your wife is as interested as you are in learning about how to be a disciple."

"I'm sure you are right."

After lunch, we sat around the kitchen table. We

could hear the shrieks of laughter from the family room as the children played together in the daycare area.

"I'm ready," Ruth announced.

"You're ready?" I asked.

"I'm ready to learn how to make disciples. It's time to quit stalling."

"I thought you were ready," Cindy said, smiling.

"Who's stalling?" I asked.

"We could hear you men talking out on the patio. Theory, theory, theory. Abstract. I'm ready to learn what I'm supposed to do right now."

"I'm ready, too, although I love talking about theories," I said.

Bill laughed. "Your wish is my command." He took four of the little brochures out of his briefcase and handed one to each of us. "You've seen these."

"Yes," Ruth said. "I like the name; JUMP stands for *Jesus Understands My Problems*."

"This is the JUMP group brochure; it's a complete discipleship system developed by David Oliver. It, in turn, is based on the *Life Transformation Groups* developed by church planter Neil Cole, who based his system on John Wesley's instructions to the small groups he called Bands. Our system fits into a brochure; Neil Cole's system fits onto a bookmark."

"Why have a brochure at all?" Ruth asked.

Bill grinned. "To make it easy to explain to people. After today, you should be able to use the brochure to explain the system to most people yourself."

"And to hand out when people are curious," Cindy said. "We wanted something more complete so that people could think about it and also pass it on to others for their consideration."

"It is pretty clear," Ruth said, looking through it.

"And simple. Not much theory," I said.

Bill laid the brochure out flat and pointed to the title column and tapped the line with a heart with his finger.

♡

Justifying

"A discipleship system is a process of grace. Prevenient grace is God drawing us to a moment of Justifying grace and beyond to a process of spiritual growth called Sanctifying grace. It is an ongoing conversion of our hearts to love and serve Jesus Christ as Savior and Lord."

Bill tapped the first of the three scriptures underneath the heart. "Take a look at these scriptures. Ruth, would you read the first one?"

"*Go therefore and make disciples of all nations, baptizing them in the name of the Father and of the Son and of the Holy Spirit, teaching them to observe all that I have commanded you; and lo, I am with you always, to the close of the age. Matthew 28:19-20.*"

"These verses at the conclusion of Matthew's gospel are called the Great Commission. We believe that they summarize the discipleship system of Jesus. It's a cycle. Going and making disciples involves cooperating with God in prevenient grace. Teaching them to observe all that Jesus commands us involves cooperating with God in sanctifying grace. John, please read the next verse aloud."

"*Why do you call me 'Lord, Lord,' and not do what I tell you? Luke 6:46.*"

"Spiritual growth is nothing more than learning to obey Jesus Christ. The quality of our spiritual life is measured by the quality of our obedience."

"What about free will?" Ruth asked.

Cindy looked over at her children playing in the family room. "When my children are young, rules are specific to help keep them safe. *Never cross the street without an adult.* As they mature, rules adjust: *Look both ways before you cross the street.* The meaning of obedience changes as children grow up; with maturity comes freedom, including the freedom to make our own decisions and learn from our mistakes. Eventually rules relax as they are replaced with wisdom."

"Just as long as I'm not expected to be some sort of robot," Ruth said.

"Unthinking obedience isn't at all what God desires, in my opinion," Cindy said. "This verse indicates the key problem in our discipleship: there is a gap between what we name - 'Lord' - and what we do. As sanctifying grace works upon us, our level of obedience improves."

"That makes sense," I said.

"Cindy, would you read the next verse?" Bill asked.

"*You then, my son, be strong in the grace that is in Christ Jesus, and what you have heard from me before many witnesses entrust to faithful men who will be able to teach others also. 2 Timothy 2:1-2.*"

"You'll notice that the Great Commission commands the disciples to teach their disciples how to obey the commands of Jesus Christ. We are not meant to teach ourselves or raise ourselves to spiritual maturity; we are not 'self-made' disciples, but someone else takes the responsibility to cooperate with God and come alongside us to help us grow." Bill tapped the verse from 2nd Timothy again with his finger. "Paul called this being a spiritual parent. If that level of responsibility seems too challenging, think of a big brother or big sister. Timothy, likewise, was to have that role with 'faithful men' who would then play that role with others. The end result is multiple generations of disciples, or as we say, *disciples making disciples making disciples.*"

"Ruth and I talked about this," I said. "Taking responsibility for others is a little daunting."

"Raising a child is a big challenge," Cindy admitted. "But if we consider what's happening around this table right now as spiritual parenting, realize that 'raising' you and Ruth is going to be a lot easier than potty training those four little savages in the other room!"

I smiled. "You're right. We're already house broken."

"What's scary to most people," Bill said, "is taking

any responsibility at all for another person's welfare. We want all the nurture to flow toward us but we resent any interference with our own freedom to do what we want. How old is that?"

"I beg your pardon," I said, not understanding.

"About 2 years old," Ruth commented. "That's when we are not aware of anyone's needs but our own."

"A lot of Christians never grow up past those self centered early childhood years," Cindy said.

"I believe I've served congregations with several hundred people just like that," I said.

"Exactly," Cindy said. "Without a discipleship system to help them to grow, most Christians are stuck in spiritual infancy."

"That's not a very comforting image," I said.

"No, it's not," Cindy said. "In a way, both of us run a daycare." She smiled at my frown.

"Aren't we supposed to get this sort of spiritual parenting directly? From God?" Ruth asked. "After all, isn't God supposed to our heavenly Father?"

"True," Bill shrugged. "We refer to God as Father, but Jesus commanded us to play this role with one another. To expect God to do it all is not only disobedient, it's a way to perpetuate our own immaturity."

"I guess what you are saying is that we delegate our task of helping others grow up spiritually to God, and then complain about the job that God is doing," I said.

"Exactly. We do delegate the Great Commission to God, but if you take the Bible seriously, it's obvious that God has delegated it to us."

Bill opened the brochure to the inside column. "This column is for Justifying Grace. It explains the system's origin and has a prayer for Justifying grace. Let's pray the prayer now." We all prayed in unison:

"Lord Jesus, today I am far less than the person I want to be or can be with your help. I ask today that you would be more and more the center of my life. Guide me to all that is good, cleanse me from all that is not. Teach me Your ways and form in me Your nature. Help me to serve you as I am gifted. Work through

me to redeem my neighborhood. I am a sinner; please be my Shepherd, my Savior and my Lord. Amen."

"It's important to remember that you can't make yourself a Christian," Bill said. "Only God can do that, but God is ready to answer a prayer like this one. It's carefully written so as to serve two purposes: to be a prayer for salvation the first time, and a prayer for rededication every other time, so that Jesus Christ as Lord can become more and more the center of our lives."

"What's the history of this prayer?" I asked.

"When Dr. Oliver was in a class for his doctor of ministry degree, the professor gave writing such a prayer as an assignment for the class. The professor was a church planter who had put such a prayer for conversion in his worship bulletin on Sundays when the church would have communion. After a while he began to notice that, when asked when God became real to them, people in his church would say that it was after praying the prayer in the bulletin. God answers this sort of prayer."

"You can write your own," Cindy said. "They ask each of us to do that. What's hard is to balance the three aspects: to pray for justifying grace, to ask for maturity as sanctifying grace, and to include prevenient grace."

I peered at the prayer. "What part refers to prevenient grace?"

"Which part seems odd to you?"

"Work through me to redeem my neighborhood."

"There it is," Bill said. "Once you've prayed and God has answered a prayer for justifying grace, you are ready to become a disciple. You've entered the part of the process which is sanctifying grace."

"When do we begin to make disciples?" I asked.

"The first part of making disciples is to *be one*. We call that the first part of sanctifying grace and give it a special name: *ascending grace*." Bill opened the brochure to the inside three columns. "There are three basic tasks in *ascending grace*. They form the sanctifying grace phase of the JUMP group discipleship system: *Partnership, Bible Reading* and *Questions* for accountability."

"That's all?" I asked.

105

"That's enough," Bill replied, opening the brochure to lay open and flat so that all three columns were visible. "The first task is partnership. Take a look at the right column - read it over."

Partnership

*"For where **two or three** are gathered in my name, there am I in the midst of them."*
Matthew 18:20

Something unique happens when we become partners in faith with one to three other people. We learn more, and we enjoy it more. Jesus says, literally, that He is present in a unique way when two or three people gather.

You can grow spiritually through your own private prayers, but your growth can be doubled if you meet with another, and tripled if you and your partner invest yourselves in a third and fourth person.

Spiritual partners meet together once a week at a convenient time for about an hour or less. During that time you answer the Questions honestly.

Here are some tips for choosing a spiritual partner:
1. Partners should be of the same sex - men with men and women with women.
2. A partnership of two will open up to include a third and fourth person, and then open further into 2 groups of 2 persons.
3. Partnerships are not forever - these spiritual friendships of two to four persons are very flexible, forming and reforming as seems to be meaningful. This allows meaningful spiritual friendships to develop with a variety of people and builds a spiritual network within the church.

If no one comes to mind as a partner for you, let me know and I will help you find one!

"The first thing to notice, of course, is the promise of Jesus: where two or three are gathered in my name, there am I in the midst of them." Bill looked up at Ruth and I.

"We have a tendency to take this for granted," Bill said. "But it's the heart of everything. Jesus said that he would be with us always - and he is. But when we are with another believer 'gathered in Christ's name' Jesus is there in an even more tangible, real manner."

"Traditionally, in prayer, you are supposed to go off alone, into a monastery or up on a mountaintop, to be isolated in order to be in touch with God," Bill said. "This statement of Jesus contradicts that human tradition: if we want to truly be with Jesus, we need to link up with one or more Christians in a small group."

"You don't think this is also true when a hundred people are present for worship?" I asked.

"It's true," Bill shrugged. "But Jesus deliberately placed the emphasis here on two or three. When Jesus sends the twelve in Matthew or the seventy in Luke out to minister, he sends them in partnerships of two. Throughout the gospels we hear of Peter, John & James; in Acts it's Paul and Barnabas plus Mark and Silas. There are too many New Testament examples of smaller groups of two or three or four people to ignore."

"I agree," I said.

"So do I," Ruth said.

"Therefore, we believe that partnerships are important. They are important enough to be specific about. The reason that Cindy and I wanted to invite you to our home today is to offer you both the opportunity for partnership."

I looked at Ruth; she nodded and smiled at Cindy. "Cindy and I've already worked it all out between us, John."

I looked at Bill. "So will we be a group of four or two groups of two?"

"We believe that two groups of two will feel more of an internal pressure to grow to become two groups of three or four."

"You also believe in men with men and women with women."

"Yes. Why would you think?"

I took a breath. "Ruth and I already have a partnership. Spouses would be more hesitant to split up; they'd want to stay together forever. So it would defeat the purpose of evangelism."

"Good point," Bill said.

"Men and women have difference communication styles and that would help people open up," Ruth said.

"We also find that to be true. Our women's groups like to visit, while men's groups rush through their meeting and then go shoot baskets ... at which time they do the same sharing that the women do."

"And there are problems when a man and a woman share deeply intimate and emotional experiences with each other," Cindy said. "A bonding occurs which is so like courting that emotions and physical feelings can get out of hand."

"What happens with people who are attracted to someone of the same sex?" Ruth asked.

"We believe that partnerships are not forever and that as new groups form, it links people together in a network. Normally, if you are a convert, you would first be in a JUMP group with the person that converted you. In the case where this is a man and a woman, the convert is referred to someone who steps in and who would be someone to whom they are not sexually attracted. As people select their partners, we trust them to police each other. If a person is hiding their sexual orientation, when they are comfortable enough to be honest, they keep in touch with their original partner but begin to work with another person where that sexual energy doesn't interfere with their spiritual growth."

"Bill, I'd be pleased if you would be my partner in this," I said.

"I'd be happy to do that, John."

"How long do partnerships normally last?" I wondered.

"It depends on the person, John," Cindy answered. "Partnerships conclude when someone drops out - they aren't ready for the level of spiritual discipline - or when two new disciples join the partnership. When you invite a third person to join the JUMP group with Bill, the process will begin for the two of you to have your own group."

"What if two people join?"

"A group of four would open further to become two groups of two. One person would go with you for partnership, while another would go with Bill."

"Let's say I get two other guys to join us for next week. What then?"

"It normally doesn't happen that fast, but if you are gifted evangelistically, you'll have a tendency to impact people that way. That's why you stay in touch with Bill."

"What do you mean by that?"

"If your own group starts very soon - 3-6 months is typical - you would probably continue to meet with me first on a weekly basis, then every other week."

"And beyond that?"

"We get together in a larger group twice a month. The Gathering is the meeting with everyone who is in a JUMP group. Solomon's Porch is a second meeting for training and is open to those who have a partner in a JUMP group."

"Are partners equals?" Ruth asked. "Wouldn't they both be at the Solomon's Porch meeting?"

"Porch is about watching over your apprentice, the person you've invited into a group," Cindy said. "While our partnerships start as peers, that won't be the case when you bring someone else in. They are there at your invitation. So in that dynamic, there is already a big brother/little brother pairing whenever disciple making is happening."

"When you invite someone into our partnership, then you will go to Porch," Bill said.

"So basically, everyone sees everyone once a month at the Gathering?"

"Yes. And the senior members of partnerships see each other twice a month, at Porch and at the Gathering."

"So even after we formed new groups, we would still see each other on a regular basis?"

"And work together on a regular basis. But you would have a focus on a new person who would need you."

"How do we reach out to other people?" I asked.

"That's for a later time of sanctifying grace which we call *descending grace*. First we learn how to live as a disciple, then we add to that foundation the way we live as a disciple maker. The first step in disciple making cannot be skipped: you have to be one."

"Cindy and I have already talked about the next step, so we are going to go in with the kids and visit," Ruth told me.

"There's going to be less theory in there, I bet," I said.

"And fewer questions," Ruth laughed.

"I'm sure you would agree with me that reading the Bible is a good idea," Bill said.

"Absolutely," I said.

He touched the column of the brochure headed by the title "Bible Reading" and asked me to take a minute to read it over.

Bible Reading

*Jesus then said to the Jews who had believed in him, "If you **continue in my word**, you are truly my disciples, and you will know the truth, and the truth will make you free." John 8:31-32*

Members of Jump Groups set a goal to read 28+ chapters of the Bible each week, an average of 4 per day. (At first this simple goal will seem impossible to achieve.) Most groups choose a book of the Bible and read it at this pace. The goal is to read these chapters every week - some weeks you might read less, but read the same chapters over and over again. Groups of 2-4 persons stay with the same book of the Bible until everyone has completed the reading. In one week with this plan you can read Matthew once (28 chapters) or Colossians 7 times (4 chapters).

This method of reading the same section of Scripture over and over has several advantages. First, you can read it like a newspaper - read over it all, but you don't need to concentrate on every word. Second, by reading the same chapters over and over you will eventually memorize them without any significant effort. Third, your familiarity over multiple readings will result in sudden insights as God opens up deeper meanings and connects the various ideas together. Fourth, you are building a good habit of reading God's word regularly.

Some people don't enjoy reading, so even one chapter a day is a challenge for them. Yet even one chapter read daily until it is familiar can make a tremendous difference in our spiritual life. ***Don't worry about it . . . just do it!***

And as your partner, I am always available to answer

questions about a Bible passage and its meaning. Just ask - but you'll be surprised how much you learn in several weeks of reading.

"Twenty-eight chapters a week," I whistled.

"It's a challenge," Bill acknowledged.

"Ruth and I read two a day and we thought we were pretty hot dog," I said.

"Actually, John, that's pretty good. There are a lot of weeks that that is my average for the week."

"We read the same chapter twice a day. Does that count as one or two?"

"It counts as two. Long as it is a whole chapter."

"We read it separately in the morning and discuss it together at night after reading it one more time out loud."

"That's a great idea that Cindy and I will have to try."

"I like it," I smiled. "It's my favorite time of day."

"Which book do you want to read?"

"We read the same one together?"

"Yes. It lets us answer each other's questions."

"We are reading the gospel of Mark now in church. Would that work for you?"

"It's 16 chapters long. Do you think we can do it twice in a week?"

"We can try."

"John, don't feel like this is something macho. I've had men drop out of meeting with me because they couldn't get all the chapters read in a week. They were too proud to tell me that they hadn't made it."

"I won't have the problem; I'm sure I won't make it. But it will be worth trying."

"We have a system on the *Question* side to try to take the sting out of it. If you read one chapter, you are in first grade; six chapters, sixth grade. Seven plus chapters, Freshman, 14 plus Sophomore, 21 plus Junior, 28 plus is Senior. This way a guy can admit how much he's done without, hopefully, feeling bad about it."

"Why don't you just decrease the goal?" I asked.

"Neil Cole originated this spiritual discipline and he's pretty adamant about not decreasing the expectation of chapters - even though he knows most men won't achieve the goal."

"What's the difference?" I asked.

Bill shrugged. "Some weeks you make the goal; that feels really good. Another reason is that these small partnerships are for pretty serious Christians, and having the self discipline to read the Bible is a good way to identify those whose commitment is weak."

"Do you kick people out for that?"

"No, we don't have to. Immature people have an ego - they will remove themselves if you give them a challenging goal to reach."

"I think - yes, Sam called that a speed bump."

"Exactly. It just helps separate those who are serious from those who are not. Neil Cole's other expectation is that there is nothing more powerful than the word of God in a Christian's life. He calls it the seed; you sow the seed and you bear fruit."

"Jesus called it the seed as well."

"We've seen amazing things happen when people become familiar with the Bible. A situation comes up in their lives and their memory dredges up a Bible verse that applies - so our Bible reading influences how we live due to familiarity. And by reading chapters in context, we learn the meaning of verses in their context. It can be life changing."

"I agree with that whole heartedly. Are we going to go over the whole book when we meet? That's a lot for a Bible study."

"Our partnership isn't a Bible study, so we don't go over it; we just ask you to read it and apply it to your life. If you have a question, you can ask it, but normally we find that people understand what they are reading."

"Some parts of the Bible aren't that easy to understand."

"That is true, but as we focus on working individually with new Christians, we don't really get to those. Some partnerships will read in the Old Testament, for example, but we recommend that people start with the gospels and learn them thoroughly. After all, Christians should focus on Christ, right?"

"I can understand that priority."

"After the gospels, Acts. Then the rest of the New Testament. It's not that common for a partnership to get into the Old Testament before it reforms with a new disciple who needs to learn the words of Jesus."

"So you wouldn't read the prophet Habbakuk, for example?"

"Probably not. The joke is that when you get to heaven, you can study Habbakuk with the help of the original author. The focus of the JUMP group is on teaching new converts to observe all that Jesus commanded; so we want them to first focus on all that Jesus commanded."

"This would scandalize some of my colleagues who think that Habbakuk is really important."

"All the Bible is important, but we give the priority to the words of Christ."

I thought for a minute. "Most of the controversial passages are outside the gospels, so that may be another advantage."

"That's true. It's kind of interesting how the gospels seem more and more relevant for today even if people want to argue with Paul about some of his issues."

"True. So we won't be studying the Bible?"

"The focus is on you applying it to your life. What you will do is answer the question about what you believe God wants you do based on what you read. We want people to be able to learn how to hear the leading of the Lord through reading the Bible to the point of familiarity."

"Any tips or tricks?"

"I keep a notebook handy to jot observations into it when I read. I also write down questions. It's funny how if I write a question about something I don't understand, in a day or so I get an answer. It just comes to me."

"So how do we get started?"

"We pick a time to meet and then you go home to read the Bible and pray. The next time we'll use the questions."

"And I know there's an assignment in here, right, Bill?"

"There's always homework, but not till after next week. And we'll start with one question the first week, and add another question each week for seven weeks. This will allow us time to talk about the purpose and meaning behind each question. We want you to consider writing your own questions, and adding one a week gives you time to think about what they mean to you. "

"And I need to write my own prayer, too."

"Sometime."

"Bill, why don't you and Cindy join us for lunch next Sunday after church? It's our turn."

"I'm sure Cindy would like that if it is OK with Ruth."

"We'll check and let you know. Gospel of Mark, twice this week, right?"

"Right. It's 32 chapters but the 16th is pretty short."

"Relax, Bill; we'll be in this book for a while."

"Nothing wrong with that; it's all good," Bill said, smiling.

CHAPTER FIVE: The Questions
Sunday - February 15

Life began to settle down into a rhythm as I practiced the JUMP group discipleship system. I still read one chapter of Mark in the morning and read it again to Ruth that night; she and Cindy were also doing Mark. At lunch and before leaving work for home, I would read two other chapters. If I missed that time, I would read them before bed and before Ruth and I talked. While I consider myself a fast reader, it really didn't take much time. Bill had pointed out that the type of reading we wanted was like reading a newspaper; don't get stuck on one phrase or sentence and stop. If one sentence did speak to us, he said, make a note and meditate on it through the day.

Previously when reading the Bible, I would start and stop in a jerky manner as I analyzed each verse in detail and sometimes each word. What else is it when you stop to look up a word in the original Greek? Reading the whole chapter in context helped me to better understand the individual verses better, and reading the whole book in a few days helped me to understand the chapters better. Learning is better in context, Bill had said. I found that it was true that reading for familiarity fed the ideas into my subconscious mind, where they would begin to link together. I began to see themes over chapters that I had missed before in the days when I studied verses rather than books of the Bible.

On Sundays, Bill and I would meet for Questions; usually after we all had lunch. After recommitting our lives to Christ with the Centering Prayer, we would go down the list of Questions.

Questions

*"**Ask**, and it will be given you; **seek**, and you will find; **knock**, and it will be opened to you. For every one who asks receives, and he who seeks finds, and to him who knocks it will be opened." Matthew 7:7-8*

1. Begin with the Centering Prayer *or one like it.*

2. What chapters in the Bible did you read? What is God telling you through what you read? What are you going to do about it?

<u>*JUMP "lite" - levels if these are too challenging:*</u>
Kindergarden   0   Bible chapters a week
Elementary: 1-6 Bible chapters a week
Freshman: 7+   chapters a week (25%)
Sophomore: 14+ chapters a week (50%)
Junior: 21+ chapters a week (75%)
Senior: 28+ chapters a week (100%)

3. What did you hear from Jesus through prayer about His will for your life this week? What are you going to do about it?

4. As a maker of disciples, who are you praying for to find Christ? How are you loving your neighbors? What conversations have you had? How has God been present? What is happening in their lives? What are you going to do next?

<u>*Questions for my own goals and growth:*</u>
5.

6.

7. Becoming like Christ: Rate yourself +/-

Love	Patience	Trustworthy
Joy	Kindness	Gentleness
Peace	Generosity	Self-control

*_____   *_____   *_____

Were you financially honest this week? (Mt 6:21)
Do you wish anyone harm?
Who needs your forgiveness?
Participate in any addictive behaviors this week?

In order to spread out the discussions on theory, we started with the second question on Bible reading and planned to add a question a week to build up speed. "It takes a little bit of time to work your way into the system," Bill said. "We're not in a hurry. What we want to do is move inexorably forward."

"Inexorable," I said.

Bill laughed. "Sam taught me that word. I like it.

Totally focused, totally intentional, unstoppable. Inexorable. When you move forward like that, but slowly, life reorganizes itself so that obstacles get out of your way." And so we moved inexorably forward in the faith.

Each week I would dutifully report to Bill that I was a "junior" - that I had read only 27 chapters - but that I had failed to read the full number we had set for our goal of 28, falling one short.

"John, you're showing off," Bill told me. "You want to stay in the same book with your congregation." He had reported the same thing.

"I like Mark. Besides, I'm doing my preaching out of it the next month. As my people are finishing it, they will be familiar with the text, so I'm going to take advantage of that." My preaching was now focusing more and more on explaining the commands of Jesus to the disciples.

"How many of your people are reading one chapter a day?"

"I don't know. A good percentage, I think; some will tell me that they are keeping up as they leave the worship service each week." We sat and thought for a moment. How could you identify who was reading and track their progress? Wasn't that the most certain way, psychologically, to help a behavior become established as a habit?

"Why don't you put out a list each week for people to sign their names and write down the number of chapters they read that week?" Bill suggested.

"I could do that."

"That would encourage them to keep up to the goal of seven in a week. Some might surprise you and read more."

"We have one couple to reads the same chapter in two different translations."

"That should count as two chapters read."

"Others are reading ahead of schedule. Others are reading any chapter they want after they read the first one."

"Nothing wrong with that. We think it's better to read it by chapters within one book so that what we read is in context. Why not count them all?"

"I like the idea, Bill."

And just as simply as that, our whole church began the process of continuing in God's word: *Jesus then said to the Jews who had believed in him, "If you continue in my word, you are truly my disciples, and you will know the truth, and the truth will make you free." John 8:31-32.* As the process solidified, we found that about 15% of my worship attenders were reading chapters in the Bible consistently. Others might also be reading and just not reporting.

"Do you understand what this means, John?" Bill asked me one Sunday.

"No, Bill, I don't really understand it. It's kind of marvelous to me; obviously I've been underestimating my people. I didn't know so many would be interested, and the names that show up on the list are likewise surprising. There's some on the list that I wouldn't expect - and others that are missing that I would have expected to be there. Some of our leaders, for example."

"So you have leaders who are not reading the Bible?"

"Yes."

"That's to be expected. I suppose it is good for you to know. But two things surprise me, and I'm going to encourage others to do this in their churches. It's a great idea."

"What two things?" I asked.

"First, the best definition of who is a disciple is what Jesus says in John 8 - that people who continue in his word are truly his disciples. As this saying occurs before the writing of the New Testament, it particularly applies to the words of Jesus. "

"So?"

"Not all people attending the temple worship services are disciples, whether that is Jewish temple services in Jesus' day or the worship services you offer each week. There are always more worshipers than disciples. In Jesus' day, it was easy to tell them apart as the ones who consistently gathered around Jesus to listen to him were most likely his disciples. But how can you tell today?"

"Tell me what you are thinking."

"In our movement, we love percentages. Did you know that on any given Sunday, according to U.S. census department time studies, that 26% of Americans will be in church worshiping?"

"That few?"

"That many?" Bill countered.

"That means," I said, pausing for a moment to do the math, "that there are over 4000 potential new church attenders in our area."

"What is that area? The village?"

"The zip code for the village and the surrounding unincorporated area."

"We use that percentage to remind people that there is always potential for evangelism when so many people do not routinely attend church," Bill said.

"Some of them will attend irregularly, so it is not as if they are unchurched."

"True, but would a disciple attend regularly?" Bill asked.

"I guess so, if obedience to Christ is a priority. Some would argue that you don't have to go to church to be a Christian, but it's hard to argue that anyone very serious about being a Christian would choose to avoid regular participation in a church."

"Being a disciple means following, which as you know, means putting Christ at a high priority in our life. That means that we follow not just when it is convenient but also when it is inconvenient."

"I agree," I said.

"And so if Christ would set the alarm, get up and go to church, you should, too. It's as simple as that."

"I agree. So what's your point?"

"When you look over the people on Sunday morning, like Jesus looked over the crowds that gathered because they wanted healing or bread or some other sort of miracle, how do you separate the disciples from the attenders?"

"One way would be a speed bump."

"And the speed bump our movement has used for disciple identification has been participation in some sort of weekly activity for learning - Sunday School, Bible study, prayer meeting. Care to guess what the percentage of attenders participate in any such activity on a weekly basis?"

"This church has about a twenty percent participation of adults in Sunday School."

"That's pretty good."

"My last church had only about a five percent participation rate."

"Wow."

"When attendance hit the high of 205, there were only eight to ten adults in Sunday School."

"And the difference between the two churches?"

"Both had good people, but this church seems a lot warmer. More accepting, and to be honest, more spiritual for that reason and less like a business organization. They are less demanding and less critical."

"Worship might draw a crowd, but it provides a weak link between people. Sunday School has a great, unrealized potential to renew a church."

"So what's the percentage?" I asked.

"Seventeen percent."

"That's about what my Bible readers are running."

"Yes, and that's interesting. Some people don't participate in an event because of they are busy, because of work or family obligations and sometimes because there isn't a group that meets their needs. These people aren't easy to identify - but they are showing up on your Bible reading list."

"So what's the other advantage, Bill?"

He smiled triumphantly. "John, you've really taught me something today that is going to benefit our movement."

"And what would that be?"

"JUMP groups are not for worship attenders; they are for disciples who are committed, growing and ready for something more - a challenge, an adventure, a chance to test their potential and learn God's will for their lives. If a committed disciple is invited to join a JUMP group and they follow the system, they will flourish. If an uncommitted attender is invited to join a JUMP group, they will fail at the system and drop out."

"They're not ready, in other words."

"No, they are not ready. Discipleship is a process of growth, so it's possible to say simply that they aren't ripe. It's not their time, and if they are picked too soon, the results are not the best."

"So what does the Bible reading have to do with this, Bill?"

"Every person on your list is reading the Bible regularly. They are continuing in the word. Therefore, they are truly disciples of Jesus Christ."

"Yes, that's obvious."

"And these are the people who are available for you to invite to be a part of a JUMP group. We've not had such a simple way to identify potential JUMP group members before. There are so many who are regularly active in worship and so many who are active in serving in church leadership positions. But those indicators don't really tell us what is happening in their spiritual lives as clearly as the indication that they are regularly reading scripture."

"I'm going to have to look over that list," I said to Bill.

"You're going to need to pray over that list. One of those people is likely to be your first partner in a JUMP group."

Ruth and I were both excited that night. I brought the bible reader list home so that we could pray over it. There was one man who listened to the Bible rather than read it. Denny worked in sales and would listen in his car going between calls and also when he exercised. The rest did it the old fashioned way, by opening the Bible and reading it.

"This is a pretty broad cross section of our church," Ruth pointed out.

"A few of them are reading more than we are."

"I wonder what they are reading?"

"I know Dolores likes the Psalms." Her totals were very high.

We talked about the day as we always did, and what

we liked about the chapter for the day. As I rolled onto my back and began to be thankful before I went to sleep, I made an interesting discovery. I realized that I really liked being a disciple. The process of being one was fulfilling me and making connections within my soul that made me feel stronger. How simple it is, I wondered, as I held my sleeping wife in my arms, to experience the bounty that comes from reading the Bible in partnership with someone.

The Next Sunday - February 22

The following Sunday Bill and I were in the living room at his house. Cindy and Ruth were in the kitchen. We began as we always did by praying the Centering Prayer and rededicating our lives to Christ.

"Have you given some thought to writing your own prayer?" Bill asked.

"Not really," I shrugged. "I like the one that we use."

"You're free to use it. But the question is whether or not it fully describes the totality of living as a Christian for you."

"My denomination would want more in there about serving - missions, feeding the hungry, helping the poor."

"That's certainly present as an emphasis in scripture."

"As a pastor, I have an interest in people discovering their gifts and learning how to use them in service - another aspect of missions. Missional."

"That's also well represented in scripture. Remember, you can write a whole new prayer or simply add sentences to the Centering Prayer."

"If I did, could I still call it the Centering Prayer?"

"We have no copyright on the term. In fact, there is a form of monastic, meditation prayer called centering prayer. So we have no claim on the name."

I had known that, having searched the internet with the term "centering prayer." Thomas Keating and Basil Pennington were the primary authors involved. "I've heard of it," I said. "But it's such a good name for what the prayer is about."

"I think so, but maybe you will come up with a better prayer. Or find something that you like that someone else has done."

"It's on my mind, but not in the forefront."

"No hurry. Let's answer the question on scripture."

I read it out loud: "*What chapters in the Bible did you read? What is God telling you through what you read? What are you going to do about it?*" This week I moved on to Luke."

"So did I. I figured you'd stay with your congregation."

"What do we do when the numbers don't nicely make up twenty-eight? Luke has twenty-four chapters."

"You do what you want. Start at the beginning or someplace in the middle and read the rest that are due for the week ... if you are going to finish."

I grinned at him. He knew what I would be doing. It would take three weeks for my congregation to make it through the Gospel of Luke.

"So, what is God telling you through what you read? And what are you going to do about it?"

"It's been a long time since I read the Bible the way I am doing now. I was preaching out of Mark and now Luke, but just to read it to let God speak to me is a new thing."

"It's a little different, I guess, when it is your job."

"That's true," I shrugged, "but it's also that in seminary you shift your focus from reading the Bible to reading what other people say about the Bible - scholars, commentaries, theologians. You read the Bible so that you can figure out how to fit it into someone else's logical configuration because that big picture will be on the test."

"Makes it seem less interesting to me."

"It's also the nature of graduate school to focus on the difficulties. What is easily understood is no challenge to a professor trying to establish his career by publishing something to draw attention to himself. For a number of years in graduate school, you would get attacked if you made a clear statement on any position - because some scholar somewhere had made his or her reputation by challenging the status quo in that area. So you learn to not make statements, but just quote scholars; that way the scholar is attacked rather than you, yourself. It's dangerous in grad school to have your own opinion."

Bill laughed long and hard. "I guess I should be very happy to have my job at the tire store."

"You could do it if you wanted to, Bill. I know from our discussions that you're pretty bright. If you wanted to go to seminary, you could."

"I could." Bill shrugged. "The idea is interesting, but only as an idea. It's expensive and would take time away from my family, but God could make a way if I were supposed to go. But it's only interesting as an idea."

"Everything starts as an idea."

"But I don't feel a sense of God wanting me to do it," Bill said. "There's an abstract curiosity about the ideas, theology and church history, but no strong pull to do it. I'm really enjoying what I'm doing now for my Lord and ready to keep on doing it."

"As you've said to me, you follow where Jesus leads you. If he wants you to go to seminary, it will happen."

"Yes, it will. And there's another problem. I don't mean to offend you, John, but I'm interested in discipleship systems. With regard to how I believe I should live my faith, I'm not certain that a seminary would have much to teach me that I would find useful in the real world."

"That's also true. Unless you want to pastor a traditional church."

"I might pastor a church someday; that's a part of our movement, did you know?"

"No, I didn't."

"But if I plant a church, it won't be a traditional church."

"Tell me more about how your movement does church planting," I requested.

"As you know, the JUMP group is based on Neil Cole's work. He is a church planter out of California of what are called 'organic' or 'simple' churches. Heard the term?"

"No."

"Some people call them house churches, but that's like considering a church to be the building where worship happens. We don't really want to buy into that imagery."

"How do you define a simple church then?"

"In the terminology we use, a simple church is the strongest possible discipleship system combined with the minimum possible traditional church temple system."

"I think I understand. No buildings, no committees, no budgets, no seminary trained clergy, no bazaars, no fund raisers, no organ, no hymnals..."

Bill was laughing as hard as he could. "I think you have the basic idea!"

"My God!" I exclaimed in staged shock. "What's left when you jettison all that makes church meaningful for us squares!"

Bill smiled. "A lot. And you know what it is: what's left after you take the temple out is everything Jesus said and did. He had none of that, and no place to lay his head."

"True," I admitted. "So tell me about the sort of church that you would plant."

"We use the discipleship system of the JUMP group to make disciples makers. The JUMP group is the leadership training system of the church."

"I take it that this is the part of the system which hasn't been explained to me."

"Correct. Disciple making is the *descending grace* part. Pastor Pam does that."

"Is it also from Neil Cole?"

"Yes, but we formulate it differently. It's not as close a copy as the JUMP group is for Neil Cole's *Life Transformation Group*. We have a specific system with steps but Neil Cole just lets it happen naturally."

"Organically," I said with a smile. "I look forward to meeting Pastor Pam."

Bill smiled an odd smile. "She's unique. There isn't anyone quite like her."

"Is she the leader of your movement?"

"What we call the movement doesn't really have a leader; we're people who are merely trying to do what Jesus did as faithfully as possible in the modern world. We have a consultant - Dr. David Oliver, you've heard his name - who is trying to get these sort of faith communities started wherever he can. And the local faith community has an organization, although we don't say much about it."

"I know you like to put information out where and when it is needed. I don't mind waiting to learn about it later."

"It's actually a Neil Cole thing, from *Leadership Farm Systems.*"

"That's an interesting phrase."

"It's his first book. With church planter Bob Logan. You can find it on the Internet if you want; the title is *Raising Leaders from the Harvest.*"

"And what was the concept?"

"It's called *just in time leadership training.* You teach something when someone is ready to use it rather than before or on some sort of arbitrary schedule."

"I can see an advantage there," I said, thinking it over.

"And that would be," Bill said, giving me time to think.

"Motivation; someone has a need and is motivated to learn how to deal with it."

Bill nodded.

"Part of this movement is letting people figure things out for themselves, too, right?"

Bill nodded, his smile widening.

"OK, then, I'll take my best shot. A motivated learner. Second, a real life situation to apply it to - and in applying it, the student not only learns but solves a problem at the same time."

Bill nodded.

I was on a roll. "They are pushed by their problem to work harder, learn faster, and get real, instant benefits from their learning."

Bill nodded, smiling.

"Fourth, because of the real life problem and the

anxiety, the lesson is very memorable. Maybe life changing, because the problem goes away."

Bill nodded, still smiling.

"It would also be cheaper."

Bill lost his smile. "How so?"

"Well, obviously, no textbooks to buy or classrooms for provide. Schools have the same administrative overload as traditional churches - their own version of the temple system."

"That's obvious," Bill said, "but nobody's ever really pointed that out before. I wonder if we will be tempted to build schools and hire teachers then, sometime in the future?"

"In two hundred years, if what Sam told me is true."

"Are you busy next Saturday night?" Bill asked me.

I ran over my schedule in my mind. "No, I don't think so. Why?"

"The Hub is meeting before the Gathering. I'd like you to come with me and talk about how you have your church reading the Bible."

I shrugged. "Sure. What's the Hub?"

"The Hub is our leadership team. They meet once a month before the Gathering and check signals at Solomon's Porch."

"And the Gathering is?"

"A monthly gathering of all people in the *ascending grace* part of the system. Those participating in JUMP groups, in other words. Or interested in them."

"What happens at a gathering?"

"Food and fellowship. Worship, prayer, testimonies of what God is doing."

"And you mentioned something else? Porch?"

"Solomon's Porch." He thumbed his New Testament open and read: "Acts 5:12-14: *Now many signs and wonders were done among the people by the hands of the apostles. And they were all together in Solomon's Portico. None of the rest dared join them, but the people held them in high honor. And more than ever believers were added to the Lord, multitudes both of men and women...*
Solomon's Portico or Solomon's Porch was an area of the

temple where the early disciples would gather. A 'portico' is a roof supported by a double row of columns placed at regular intervals. It ran along the eastern wall of the Court of the Gentiles of Herod's temple. If you needed to talk to the apostles for any reason, you would find them there."

"I don't think I've ever heard of it."

"We believe that it's the missing piece of the understanding of the church of Acts."

"Now you've totally lost me."

"Have you heard of the cell celebration model?"

"Those words aren't really familiar. Maybe."

He opened his New Testament again and read to me. "Acts 2:41-47: *So those who received his word were baptized, and there were added that day about three thousand souls. And they devoted themselves to the apostles' teaching and fellowship, to the breaking of bread and the prayers. And fear came upon every soul; and many wonders and signs were done through the apostles. And all who believed were together and had all things in common; and they sold their possessions and goods and distributed them to all, as any had need. And day by day, attending the temple together and breaking bread in their homes, they partook of food with glad and generous hearts, praising God and having favor with all the people. And the Lord added to their number day by day those who were being saved.* There were 120 people in the upper room; we call that the base congregation, which I think is a term that comes from Bill Beckham. The next day there were three thousand Christians baptized and all were cared for by the original base congregation of 120."

"How did they do that?"

"Would you be ready if 3000 new people came to your church tomorrow?"

"No," I said honestly. "Three hundred new people would overwhelm us. Even one hundred."

"They were ready - after all, they had been trained for this moment by Jesus for three years. That's why we are so adamant about following the pattern of the gospels. We consider the Gospels to be the training program for leadership in the church of Acts."

"OK. So how did they do it?"

"The standard idea is 'cell celebration.' In other words, those three thousand people were divided into small groups. That's the cell."

"How big were these small groups?"

"It doesn't say, but Jesus chose twelve disciples. If you divide those three thousand people into 120 small group leaders, you have each small group leader leading 2.5 groups of twelve."

"Some lead two, some lead three? That's doesn't seem so hard."

"Or two partners lead five groups. Remember, these people didn't have television and their kids weren't in soccer leagues. We know from 1 Corinthians 11 that they would share the evening meal in their home meetings."

"So that's the cell?" I asked.

Bill nodded.

"What's the celebration?"

"Even in the avant garde, wild and crazy wing of the church you have to make the temple system happy. It's not terribly accurate biblically, but the 'celebration' is the idea that the disciples, all 3000 of them, attended the worship services of the temple."

"What's not accurate about that? If they did, they did."

"What's not accurate is that this is used as a justification for preachers doing large services of worship in megachurches - the modern version of the temple system. In the cell celebration model of the church, the church is found in either small groups or in a large group - the celebration. And the large group attends worship together .... in as large a group as possible."

"Again, what's inaccurate about that?"

"Remember, the temple system needs to justify its existence biblically. So to them this attendance at the Jerusalem temple service - with dozens of different services offered in the temple each week - is considered the equivalent of 3000 people gathering for one service at one time in a megachurch to hear the senior pastor preach. It's not a match."

"I guess I see that."

"Additionally, Jesus drew large crowds. The perception is that Jesus conducted worship in front of those large crowds with everyone sitting in rows facing him - a celebration. In fact, there is no example of Jesus doing what we would call worship - a prayer, liturgy, or even a hymn, with a group larger than the twelve. What's more common is Jesus disrupting the temple worship."

"Can you give an example?"

"John 7:37-38: *On the last day of the feast, the great day, Jesus stood up and proclaimed, "If any one thirst, let him come to me and drink. He who believes in me, as the scripture has said, 'Out of his heart shall flow rivers of living water.'"* One theory is that this disrupted the services at the Feast of Tabernacles. Jesus taught in the temple, and again we have that image of him in front of a large congregation; but it's not there in the Bible. They sing a hymn - once - after the Lord's supper."

"Only once?"

Bill nodded. "There is no other mention of singing or hymns. Music is mentioned in the Parable of the Prodigal son. Jesus never preaches in the temple. Jesus never leads worship in the temple. Jesus never functions as a priest in the temple. Jesus never leads singing in the temple or plays guitar in the temple praise band... but all of that is assumed to be the biblical model in the cell celebration model. In fact, the worship in the temple was never worship of Jesus and it's likely that no aspect of Jesus' teaching was mentioned."

"How can you prove that?"

"Look here in Acts 6:7: *And the word of God increased; and the number of the disciples multiplied greatly in Jerusalem, and a great many of the priests were obedient to the faith.* Notice that a number of the priests are becoming Christians? What naturally flows from that is an attempt to change the worship forms of the temple to reflect the teachings or even the existence of Jesus. What immediately happens? Persecution, and they are driven out of Jerusalem."

130

"That makes sense."

"Everyone loves the church of Acts and everyone wants to emulate it, but you can't make the case that the apostles had anything to do with worship in any form whatsoever. There were no," Bill said as he fixed me with a glare, "no contemporary forms of worship whatsoever in the book of the Acts. It was the same old Jewish worship, Jewish traditional worship, that the disciples attended."

"Wow."

"Likewise," Bill said, "we therefore don't believe it's necessary to offer any sort of special worship to make disciples - the same old traditional worship was good enough for the church of Acts. In fact, we don't believe it is necessary for us to offer any worship at all."

"That makes no sense."

Bill was sure he was on solid ground. "Think through the gospels as you read them. There was a temple system; Jesus and the disciples participated in it and even challenged it, but they were never in charge of it and never had any control of it. You agree there was such a temple system in the New Testament?"

"Sure - they even had their own temple to play with as well."

"So if the purpose of Jesus was not to run the temple system, what then did he do?" Bill asked.

Suddenly it was clear. "Jesus created and ran the discipleship system apart from the temple."

"Exactly. So therefore, we believe that we can do what Jesus did within any earthly temple. Catholic, Pentecostal, liberal, Quaker or Baptist worship - it doesn't matter, because it's not the temple that matters when you are making disciples - it's doing what Jesus did."

"So why does a discipleship system need a temple?"

"It doesn't. And that's the basic simple church concept. All disciple making, and whatever minimal sort of temple the people need, including none at all."

"How do you have no temple at all?"

"You can do your worship in your cell or small group; that's what most of simple churches do. In our movement, we don't see the need to recreate the wheel or provide even that much of a temple system. We can just as easily utilize your temple. Instead of developing our own worship service, we just go to yours. We're welcome to attend and give and work as long as we don't attempt to change anything. And guess what?"

"What?"

"We don't need to change anything about the temple. It can be as it always has been. You can make disciples within any church by operating a discipleship system."

Ruth appeared in the doorway. "Are you guys having a fight?"

"No," I said to her. "Bill's just getting excited."

"He does that," Cindy said from behind her. "What's he excited about this time?"

"I'm not sure. I think it's that he doesn't have to take over my church in a power struggle in order to make disciples."

"Oh," Cindy said, "the whole temple thing."

"We covered that hours ago," Ruth said. "You guys get stuck on the weirdest things."

Cindy fixed Bill with a chilling glare. "You're supposed to be talking about prayer this week. Ruth's been telling me about how John organizes his prayers and you need to learn something about what he's doing. It's pretty neat. You just leave that temple behind you and focus on disciple making. You're going to fall behind."

"We're on a schedule?" I asked.

"Not at all, but Mr. Superior here tends to go off on tangents sometimes."

"I like tangents, too," I admitted.

"Don't let him lead you astray, John," Cindy told me.

"Don't let him tempt you with his theories, Bill," my wife said to him.

"I think we've just been made fun of," I said to Bill after they left the room.

"Won't be the last time, my friend," Bill said.

Bill and I ran out of time to talk about prayer on Sunday so we met for breakfast on Monday morning.

"It's not that easy for the kids when I have to work an

evening, but it makes it easy to meet you when I'm free in the morning," Bill said.

"It's convenient for me," I said.

"Cindy keeps telling me that you have a system for prayer that I have to hear about."

"It's not really a system for prayer; it's actually a form of spiritual time management."

"Now you've intrigued me," Bill said. He took his spiral notebook out of his briefcase and laid it on the table to take notes.

"Basically, three years ago I was burning out trying to make everybody happy. I was pulling away from my wife and running away from stress into activities that were basically worthless. Channel zapping late at night."

Bill nodded.

"One night I just hit a crisis; I woke up and could not stop crying. Ruth held me and comforted me. What I realized that night was that I could no longer live as I had. And one key was that I realized that life was too hard to do alone. My brother in law, Frank, is personnel manager of a large company up at the state capital and he encouraged me to come to his church and talk with his minister. It's his system I'm using. He calls himself a *One Minute Minister*."

"What an unusual title. What does it mean?"

"It means that if you take control of this minute, you can change your life almost instantly by how you choose to invest your minutes. Basically, it's sowing and reaping; if you sow the right minutes into the garden of your life, then the right things begin to grow there."

"That's biblical. Where is that?" Bill asked.

"Galatians, chapter six, I think. In the context it also refers to how we invest our resources, including time."

Bill thumbed through his New Testament, looking for the verse. "Gal 6:6-10: *Let him who is taught the word share all good things with him who teaches. Do not be deceived; God is not mocked, for whatever a man sows, that he will also reap. For he who sows to his own flesh will from the flesh reap corruption; but he who sows to the Spirit will from the Spirit reap eternal life. And let us not grow weary in well-doing, for in due season we shall reap, if we do not lose heart. So then, as we have opportunity, let us do good to all men, and especially to those who are of the household of faith."*

"That's the verse. You need to think about what you are sowing into the time of your life."

"So how does the system work?"

"Basically, it applies the Pareto principle - the 80/20 rule - to time management. One fifth of what we do generates four times the investment. The other 80% of what we do generates a loss - one fourth is returned for every unit we invest. Time management is to invest in that which is in the vital 20%."

"We use the Pareto principle at work; I hear it repeatedly in the managers' meetings I attend. What else is in the system?"

"The system involves three parts: *paperwork*, *peoplework*, and *prayerwork*. Since this is spiritual time management, the highest priority is to plan the time we invest with God, which is *prayerwork*; if we had a senior partner, we would work things out with our partner first. Why would you ever want to do something without praying about it first? We learn to pray over our day, our schedule, write out what's important and get clear in prayer before we act. Writing till we are clear is called *Journal Clarity*."

"I like it."

"The second highest priority is people; most problems come about because of an imbalance with people. When you invest in relationships, other problems tend to fall in place. So during *prayerwork*, we focus on planning our *peoplework* - what we need to do with people in our lives. The discipline there is called *Network Elements* - seeing how all the people are linked together, how they are connected to one another in the network."

Bill nodded.

"The last priority, of course, is *paperwork* - but it's essential," I said. "Paperwork refers to the work necessary to finish things and get closure. 'Work is not done until the paperwork is done.' It's how we deal with the 80%

that's left. There's more to it, but that's basically the gist of it."

"I can see why Cindy is interested in it; she is more naturally organized than I am. I like the way you talk about *prayerwork* and using prayer to organize your day."

"That's how all this came about. I sit in my sanctuary first thing every morning with my organizer and I pray through my day, focusing first on God, then people and finally things. The rest of the day, I just go through what I prayed about."

"It sounds like it would really result in your prayers being focused."

"They do something like Solomon's Porch up at their church, too. That's where we had the meetings. The focus is different, I think; they bring all the leaders of their church together once a week to work together. Committees can set a meeting date on another night, but the minister won't be there. It really helps him control his schedule."

"I like it," Bill said. "In a sense, it restricts a lot of the busyness of the temple system to one night a week."

"You're right."

"David Oliver pulls his ideas from all kinds of places; maybe there's some connection. I'll have to ask him."

"What's your Solomon's Porch like?"

"The Gathering brings everybody together who is in a JUMP group for fellowship and inspiration. Since we want the groups to proliferate and want to organize so that nothing gets in the way of that, the Gathering is like a reunion with anyone who has been in a JUMP group with you before. There's an hour of fellowship and then an hour of sharing. The fellowship gets longer because some people come up to two hours early, which leads to three hours of just visiting. But that's the way it is."

"And we're going to do this Saturday?"

"Yes - the Gathering is after the Hub."

I got out my organizer notebook and opened it up to the calendar section. "What are the times?"

"And Hub is at 5, visiting at 6, inspiration at 7."

"And where is it?"

135

"We're meeting at Murphyville this month. It moves around from temple to temple."

"Now that's a pregnant phrase. What do you mean - temple to temple?"

"The Gathering is for everyone who's ever been in a JUMP group. Because we are totally disinterested in setting up our own temple system, our people attend all sorts of churches. Many of them go to the church they hated before they got saved."

"I'll bet that makes their parents happy."

"Makes the pastor happy also, because we make very hard workers and we tithe. Generally their only frustration is that we won't let them put us in charge of anything - we'll help out but we won't chair or serve on a committee."

"I'm still not in agreement with why you do that. What harm could it do?"

"It's not a matter of harm; it's a matter of principle. Serving is a 'follow Jesus' thing and an important part of *descending grace*. So is using your gifts. But being in charge of something means being in charge of an element of the temple system. Serving on a committee is the same thing. We keep ourselves free to follow Jesus and won't take on obligations in the temple system."

"How about preaching?"

"We believe that each person has a gift that they are obligated to use. You can use it in the temple, including preaching; that's where most of those gifts are intended to be used. But you don't want to get to where you are stuck in the temple as an obligation; you need the freedom to be able, at any given time, to do something your Lord wants you to do. And our primary goal is to make disciples, and that is done through the discipleship system, not through any temple type program."

"I guess what that means, based on how you look at it, that the temple stuff is in the 80% that doesn't result in much return on investment."

"That's the perfect way to express it," Bill said. "Disciple making, for us, is in the vital 20%. And, as in the system you described, it focuses primarily on prayer, on people and on being faithful to the need to achieve closure. Closure being first a disciple ..."

"*Ascending grace*, right?" I asked. "The first step in disciple making is to be one?"

"Yes. And then a disciple maker."

"And that's *descending grace*."

"Right."

"Why don't you combine the two and mix them all up?"

Bill looked at me like I was insane. "That would be like giving a 9 year old keys to the family car. That would be like forcing a teenager to wear diapers because the baby needed them."

"That's an odd analogy."

"Not the way we look at it. In the discipleship system, we believe that growth occurs in sequential stages. In the temple system, things cycle and every one is considered to be at the same level. It's how you tell the two apart: sequence or cycle."

"So my comment - mix them up - only works if every one is at the same level."

"Exactly - and we believe that people aren't."

"So that's the temple assumption."

"The temple virus; it infects everything with the intent of keeping everything the same, everyone together, everyone in a unity of the same direction. That's why there is conflict, sometimes, with the discipleship system."

"I'll be that's another reason why you won't let your people chair committees."

"It's not that we don't let them; most of them are trying to get away from that sort of stuff."

"Committees?"

"No, John. From the manipulation in the temple system. They'll put you in charge of a committee - but then try to control what you do or what you can do. If you don't do what is expected, there will be strife to get you back into line. People will find fault and criticize. If you keep on your purpose, people will get nasty. And if you are really adamant about obeying Jesus, then you might even enjoy what they gave the founder - three nails and a view

137

from above."

"You're right; there is a lot of manipulation."

"That's why we ask our people to do what they feel led to do ... but to not accept commitments where they would need to compromise. Everyone is happier that way."

"There's not a lot of desire in people to serve on committees today."

Bill snorted. "And that's why. Not much return on the investment and way too much manipulation."

"So when do I get to graduate to *descending grace*?" I asked Bill.

"You could probably do it now, but why don't you wait until the Gathering and meet Pastor Pam? Then you can get on her schedule. And we need to finish working on the questions."

"That works for me."

"And now, back to prayer."

"Prayer."

"What is God telling you through prayer and what are you going to do about it?"

I tapped my organizer. "God is telling me what to do today after I leave here."

Bill smiled. "We're looking for a bigger picture. Being in the discipleship system, we believe that God is teleological. Everything has a purpose and every thing moves you into a direction."

"Does it have to be that?"

"You like your cycles, don't you?"

"I do work in the temple system."

"God also works through cycles. But the inspiration for us boils down to just two little words: *Follow Me.* That's a direction."

"One direction ... how can that not be controlling?"

"Ho, ho, ho," Bill said.

"I just walked into another *just in time* lesson, didn't I?"

"Yes, you did, grasshopper. I am very pleased. Do you have your New Testament?"

I fished around in my coat pocket and found it. "Where to?"

"John 3:16. Know it?"

"Yes."

"Know what comes after?"

"I think. Maybe."

"Read it for me please. Keep going till I stop you."

"For God so loved the world that he gave his only Son, that whoever believes in him should not perish but have eternal life. For God sent the Son into the world, not to condemn the world, but that the world might be saved through him. He who believes in him is not condemned; he who does not believe is condemned already, because he has not believed in the name of the only Son of God. And this is the judgment, that the light has come into the world, and men loved darkness rather than light, because their deeds were evil. For every one who does evil hates the light, and does not come to the light, lest his deeds should be exposed. But he who does what is true comes to the light, that it may be clearly seen that his deeds have been wrought in God."

"Stop there. See the direction?"

"The light creates a center. Ah, the Centering Prayer."

"You are good, grasshopper. Now bring in the diversity."

"From where you are, wherever that is, for each person there is one and only one direction toward the light."

"Does it matter that it's a different direction for each person?"

"Not if the priority is following Christ."

"Exactly. Now what if Christ is moving - if Christ is teleological, if Christ has a direction, and if Christ calls us to follow him?"

"There's still only one direction."

"That's the unity; all directions point to Christ. Now here's something cute. What happens when people get closer to the light?"

"Who they are and what they've done become visible?"

"Would that be comfortable?"

"No," I said. "No one likes to be exposed."

139

"So coming to the light has a cost."

"It does."

"What do people do who don't want the exposure and don't want to pay the cost?"

"They move farther back into the darkness to hide what they do."

"And that's called ..."

"Dishonest?"

"Think a bit harder, grasshopper."

"Denial?" I asked.

"Exactly. In order to preserve an image of ourselves as someone better than we truly are, we are in denial and attempt to hide the truth about ourselves by hiding in the darkness."

"So there is some discomfort in coming into the light. And way too much comfort in most churches. Do we feed the denial that people have that they don't need Christ?"

"You'll have to answer that for yourself," Bill said. "Balancing systems cycle to keep everything happy and running smoothly; reinforcing systems bring change, and change isn't always comfortable."

"You're right; no matter where you are, there is only one direction toward Christ, wherever he is. And it doesn't matter that the direction is different for each person."

"That's the freedom in differentiation. The unity in our movement comes not from conformity, but from moving in the same direction - toward Christ and ultimately in the direction that Christ is moving."

"So what happens with leadership?"

"Oh, grasshopper, you are just too perfect today. Leadership is irrelevant."

"How can this be, O wise one? All the books say that everything turns on leadership."

Bill turned to a new page in his notebook and drew an arrow horizontally across the page. "This, grasshopper, is leadership. On this end, you have the children of Israel in Egypt, in slavery and in misery. Making bricks without straw."

"OK."

"And on the other end of the arrow is the promised

land. Milk and honey and prosperity. A chicken in every pot. And who is the leader of this little excursion?"

"Moses."

"So let's write the name of Moses here. Poor Moses. Did anyone suffer like he did?"

"Suffer?"

"So, grasshopper, here is the definition of leadership. Something bad leaves the people in misery. God sends a leader to bring them into the perfect place. And what is the result of this leadership?"

"I don't know what you mean. What are you looking for?"

"Was the Exodus a success or a failure?"

"Please, tell me, master, the grasshopper waits."

"They all died. They fought Moses every inch of the way. They constantly complained, God's people did. Built a golden calf to worship when Moses left them alone for a few days. And they all died, except for Caleb and Joshua. Because, although they were slaves and constantly forced to obey their masters, they were unable to obey God. That's the problem with leadership; it looks simple to take a group of people in one direction from a bad place to a good place. In reality, it fails all the time. It's like herding cats."

"It is exactly like herding cats. I work with some of those same people."

"What you can see when you look closely at this is the failure comes from the need to get everyone to conform, to all go in the same direction at the same time in a helpful cooperative way."

"So how does that mean that leadership is irrelevant?"

"Leadership is teleological; it moves in a direction. But all of the resistance to Moses is cyclical - over and over again. Leadership pushes against the balancing cycle and it loses. When the discipleship system attempts to lead or control or manipulate the temple system, the temple system swats it down."

"Now I'm really confused," I said.

"The discipleship system can live with the temple

141

system, live within it actually; it just can't control it. Leadership doesn't run the balancing system, management does."

"Before I'm totally confused, can you explain what you mean?"

"The only person you can truly lead is yourself. Someone can choose to follow you, but you can't really make them. You don't have the power you need to control others. But you can focus your control on yourself, find the direction to the Savior, and travel that way."

"That I can do."

"You have a good system for prayer." Bill touched my organizer. "It works because you are learning how to lead yourself." He leaned closer to fix me with his gaze. "But the issue is whether or not you understand where you are going in the bigger sense. Otherwise your *prayerwork* just keeps you moving in very efficient circles. Daily circles, if I understand you right."

"So what do you mean?"

"John, do you know what you will be doing in a year? Other than having the same sort of days over and over again."

"If I'm still the pastor here, then ..."

"There's a cycle. But God has a direction, John, and Jesus is moving to perfectly fulfill God's will. If you want to follow Jesus, you will find him in the direction you are supposed to go. And what is that direction?"

I had no answer that would satisfy him; that was the point. In my job, we did not make plans; we coped with what was happening, day after day and month after month.

I didn't know what to tell him. Everything I knew - that I loved my wife, that I loved my son, that I loved my job, that I loved my church - they were no new direction, no change, they were just more repeating cycles of what I had now. I was more than comfortable; I was stable in my comfort.

"I know that I want to follow Jesus," I finally told him.

"That's the right answer," he said. "That will lead you

142

to change."

"I know."

"And what will change?"

"I don't know that. But I know I want to learn how to be a disciple maker. And I believe that I can learn that from you and the others."

"I believe we can teach you that. And when we do, everything will change." Bill smiled. "And nothing will change. That's the paradox of faith."

I was confused, but I didn't care. If I followed Jesus, the confusion would decrease as I came more and more into the light.

That night I tried to explain my confusion to Ruth. She just laughed. "Cindy told me he would lay the Moses rap on you. He loves it, she said."

"It's weird. It's like, I know he is right; I just don't understand why or how he can be right."

"Cindy told me how to deal with that, John," she said.

"And how do I deal with it?" I asked.

"You," she said firmly, poking my chest with her forefinger, "need to follow Jesus and stop worrying about anything else. Including your need for it all to make sense. If you know the next step, that's enough. If you only know one step, if you take that step, you will learn the next step."

"Ummm."

"Stop thinking about it." She poked me again with each word. "This is kind of fun," she giggled, poking at me again. "It takes feet to follow Jesus. Just do it."

Just do it. Maybe that will work better than attempting to understand everything. Perhaps understanding everything wasn't necessary if I was able to do what was needed to follow Jesus.

CHAPTER SIX: THE Hub
Saturday, February 28

Bill arranged to meet me an hour before the Hub meeting so we could move a little farther through the questions.

"Earlier this week we talked about the temple system and how it cycles - it just repeats forever."

"We did. You pushed me to be teleological," I said.

"That's right - because we have two teleological questions coming up - #5 and #6. We skip #4 until you enter *descending grace* with Pastor Pam. You get to write these questions yourself. They are 'questions for my goals and growth' and there are two of them. Usually that means one for spiritual goals and one for life goals ... or one for work goals and one for family goals."

"Which is more typical?"

"Everybody's different, John."

"I'm not sure what mine are. I've come to realize that I don't really have any long term goals."

"You will. Most people in the pragmatic majority don't have goals; they are into maintaining their cycles. But you will."

"Why do you think you can say that?"

"It's not arrogance; the questions will bring them out. It's just that in this process of discipleship, you are talking about following a teleological God. God has long range goals for you; you just don't know them."

"Well, I guess that makes sense," I said. "But it would be nice if God would let me know what they are."

"It would. And just how do you believe that God would choose to do just that?"

"Is this another trick question?"

"Maybe. It's obvious when you think about it. Take a minute and think and let's see if you can guess the answer."

I sat and thought over everything I had learned since I had decided to learn how to make disciples.

"I know I want to learn how to make disciples," I said.

"I know," Bill said, "but the question is how you

144

would learn God's goals for your life. Think on that. How would God communicate these to you?"

"How about a hint?"

"OK, then, when would God communicate these goals to you?"

I thought a bit more about when I had heard from God and suddenly it was clear. *"Number 2. What chapters in the Bible did you read? What is God telling you through what you read? What are you going to do about it? Number 3. What did you hear from Jesus through prayer about His will for your life this week? What are you going to do about it?"*

"Exactly," Bill said. Your answers to those questions - on a bigger scale than you are used to - point toward your two goal questions."

"What do you mean by 'on a bigger scale?' I don't understand."

"You already practice a system of prayer I sincerely admire. In fact, you are going to teach it to me. You call it *prayerwork* - where each morning you pray in order to get the details of your day right, what God's will is for each of your hours, in focus and written clearly. The rest of the day is execution of the tasks on that list."

"That is what *prayerwork* is all about."

"But, still, it's a focus on the details. These questions look at the long view. You need both kinds of vision - up close and far in the distance."

"That makes sense. But how do I know?"

"One thing we offer to people who don't know are Covey's Questions."

"Stephen Covey? *The Seven Habits of Highly Effective People?*"

"That's the book; millions of copies sold. Here is the first question: *What one thing, if you did it consistently, would significantly increase the quality of your professional life?*" Bill waited for a moment. "Any clue?"

"What comes to mind is to keep on with what I am doing."

"The JUMP questions focus you on something new; it's possible that nothing new will come to mind. Ready for the second Covey Question?"

"Sure."

"*What one thing, if you did it consistently, would significantly increase the quality of your family life?*"

"I need to spend more time with my son," I said automatically.

"There you go," Bill said. "Sometimes it just comes to you. So, now you write a question that reflects how you should spend more time with your son. I'll ask that question to you each week and hold you accountable."

"Something more specific than just spending more time with him?"

"We're measuring behavior here, so it should be more specific. I can ask you what you did with him, or if you want to build a habit, I can ask you how many days you read him a bed time story. We can identify any kind of behavior you want to strengthen - or any kind of behavior you want to reduce."

"I can see that this might have some power once you could organize it to focus on something you need to change."

"So what do you need to change, John?"

"I need to talk with my son at least 15 minutes each day and listen to him tell me about his day."

"Phrase it as a question I can ask you."

"How many days this week did I visit with my son?"

"Want a suggestion?"

I nodded.

"What days did I visit with my son and how did it go?"

"I like that one better."

"Phrasing the question this way allows the question to function as it should. It's a chance to confess your sins - to describe your life accurately - and in so doing find forgiveness and cleansing for change."

"There's a verse for that, I'll bet."

"1 John 1:9. Remember how we talked in John 3 about how coming into the light exposes what is truly happening in our lives?" Bill opened up his New Testament.

"Yes."

"Listen to the parallel - 1 John 1:9 in context: *1 John 1:5-10 This is the message we have heard from him and proclaim to you, that God is light and in him is no darkness at all. If we say we have fellowship with him while we walk in darkness, we lie and do not live according to the truth; but if we walk in the light, as he is in the light, we have fellowship with one another, and the blood of Jesus his Son cleanses us from all sin. If we say we have no sin, we deceive ourselves, and the truth is not in us. If we confess our sins, he is faithful and just, and will forgive our sins and cleanse us from all unrighteousness. If we say we have not sinned, we make him a liar, and his word is not in us.*"

"I guess there's a lot more benefit in the details than just a number - 5 nights."

"I don't need to know the details, but you do. If you talk them out with another person, you gain a lot more self understanding and it's a lot harder for you to hide in denial."

"I didn't really catch that the questions were about confession."

"Ours aren't - but that's right where Neil Cole's *Life Transformation Group* questions focus: *James 5:16 Therefore confess your sins to one another, and pray for one another, that you may be healed. The prayer of a righteous man has great power in its effects.* That's Neil's focus: confess your sins one to another."

"I don't think I'm quite ready for that; I like the emphasis on growth in our questions."

"I do, too. But questions that lead to confession are more powerful for change. They are more intimidating, but that's because of their power."

"I'd prefer not to be intimidated, thank you."

"That's why we changed them," Bill said. "We were concerned that the original questions would drive people off before they learned the power of the system. You're welcome to try Neil's questions. Some groups do for a period, like Lent, but usually only for a specific, limited time."

"If confession questions are more powerful, why would you limit the time to use them?"

"You know that answer, John," Bill said. "It's the same for everything we do."

"Using the simpler questions facilitates disciple making?"

"Exactly. We don't want to adjust the system to move away from the people we are focused upon drawing into the system. So we keep the same system and keep it simple, and try our best to remember that this is not for us, it's for new disciples."

"So I have one question. Got any other tips?"

Bill sniggered. "When a man's poor brain runs out of possibilities, there's one answer that never fails. Go ask your wife where you should improve and you will get an immediate answer to turn into a question."

"That is funny," I said. "Like a flat tire."

"If you don't come up with an answer for yourself, that's the alternative that is left. And that alternative never fails."

"What do you do if a JUMP member is single?"

Bill waved it off. "The women are always glad to help any poor man who asks them to improve himself. They are very generous with their analysis."

"So I'll ask Ruth tonight."

"I'll bet she has an answer for you."

"I'd bet the same way."

"Only one question to go," Bill said.

"I think my brain may have had all it can take today. Can we do it tomorrow?" I asked.

"Sure. What do you want to do now?"

"I feel..." I stopped for a moment to assess my feelings. "I feel like I need to pray and read the Bible for a bit. How much time do we have before we have to leave for the meeting?"

"For the Hub? Half hour."

"That's what I want."

"I think I will do the same."

I went for a walk with God. I wasn't following, just meandering. But I felt a comforting presence none the

148

less. And as I walked, I pondered my answer to the third question.

The first person I saw at the Hub was Sam. He hugged me like an old friend and I certainly was glad to see him.

"How has Bill been taking care of you?" he asked.

"It's been great, Sam."

"Wonderful. Come on inside; I want you to meet some folks."

I finally met the famous Pastor Pam; she was not tall, but I could feel the compressed energy about to explode. Her hair was a deep, bright auburn, a red one rarely sees on a human being without the aid of assistance. She had the peaches and cream complexion of a genuine red head and simply glowed with good will, enthusiasm and energy.

"I've heard a lot about you, John," she said. "When are you going to be ready to descend into grace?"

"Whenever you are ready," I said. "I just follow around here."

"Hmm," she smiled. "You seem to have gotten off to a good start. Following is more important than anything else. Except possibly love, joy and peace."

"I'm glad to meet whenever you and Bill are ready."

"Let's figure it out. I love talking about *descending grace*."

Sam then introduced me to Deb, who he introduced as the 'wonder girl.'

"I'm not that," she said. "I am the administrator."

"What's an administrator do with this group?"

"Oh, I'm a volunteer like everybody else, but the administrator does what every administrator does when surrounded by all sorts of theological and creative types."

"You administrate?" I said.

"You got it. Someone has to see to the details around here and keep people on some sort of schedule."

"Sometimes I need that myself."

"It comes natural to her," Sam said, laughing. "If you spend much time around her, you will be purpose driven for sure."

149

"With the emphasis on the driven," Bill said.

"I don't know how to handle all this positive affirmation," Deb said. "If I start blushing, would y'all throw some ice water on me?"

Sam introduce me to Diane, Fred and Louise as we all sat down around the table. Deb set up a laptop and prepared to take notes of the meeting.

"Welcome to the Hub, John," Sam said again. "We want to hear more about your spiritual disciplines after a time of prayer."

The room grew quiet as we all prayed, with Pam closing out the time with a short prayer. I not only felt welcome; I felt at home here. Sam nodded to me to begin my story.

"Three years ago I was close to burnout and the love of my wife and the wisdom of several of my colleagues saved my life. Certainly my spiritual life. They taught me a system of managing my time - the details of my time - so that I had room in my life for what was the most important." I described the three secrets and three principles I had heard and that had helped me so much. They listened and asked questions, and a half hour went by very quickly.

"Thank you, John. Would you like to stay and sit with us or would you prefer to wander around?"

"I'm happy to stay, if it's all right."

"Let's do check in. Bill, why don't you go first?"

"I've been working a JUMP group with John here for the past three weeks. We're having a great time. We're at the goal questions right now. Cindy is working a JUMP group with John's wife, Ruth; they've worked through all the questions and Ruth is more than ready for *descending grace.*"

"Great," Pam said with enthusiasm.

"John and I are close. We have a tendency to go on tangents. Our other partners, Phil and Jenny, are doing well in their JUMP groups. Total spoke: 8."

"Excellent," Sam said. "Pam?"

"Deb and I are still meeting. My five other partners are doing well in their JUMP groups. The newest one,

Jill's, is ready to multiply; she's had four for about three weeks now."

"Jill has the gift, doesn't she?" Bill said.

"She does, but while she can get them started in the system, she's not the maturer that her partners are. They are picking up the work where she is weak and it's going to work well. She'll be ready to join the Hub soon herself. Total spoke: 14."

"Pam, I don't have the contact information on the fourth member in Jill's group," Deb said.

"I'll either get it from her or send it in myself."

"We keep in contact via email and the internet between meetings," Bill whispered to me. "That's why Deb is so helpful. She keeps us all connected and on schedule. She's the manager for this group of leaders."

Sam turned to the others and they made their reports, each reporting a number for "total spoke." I wanted to ask what that was but would wait until the meeting was over.

THE GATHERING

The Gathering was a surprise. This wasn't difficult because Ruth and I had no idea what to expect. Anything would have been a surprise.

The Gathering was held at the Murphyville Church, Sam's home congregation. Bill and Cindy had worshiped there until they started attending my church. It was a large, older, 'first church downtown' type congregation with a few distinctions to differentiate it from the church it had been in the 1950s. There was an elevator now, with a remodeled entrance to support it. There was also a projection screen in the sanctuary, installed by the current pastor's predecessor who had brought a wave of change to the staid congregation until finally leaving after four years of turmoil.

The time of change had not been comfortable. The current pastor was more traditional and more a match for who the congregation was in the present day. I'm not sure what he thought about Sam's little group or even what he knew about them. The movement, as they called it, was so

151

decentralized that there wasn't much that was visible. Just a bunch of people walking the neighborhoods and drinking coffee at Starbucks, as Bill had characterized it in fun.

So I was surprised to find about eighty people at the Gathering. We were greeted at the door and given name tags with simple instructions. "Put your first name in big letters and the name of your circle or the full name of your sponsor underneath it." Her name tag said "Denise" in big letters and underneath "Pam Clancy."

"So you are one of Pam's people," I said.

"Absolutely," she smiled with a lot of bright energy.

"She could give me a headache after a while with all the cheerfulness," Ruth said after Denise made her way to greet the next arrival with a hug and a name tag.

"I know what you mean," I said. "Who exactly is our sponsor?"

"You are in a JUMP group with Bill, and I'm in a JUMP group with Cindy. That's who our sponsors are."

"What are circles?" I asked.

"I don't know," Ruth said. "I just know that we aren't in one. Maybe you will be able to tell from the other name tags."

We adjourned to a room filled with exuberant, happy people enjoying refreshments.

"I know you don't know very many people here, John," Bill said, "but I'll stay with you and introduce you to anyone who comes up.

I met Phil and Jenny, the other two JUMP leaders related to Bill and their partners. Jenny brought another woman who was brand new to their JUMP group. Ruth and Cindy came in and I got a big hug from each of them.

"Bill, what's a spoke?" I asked when we had a minute.

"I'm a member of the Hub because Phil and Jenny started their own JUMP groups. I'm a spiritual grandparent now, in other words. We're in the 'build the clock' phase of growth right now. A *spoke* is a group of related JUMP group people linked in a chain to a person in the Hub. *Building the clock* means that we are working to build twelve spokes, like the numbers on a clock. We have six now: Sam, Pastor Pam, me, Diane, Fred and Louise. When we have twelve, our emphasis shifts to *building the wagon wheel.*"

"Sounds kind of strange."

"It's just our terminology. It takes a while to grow on you."

"It's like a bad case of mental fungus, John" a voice said from behind me. "Once you get into the terminology you can't let it go." It was Pastor Pam.

"You aren't the first group to develop their own code language," I said to Pastor Pam.

"I just love secret codes," she joked.

As we circulated and met people I did find out about the circles. There were Bridge #1 and Bridge #3, Gin Rummy #1, Saturday Quilters, Tuesday Walkers and a variety of other activities. Some just had names with circle appended: Ruth Circle, Gideon Circle, St. Stephen Circle.

I filed my questions away for later answers as we milled around the room and greeted people. The two bridge circles turned out to be card games. The circles with names involved people talking about Bible study, so I assumed that they were more focused on spiritual activities than recreation.

As we made our way around the room, we met Bill and Cindy's other spoke members. Phil and Jenny were a young couple the same age who had a daughter in Cindy's day care. They were Catholic but were obviously as enthusiastic about the movement as Bill and Cindy. I asked him about the support of his priest.

"Father Jim appreciates the hard work we do in the parish; while we are not poster child Catholics, we do set a good example, so he is happy to ignore the little differences. After all, why not? We are consistent, faithful, joyful, happy Catholics. We are at mass every week and on all special holy days."

"So you don't have any difficulty living your life as a disciple in the Catholic church?"

"Why would I, John? You think being a disciple is a Protestant specialty?"

"No, not at all," I apologized. "I'm just wondering if

you have people in your church hassling you for how you practice your faith."

"Not at all. It's because we are making disciples as a part of a system, John. And it's not a system where we confront people or preach to them. Nor do we make anyone feel inferior or unspiritual."

"Please explain that to me."

"People are so tired of the 'I'm spiritual, I'm superior to you' attitude. What I love about this movement is the respect that it shows for people in their situation. God loves them where they are, so why can't we?"

"I'm just getting started, so I want to learn more."

"You will," he said. "The discipleship system we practice will make disciples within any formal denominational church because it doesn't attempt to change the status quo of the church. It just makes disciples the way Jesus did."

"Jesus was trying to change the world," I said.

"He was? I'm sorry, I didn't read that in my New Testament. Did Jesus ever state that this was his purpose?"

I was at a loss for words. "It's assumed I guess."

"It is assumed. But he did change the world; I'm just arguing about whether that was his primary purpose. What's the saying - they made me memorize in parochial school in 5th grade..." He took a deep breath and recited: *"Let us turn now to the story. A child is born in an obscure village. He is brought up in another obscure village. He works in a carpenter shop until he is thirty, and then for three brief years is an itinerant preacher, proclaiming a message and living a life. He never writes a book. He never holds an office. He never raises an army. He never has a family of his own. He never owns a home. He never goes to college. He never travels two hundred miles from the place where he was born. He gathers a little group of friends about him and teaches them his way of life.*

While still a young man the tide of popular feeling turns against him. The band of followers forsakes him. One denies him; another betrays him. He is turned over to his enemies. He goes through the mockery of a trial; he is nailed on a cross between two thieves, and when dead is laid in a borrowed grave by the kindness of a friend. Those are the facts of his human life. He rises from the dead. Today we look back across nineteen hundred years and ask, What kind of a trail has he left across the centuries? When we try to sum up his influence, all the armies that ever marched, all the parliaments that ever sat, all the kings that ever reigned are absolutely picayune in their influence on mankind compared with that of this one solitary life . . .

He has changed the moral climate of the world, and he is changing it now, and will continue to do so until the kingdoms of this world shall become the kingdom of our Lord and of his Christ. I ask you to pause a moment and think of this thing which Christians believe. We are talking about great adventures. I remind you that there must be a great adventure in faith before there can be a great adventure in action. No man has ever done a great thing until he has first believed a great thing." He grinned. "That's what this is John. It's an adventure. You are following Jesus in your church setting and I am following Jesus in mine."

"More power to you then," I said, meaning it. "Change is hard."

"Are your people hassling you for being a disciple?" Phil asked. "Why would you assume that there is persecution?"

"Maybe that's a Protestant thing, to assume that there has to be confrontation and conflict if you are doing it right."

"There are at least two separate places in the New Testament where it is said that the early Jesus movement held in high esteem by everybody. Why do you think that is?"

"You tell me."

"Jesus treated people with respect and helped them. He helped them with physical healing; that drew a crowd. Who's going to object to that? Then he helped them with emotional healing, psychological healing and spiritual

155

healing. The good fruit, the good results from what Jesus did were obvious and they were everywhere."

"I guess there was some jealousy because of his success," I said.

He grinned. "We haven't seen that sort of jealousy yet. Maybe that's a sign of how bad things are in churches that any positive change is welcome."

"You're probably right." I marveled again at how much of the activity of this group was like an iceberg, below the surface and not noticed; they didn't want attention or praise. I wandered off to find Ruth who was talking with some members of one of the walking groups about how they organized their exercise time. I stood next to her and used the quiet moment to listen and look over the crowd that gathered.

A few minutes later Pam walked through the crowd ringing a handbell and people began filing up the stairs and into the sanctuary. When I came up the stairs she pulled me aside.

"John, we have a tradition with pastors who participate. Would you be willing to help with communion this evening?"

"Sure," I said. "What do I do?"

"We usually have the celebrant be of the same denomination as the host church, so that's both you and I. Since this is your first time, why don't you follow my lead? I'm an elder, so there's no ordination conflict."

"How do you do the Lord's supper in this setting?"

"Normally by intinction. We follow the shorter service right out of the hymnal with all the standard readings and responses. When I ask you to come forward, I'll give you the bread in a cloth to hold. You'll stand about 4 feet away from me so that we can each serve one person at a time. They come down the center aisle and then out to the side."

The worship service was relatively short and informal. Sam started things, calling up people to share answers to prayer and prayer requests. People were called up in four separate groups - 25 percenters, 50 percenters, 75 percenters and 100 percenters. And each time two or three would assemble in the front to say a few words about the Lord and what they were learning.

I need to ask Bill what this means, I thought. The entire community applauded vigorously after each person's statement.

An appeal was made by a bearded young man for help building concrete benches for urban street corners. Three women talked about a trip to Tipp City, Ohio - wherever that was - and what they had learned about ministry at a workshop there; it was something about opening after school centers in the inner city to tutor elementary school children in reading. They also asked for volunteers. Two college age young men told about a mission trip to Costa Rica; an older man stood with them but didn't say much. I gathered he was the leader but that the purpose of the time was for them to talk about how their lives had changed. Leaders certainly were different in this movement. The two young men were interested in vaccinating children against diseases and had done that work on their mission trip. Two older women talked about how they were forming a 'circle for study' at a coffee shop near their home geared for retired women. The whole room cheered them on and Sam invited them to tell their progress next month.

There was a vast silence as the community prayed. Sam started the prayer time and sat down. Pam walked to the front and concluded the prayer time.

After asking everyone to turn in their hymnals to the communion liturgy, Pam told them about me. How as a pastor, God had turned my curiosity to disciple making and that I was learning the customs of their movement in a JUMP group with Bill. Many warm smiles were sent in my direction. She announced that I would be assisting with communion that evening.

As the liturgy began, I found myself at peace in the midst of the familiar words. When Pam broke the bread, I walked to the front without her needing to invite me to take the broken bread from her hands.

As the liturgy concluded and the people came forward, many of them looked at me as they tore off a piece of bread. Some whispered the words "thank you,

John" and others, "I'll be praying for you, John." Rather than odd, it seemed as if I was being welcomed by the entire community to be one with them. When Ruth came forward, she laid her hand on my arm for a moment in silence. It meant very much to me. I noticed that Bill's other partners, Phil and Jenny, participated in communion with us without any hesitation.

As the last person had been served, I turned and handed the bread to Pam as she served me. I took the bread and dipped it in the cup as the others had done while Pam spoke the words to me: "the body and blood of our Lord and Savior Jesus Christ." And then I held and served her with the same words. We then held hands in a large circle that had formed as each person had come forward for communion, and we ended the service with the Lord's Prayer.

Pam hugged Ruth and I enthusiastically and introduced me to her husband, Bill Clancy. "I liked how we were served last," I said. "It's how I normally do it."

"It's how we always do it," Pam said. "We believe that should be the way because Jesus taught that the first shall be last and the last first. So those in leadership serve others until everyone has been served and then it is their turn."

That night at bedtime, Ruth told me that had Pam not been there, Sam would have asked me to serve communion with his help.

"I'm surprised that the host pastor wasn't there," I said.

"My impression is that he's not that interested in what they are doing. That he was quietly invited in a way that allowed him to beg off, and he usually has."

"That seems to fit with their no pressure style."

"I like it," she said.

"I do, too," I said. "What would you feel if I became a leader in this community?" I asked.

"I'd like it," she said. "There's something about it that feels genuine. It feels right, quietly, calmly right."

"Affirming," I suggested.

"Yes, affirming," Ruth agreed.

"Do they have other pastors?" I asked.

"I think there is a Baptist pastor and a Pentecostal lay pastor that are active. But if they meet in a building and there is a pastor of that denomination present, that pastor conducts the communion service. Cindy says it is a matter of respect for our hosts."

"So Pam and I are the only pastors from our denomination?"

"I think so," she said. "At least locally."

"I could get some of my friends involved," I said. "They would do it for me."

"But would that be right?" she countered. "Remember - calm affirmation rather than pressure? Would any of your friends really want to do this?"

"I guess not. It's Saturday night after all."

"They'd want to be with their families," Ruth said.

"Or make the sermon longer," I said.

She laughed softly. "I love it how you think you are funny."

"I'm not?" I protested, pretending to be offended.

"Clueless you are," she said in her best Yoda accent. Then we were quiet for a while.

When I lay back later to give thanks, I found myself being thankful for these new people that had become, so gently, a part of my life. I was very grateful, I found, for the gentleness of this new community.

Sunday, March 1 - The last question

"OK, Bill," I said. "Let's get the last question done so I can move on to *descending grace*." We had decided to set the goal questions aside to give me more time for prayer and discernment.

Bill sat up a little straighter. "You'll never really be done with *ascending grace*, John. It is a never ending process and like math, each new lesson builds on what happened before. So the three basics still need to be a part of your life as long as you follow Jesus."

"It makes sense that I'll still be partnering, reading

scripture and answering questions."

"Exactly. Please read the last question for me."

"*7. Becoming like Christ: rate yourself plus or minus. Love, joy, peace. Patience, kindness, generosity. Trustworthy, gentleness, self-control.* There are then three blank lines followed by four questions. *Were you financially honest this week? (Mt 6:21) Do you wish anyone harm? Who needs your forgiveness? Participate in any addictive behaviors this week?*"

"Did you catch where the list of characteristics comes from? I think so, because you read them off in columns rather than horizontally."

"Yes, I recognized the fruit of the spirit from Galatians 5:22."

"So rate yourself. Did your behavior this past week exhibit those characteristics?"

"How exactly do I rate myself?"

"Basically, there are two methods. The one you use is up to you. The first method is to give your week an overall assessment of a plus or minus in each of the nine categories."

I marked on the piece of paper. "OK, now what?"

"You read off the pluses and share any details you want about the high points of your week. Then you read off the minuses and share any details you want about the low points of your week."

"What's the other method?"

"The other method is more detailed. Some people like to call it an inventory. The problem with the plus or minus method is that you can't always remember the details of your week. If you are optimistic, it's all pluses; if you are pessimistic, it's all minuses. It's not really very accurate."

"So how does the inventory work?"

"Have you every heard about Ben Franklin's thirteen virtue system?"

"No, I don't think so."

"Franklin made a list of thirteen virtues - qualities of excellence, like the fruit of the spirit. Then he made a grid - seven days by thirteen virtues. Each day, if he violated one of the virtues, he made a black dot for each

160

occurrence in the proper square on his form. And each week he would emphasize one virtue and attempt to practice it very carefully. Thousands of people have followed the same practice; tracking behavior is one of the more effective means of building a habit and changing behavior - if you are honest."

"Seems like more work than I want to put into it right now. Is the simpler one all right?"

"It's your decision, John, based on what you need. I'm your partner, not your boss. By the way, if something is neutral, you can say it's neutral."

"It was a plus week for love, joy and peace. It was neutral for patience, kindness and generosity - and by the way, isn't that word translated as goodness?"

"It means the same thing, and generosity is easier to identify than goodness. Likewise, trustworthy is often translated faithfulness. We just think the other words come closer to the intent."

"Minus then on trustworthy, gentle and self-control. Nothing really worth reporting, just that when you are keeping track you are more aware of problems than you might otherwise be."

"OK, that's your report. What is God telling you through your self evaluation?"

"That I'm not used to keeping track of anything. What are the blanks for?"

"There's not much that isn't covered by the fruit of the spirit, either directly or indirectly. But if you feel God urging you to develop a virtue, you can add that to your list."

"Do you have a list?" I asked.

"I've added 'listens' and 'organized' to the list as qualities I want to develop."

"I'm not sure what mine are."

"Take your time, John, and pray about it. If you ever get stuck not knowing how you should improve, ask your wife. That always gets a quick answer."

"Har de har har. You been talking to my wife?"

"No, mine has been talking to me. Read the next question and answer it."

"*Were you financially honest this week? (Mt 6:21)* I was, unless this is a trick question."

"It is a bit tricky." Bill handed me his New Testament. "Look up the scripture and read it, please. Matthew 6:19-21."

"*Do not lay up for yourselves treasures on earth, where moth and rust consume and where thieves break in and steal, but lay up for yourselves treasures in heaven, where neither moth nor rust consumes and where thieves do not break in and steal. For where your treasure is, there will your heart be also.*"

"The test in the question is whether or not in the past week money, or mammon, was ever a higher priority in your behavior than obeying Jesus. It's OK to be tempted, but did you yield?"

"I don't think so," I said hesitantly. "It's another thing to keep track of."

"There is one aspect of it that is not immediately obvious. Do you and Ruth tithe?"

I took a deep breath. "No, but we're close. It's always bothered me. What do you think about the controversy between tithing on the gross or the net?"

"That's something for you to work out with God. Cindy and I tithe on the gross of my salary and the net on her daycare."

"The topic is virtually ignored in my church."

"It is virtually ignored among all non-tithers because they feel guilty about it. Unless they are harassed by non-tithers, tithers never mind talking about their giving. They care, they give, and they care about what happens to their giving."

"To whom do you tithe?"

"Most of it goes to the local church, but some of it is reserved each month for special mission projects. For example, do you know that for $20 you can provide a pastors salary in Liberia, Africa, for a full month and feed his family?"

"No - that's incredible."

"It is," he nodded. "Cindy and I send $20 each week for this purpose. It frees the pastors to do their pastoral

162

work in the villages rather than having to farm just to grow food for their families. Because of the nature of the project, it comes out of the tithe."

"What's the negative for me from not tithing?"

"Nothing from us, John, except that you won't be able to start a Quest until you either tithe or have a rock solid plan to develop tithing."

"I know you'll tell me about a Quest later and refuse to tell me now. So what happens now?"

"Now you read the Bible, focus on improving your spiritual life by working at it each day, through the questions and with the help of a partner. And you can also learn how to fish for fish instead of someone giving you a fish today."

"Is that about dependency?"

"Our goal is to make disciples and then make disciple makers. With a child, you have to feed them for a while, but eventually they learn to feed themselves. Most traditional church approaches have the children gather for a spiritual meal but don't really teach them how to provide for themselves."

"That's an important distinction, teaching people to provide for themselves spiritually."

"We think so. The question we like to ask pastors is this: what would happen if God took all the pastors up to heaven and left the churches to fend for themselves?"

"Smaller churches are pretty self sufficient; they'd find some way to get things done. Larger churches are more complex organizations."

"It seems to us that a lot depends on the lay organization; churches that have ordained laity, such as deacons or elders, the provide pastoral care, would tend to do better than churches that don't."

"Our churches aren't organized that way," I said.

"You would know best. Who would step up and give the sermon on Sundays?"

I thought for a minute. "Oscar. Ross. Diane, anytime; Bill, in a pinch. They've done it before."

"Are they lay speakers?"

"Oscar was, and Diane was. Years ago."

163

"The New Testament was written in a time of persecution. They never knew whether they would experience what Jesus did - martyrdom was a constant possibility. So what we read in the New Testament expects us to create organizations that do not depend on the continuity of human leadership."

"I agree."

"Do you build that sort of organization?"

"Not as much as I like," I sighed. "Not as much as I am going to in the future."

"What's the next question?"

"*Do you wish anyone harm?*"

"This one goes with the next one."

"*Who needs your forgiveness?* Well, I don't believe that I wish anyone harm."

"Does anyone need your forgiveness?" Bill asked.

"I don't know. I'm not sure."

"There's two sides to forgiveness. One has to do with your forgiveness, where Jesus warned that if we do not forgive, we will not be forgiven."

"People have offended me. People have even harmed me. In this job, you learn to take it in stride."

"You mean, 'turn the other cheek'?"

"Not so dramatic as that. It's like the rain; it's going to rain some days, why complain about it?"

"So you tolerate abuse."

"I answered that question already."

"So, if you don't consider it abuse, or call it abuse, it's easier to take?"

"Not everyone is going to agree with me; you just take it in stride."

"So you don't wish harm to anyone?"

"No."

"And no one has ever wished harm to you?"

I shook my head. "Why am I getting so uncomfortable with this topic?"

"Usually," Bill said, taking another sip of coffee, "because people have harmed you and you have dealt with it by being in denial. By ignoring it."

I felt a flush of anger. Where had that come from?

164

"There must be something to what you say; I'm feeling anger about something."

"Let's pray about it." Bill took my hand across the table; it's measure of how much my life had changed that I didn't even flinch at the possibility of being seen holding hands with a man in public.

"Lord, Jesus," Bill prayed, "I thank you for the love and grace you have for all of us, including those who have harmed my brother John. I ask now that you would bring to his memory what is buried in his heart, so that your grace may again flow freely through him to those who need it. Amen."

"Amen."

"If we sit in silence for a moment, you are likely to remember."

We did.

"Harry," I suddenly said.

"Harry," Bill repeated gently.

"Harry did lots of things," I said. It was all coming back to me.

"Like what?"

"This was over ten years ago."

"So it's been buried a long time."

"Yes."

"What sort of things?"

"Well, he was pretty blunt. He was the church treasurer and financial secretary. I put out a checklist each year to every elected leader so that they can tell me what the want to do with regard to the position they serve."

"Harder to tell you face to face?"

"Exactly. Harry checked that he'd like to be relieved from the work of treasurer 'if I could find someone.' I did, and the new treasurer, an accountant, took over in January."

"And what happened?"

"Harry claimed at the first board meeting after that people didn't like it that I had taken the treasurer job away from him."

"What did you do?"

"I excused myself for a moment, walked back to the

office, got the file on nominations and brought it back to the meeting. I pulled out Harry's checklist and passed it around to him," I said. "There's a space at the bottom for their signature; I was awful glad I had added it, because he had signed it and couldn't deny it."

"So what happened?"

"Nothing much. People reminded him around the table that he'd been complaining for years that none of the young folks would do the work."

"So you called his bluff, basically."

"I damaged his ego, perhaps. What I actually did was just follow his instructions."

"You had no intent to do him harm, then?"

"No. There were times after that when he made me angry. But we had a grudging respect for each other. Except when he chose to be disrespectful."

"Such as?"

"He was a clock watcher. The service started at 10:45. At noon, he would get up and leave. It didn't go that late very often, but if it did, he was gone."

"So what do you feel when you think of him now?"

"Pretty much what I felt then. I'm disappointed in him. I believe he could have behaved in a much better way."

Bill rubbed his chin, lost in thought for a moment. "Do you think God ever feels disappointed in us?"

"I do."

"Even if God is omniscient and knows when we are going to screw up?"

"I think disappointed is not about being unsure of the outcome; I think it is about hope. I'd like to think that God has hope for us."

"I do, too. I'm pleased that you feel disappointed; it's more godly, certainly, than merely being furious."

"I couldn't do this work if I let myself get furious."

"So, have you ever forgiven Harry?"

I had to think about it for a minute. "No, actually, I don't think that I have. I did stop myself from getting angry, but I'm assuming your wanting me to understand that not being angry is different from actually forgiving

166

someone."

"We believe that God chooses to use human beings as channels of grace. God can bless us directly, but it seems that when God flows through you to me, we both are blessed."

"I agree."

"So by being in this state of unforgiveness..."

"I don't believe that God hasn't forgiven him for a minute."

"I don't either. But we're working on a different premise here - there is a text that says that what we bind on earth will be bound in heaven ..." He thumbed through this New Testament. "Ah, here it is: Matthew 18:15-20 *If your brother sins against you, go and tell him his fault, between you and him alone. If he listens to you, you have gained your brother. But if he does not listen, take one or two others along with you, that every word may be confirmed by the evidence of two or three witnesses. If he refuses to listen to them, tell it to the church; and if he refuses to listen even to the church, let him be to you as a Gentile and a tax collector. Truly, I say to you, whatever you bind on earth shall be bound in heaven, and whatever you loose on earth shall be loosed in heaven. Again I say to you, if two of you agree on earth about anything they ask, it will be done for them by my Father in heaven. For where two or three are gathered in my name, there am I in the midst of them.*"

"And your point?" I asked.

"When you forgive him, grace will flow more richly toward him. That will benefit him and you. Both of you."

"But I don't feel anything for which he should need my forgiveness. Why would I need to forgive him?"

"So, we are back to your feelings? We've already talked about how you prevent yourself from feeling them. And who are you to judge that, because you aren't angry, how he treated you wasn't a sin?"

"So I'm preventing God from forgiving him? I'm not that powerful, Bill."

"No you're not," Bill laughed. "But when God looks at Harry, what if what Harry has done to you is between them? Take it out of the way, John. Forgive him."

"I'm not withholding forgiveness, Bill."

"No, you're not. Forgive him anyway. Send grace toward him."

"I don't know if he is even alive. This was years ago."

"If he's dead and in heaven, he'll appreciate it. God knows where he is; why would you need to know his address to forgive him?"

"I feel foolish doing this," I grumbled.

"That's probably a good thing," Bill said. "I try to be foolish at least once a day; it keeps me flexible and young."

"All right, I'll pray."

"Please pray out loud so that I can agree with your prayer."

"Why would you need to do that?" I asked.

"Makes the prayer more powerful, John. We just read the verse on that."

I took a big breath and allowed myself to feel foolish. "God, I forgive Harry for everything I can remember and everything I can't remember. I ask that you would bless him and help him. In the name of Jesus, amen."

Bill looked up from his folded hands. "How do you feel?" he asked.

"The same," I said. I shrugged. "No, I feel better. Not a lot, but a little."

"It's a good thing to forgive people."

"I'll have to do it more often," I joked.

"Seriously, John, some day you should make up a list of people you've harmed and a list of people who've harmed you. Then, beginning where you feel ready, ask God for forgiveness individually, for each thing that you've done, and ask God to forgive each of those who've done things to you. There is a power in the emotional closure when we ask for healing where we are wounded."

"I'll do that sometime."

"You'll know the right time. And the last question?"

"Participate in any addictive behaviors this week?"

"Well?"

"How do you define addiction? I'm not into heroin much lately."

168

"Anne Wilson Schaef once said that an addiction is anything an addict says it is. In other words, if you believe it's an addiction, it is."

"Would you buy that definition?"

"We have one we think is better. First, an addiction has a pay off. There is some benefit or pleasure to the addict, although sometimes it is pretty sick, like taking pleasure in the misfortune of another. Second, we feel that an addiction does harm, whether to the addict or others around the addict. Third, we believe that an addiction is attractive, even compulsive - that a person is drawn to it, even when they recognize that it harms people. Fourth and finally, we believe that an addiction usually involves denial. That a person exhibits dishonesty, lying about some aspect of an addiction: that it isn't pleasurable, that it doesn't harm anyone, that they can quit any time they want to or that they are not being dishonest."

"That's a long list."

"Pleasure, harm, attraction, denial equals P-H-A-D. Phad."

"I can't think of anything. I used to sit in front of the television set and zap through lots of channels at night instead of sleeping."

"Let's test it. Pleasure?"

"Not sure. I was avoiding something - going to sleep."

"Let's come back to that one. Harm?"

"I wasn't getting sleep, and that was stressing me out."

"That's one. Attraction?"

"I feel foolish admitting it, but it was sort of a compulsion. I can't think of why it was attractive, but it was. I couldn't really stop it once I started."

"That's two. Denial or dishonesty?"

"I argued with Ruth about it a lot, claiming that it did me no harm."

"That's three out of four. But one would have been enough. Let's go back to pleasure. Why were you doing it, if there were no positive benefits for you?"

I thought about it for a moment. "The only benefit I can think of is that I was avoiding something."

169

"What?"

"Facing some problems in my life."

"So it was more pleasurable to avoid those problems than it would have been to honestly deal with them?"

"Well, yes. This was back when I reorganized my life to become a *One Minute Minister*. I didn't like the way I was living and I took action to change it."

"That's good. This is a little addiction, but some are worse. We ask this question because a lot of people deal with addictions and need a question for it on their page."

"Why can't dealing with the addiction be a goal question?"

"It could," Bill said. "But if they move on to other goals, they might not notice the addiction building back up on them. If they slip back into an active addiction, it's harder to get sober again; so the question is always there."

"This JUMP question is harder than the others."

"This question is about repentance; the others are positive in focus. This one involves you looking at aspects of your life that you might rather avoid."

"Didn't you say that Neil Cole's original questions were all like this?"

"Yes. That's why we simplified them; we felt that if people moved first toward the positive by reading scripture, focusing on prayer, reaching out to the lost and living their goals, they would have more power to let go of the aspects of their life that were holding them back."

"It's not really much of a list of sins, though, is it? What about the ten commandments? They're pretty blunt."

"You could keep the ten commandments and still not be patient or generous. These are simpler and more positive but they are still harder." He grinned. "You'll see what I mean when you review your week using them, week after week."

That night I went over the list of virtues with Ruth.

"You're a pretty good guy," she said affectionately. "I don't have any complaints."

"What about down here," I said, pointing to the blank

170

lines. "Bill said that if I didn't have any areas where I knew I needed to improve, that if I asked you, you would know immediately."

She chewed her lower lip in thought. "I'll stand by what I said, big guy. You're pretty good."

I looked at her. "You're hiding something."

She looked away, tried to control it, and finally burst out laughing. "So what! Better take your good guy badge and keep it! I don't want to get in the habit of criticizing my husband who I think is wonderful."

"I'm glad you think I'm wonderful," I said, pulling her to me and kissing her. "This is not about criticism. If I have a weakness, Bill said, you can help me make it more of a strength."

"Not criticism? I don't want you ever to think I'm a bitch."

"Honey, you could never be a bitch."

"OK." She paused as if hesitant to speak.

"There is something. I knew it," I said.

"It would be better to say, now that you insist that I think about it, that something does occur to me."

"I asked for your help," I said. "I'd be a fool not to accept it."

"Well," she said, watching me carefully. "There are times that you are rather argumentative."

"Can we argue about that?"

She giggled. "Later, maybe."

"We have to put down the positive. Wouldn't argumentative be covered by patient, kind and gentle?"

She nodded. "But it's more than that."

"What does it not cover?"

"The problem with argumentative is not that you are impatient or unkind; it's more like it's too much, that you don't know when to stop."

"Say more."

"After you make your point, you just pile on more and more facts and points."

"I don't think I can say that in one word. Know when to stop?"

"Brevity?"

171

"You always know the right word, sweetheart. I have two more lines to fill."

"I know." She looked closely at me. "Are you sure you want to do this?"

"What, am I going to be defensive? After my wife tells me that I'm wonderful?"

"Sometimes you get overly absorbed in something and don't really listen to me."

"Distracted?"

"More like ignoring me."

"Do I really?" I asked, drawing her closer to me.

"Not that much."

"Be honest."

"Not as much as you used to."

"That's better. I'll use the word 'attentive.' And number three?"

"You could be a little more romantic. A girl could get used to that."

I began to cover her with kisses. "It's now my highest priority. I'm a fast learner."

"I think I'm going to like this," she said.

Much later that night as I took time to be thankful, I was quite pleased with myself. Virtue could be a very good thing, and I truly intended to be a much better person. With my wife's eager help, of course.

CHAPTER SEVEN: Confirmation Class
Sunday, March 15

The door to the fellowship hall opened and three people entered, Sam, Pam and a third man who had to be the consultant, David Oliver.

"I'm pleased to finally meet you," I said to the tall, wide and smiling man. He was dressed in blue jeans, a blue oxford cloth button down dress shirt and Birkenstock sandals. He carried several file folders in one hand.

"John Adams, right?" he smiled, shaking my hand. "Where would you like to sit down?"

"Let's go over here," I said, indicating where two tables had been set together to form a square for conversation. "My wife, Ruth, and Cindy are picking up pizza on the way back from dropping off the kids with a baby sitter." We had decided that the church basement would provide a more quiet environment for conversation than our regular lunch spot in Bill and Cindy's family room.

"Great," the big man said and settled into a chair. "I'll just sit here and play with my papers while you finish getting ready."

"What would you like to drink? Bill is making a pot of coffee, but we've got tea we can make. And there's all kinds of soda pop in the machine."

"Any Diet Dr. Pepper?"

"The only diet is Diet Pepsi," I said.

He shook his head in mock disgust. "A glass of water will be fine." He opened a file of what looked like correspondence and began making notes right on the letters and occasionally on sticky notes. Bill arrived with the coffee for he and I.

"Hello, David," he said politely.

"Hi, Bill. John, tell me how the two of you got connected."

I reminded him about the day I prayed about disciple making last January 28 and how it lead to emailing him, then the week spent with Sam on basics, followed by the weeks where Bill and I did one of the questions each week as an orientation to the JUMP groups.

"Is he on the four by twelve, Bill?"

Bill shifted in his chair. "No, David, we found that John is a regular reader of scripture, so it wasn't much of an adjustment for him. He was already reading two chapters a day before we started and easily boosted it up to four."

"Staying in the gospels?" David asked.

"Yes. He agrees with our position that the words of Jesus are the most important."

"What's the four by twelve?" I asked David.

"As a means to help people get oriented to the habit of reading scripture and become familiar with the gospels, we recommend and celebrate people reading the four gospels through twelve times. We write it '4x12' and celebrate it at the Gathering."

"I remember now," I said. "People were applauded for 25%, 50%, 75% and got a certificate for 100%."

Bill nodded. Sam and Pam brought their coffee in as well. David continued to read and work on his correspondence. When Cindy and Ruth brought the pizza in, he stood up and walked over to my wife.

"You must be Ruth," he said, taking the pizza and setting it on the table behind him and then shaking her hand. "Cindy is very proud of your progress."

"Thank you, Dr. Oliver. I'm very pleased to meet you."

"Please, just David." When Cindy and Ruth had taken their coats off, Sam nodded to Pam and there was a prayer for the meal. We each pulled slices of pizza onto paper plates.

"Well, John and Ruth, what would you like to talk about?" David asked when everyone had started on their pizza.

"I understand that you have a lesson to teach us," Ruth said.

"There's always time for questions. Before, during, after."

"Bill told us that this session had a name - what was it? - oh, yes, 'Sugar Packet Theory.' My curiosity has been killing me."

"Bill, do you have them?"

"Sure, David." Bill reached into his pocket and withdrew four packets: one white sugar and three kinds of sweetener, blue, pink and yellow. And a small package of Saltine crackers.

"A ritual has developed around this session, John and Ruth. With titles and terminology. Even the sitting is predetermined." Ruth and I sat across from him, with Cindy and Bill to our left and Pam and Sam to our right.

"Titles?" Ruth asked.

"You and John are called pilgrims. Bill and Cindy are your sponsors. Sam is the lay director and Pam the spiritual director; those are actually their titles in the movement."

"How exciting," Ruth said.

"So you and Cindy went through the same thing?" I asked Bill.

"Pretty much. Sam was the lay director. Pam and her husband Bill were our sponsors."

David laughed. "The other custom is the sugar packets; they are brought by the sponsors and taken home by the pilgrims."

"It dates back to the first time David gave this talk," Pam said, "back in a restaurant in South Carolina. He was looking for something to use as examples and pulled these out of the tray in the center of the table. There's a couple of other traditions. As this talk evolved out of questions being asked, it always starts with questions."

"So what would you like to know?" David asked us.

We looked at each other. I knew that Ruth would prefer that I, as the extravert, did most of the talking. She would interrupt if she had anything to say. I felt her hand rest on my leg under the table, stroking my thigh, but I wasn't sure if she was seeking comfort or attempting to give it.

"First question, then," I said. "You keep referring to a movement, sometimes 'the' movement. Does this movement have a name?"

"Not officially. People who make fun of us usually make some sort of pun on the JUMP group - Jesus

175

Jumpers, Holy Hoppers, jump for Jesus, are you going jumping with me, etc. Stuff like that. Most of the time when a name is needed, people use the name off of my website - *disciplewalk*. But there is no official name because we are pretty much a decentralized, leaderless network of people who are all trying to learn how to follow Jesus."

"So you are not a church?"

"Not a church, not a cult, not a faction, not incorporated, not a 501c3 charity. We don't accept donations for our work and whenever possible we give it away. We exist to help people follow Jesus."

"Is there a meaning to the term 'disciple walk'?" Ruth asked.

"In Australia they have a rite of passage called a 'walkabout' where youngsters leave the village as children, go on a spiritual journey of discovery, and return to the village as adults. These journeys are largely unsupervised. The young people are expected to find their own way. So a disciple walk is meant to be a walkabout where a person encounters Jesus as a spiritual child, follows Jesus, and returns home as a spiritual adult. In most primitive cultures, the rite of passage into adulthood is supervised by the grandparents of the village. We have grandparents, in a way," he said, smiling at Sam and Pam.

"So there is no actual disciple walk?"

"We have a process which we call Quest if people want to go through a systematic journey of growth. It's up to the individual and the community."

"I'd like to know more about it," Ruth said.

"It's on the website, in Seminar Three. And your partners will go over it with you when you've completed *descending grace*, if you are still interested.

"So this is another idea from your online dissertation?" I asked.

"Yes. As people make suggestions, the document is evolving. There is a link to the original doctoral project, but we've been editing and updating the basic files for several years."

"How many years?" I asked.

"I posted the original online in the fall of 2007. It was a convenient way to ask friends for feedback and proof reading. But I had always intended to share it widely and for free."

"Did you have a website before?"

"No, I learned how to put one together for that specific purpose. Of course, it has grown far beyond my original expectations."

"What lies ahead?"

"That depends on my partners," he said, nodding at Sam and Pam. "They are also contributing material. Another partner in New Jersey is setting up an online community that will handle email, downloads, personal sections, and a discussion board."

"Personal sections?"

"Like 'mydisciplewalk' - photo, contact information, email, links, uploads, downloads, etc. Once we have the discussion board up we can use it to teach online classes."

"I've not really heard of anything like this."

"It's not original with us," David said. "Church planter Bob Logan organized www.coachnet.org to help widely separated church planters learn from and support each other. It's still the premier example of its type."

"I'm sure I'll think of other questions," I said, looking at Ruth. She shook her head.

"We'll be happy to try and answer them," he said. "Ready to start?"

We nodded.

"I assume you are familiar with the statistics on church membership decline."

"I've heard too much about them," I said.

"I've become a collector of them," David said. "They are a symptom of a system coming face to face with its own mortality. Usually they are pulled together by the visionary minority in the hope of shocking the pragmatic majority into action. Unfortunately, when you attempt to pressure or scare the bureaucracy, you ensure that they will cling even more tightly to the customs that are bringing about their own destruction."

"The gospel enters human social networks in four

177

basic ways." David continued. "Traditional church growth theory advocates a "person of peace" approach along networks of family and friends. Two other forms of kinship networking are shared interests and geographical proximity, which is kinship between neighbors who live close together. A fourth approach, the diffusion of innovations, explains how these social networking strategies function and why they succeed. The diffusion of innovations is concerned with 'how to bring about change in a social structure and how to speed up the rate of adoption of that change.'"[2]

Our approach is based on two theories of systems which we believe describe the same reality. One is the diffusion of innovations, which is the study of how positive change in the form of innovation is brought into cultures that normally resist change. As following Jesus is a huge change, it's going to be strongly resisted. We believe, therefore, that the diffusion of innovations gives us a valuable strategy for evangelism."

He produced another handout, a graphic with a parable under it. "This graphic is what we call the adopter framework. When change is brought to a culture, some adopt it more openly while others resist. There are five distinct groups distributed in a standard bell curve. The percentage for each of the five groups is consistent: innovators are 2.5%, early adopters are 13.5%, middle adopters are 34%, late adopters are 34% and laggards are 16%. We find it helpful to refer to the first two groups as the innovative minority and the last three groups as the pragmatic majority. Diffusion of innovations theory suggests that these grouped responses to change are universal in human cultures. As we know who we are around the table, we'll read our parts and act out the parables. Ruth, will you be the narrator and read out the chairman's part?"

"All right," Ruth agreed, and began. *"Parable: The Stainless Steel Church. The Chairman of the Administrative Board called the meeting to order. 'We have a problem,' he announced gravely, 'with mice. They are gnawing holes in the wood and getting into the church.'"*

David read next. *"The innovator had an unusual idea. 'If we tore down the old church and built a new one out of stainless steel, the mice couldn't gnaw their way in.'"*

Sam read next. *"The early adopter saw the advantages. 'We would certainly be in the forefront of all the churches in our conference in using this new material to build a church. Just think: it would never rust, never need painting, and last forever.'"*

Across the Diffusion of Innovations Adopter Framework

Who do you know in this adopter category, inside or outside the church?

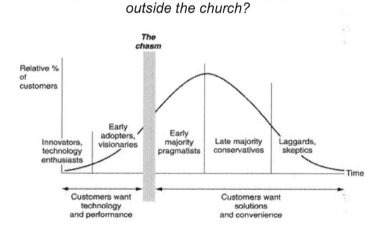

Bill read next. *"The middle adopter was practical. 'Wouldn't it be very hard to work with steel as a building material? You'd have to weld everything. And it wouldn't be cheap.'"*

Cindy read next. *"The late adopter was nostalgic. 'I would miss the old church of wood. It seems so comfortable and warm to me. Wouldn't steel be expensive to heat in winter?'"*

Pam declared, "I'm an innovator, but I love reading the negative part." She cleared her throat noisily. *"The laggard harrumphed. 'My sister has too many cats on her farm. I'll bring one over tomorrow and it won't cost us a nickel.'"*

Ruth finished the parable: *"'Well, I see we've solved that problem,' the chair noted. 'Now, on to the next problem.'"*

David smiled. "Do you see yourselves in the mix?"

"I think I'm an early adopter," I said.

"I agree, honey," Ruth said. "You are always asking questions just like that, trying to figure out the best way. I think I'm a middle adopter. John is high tech and I'm low tech. Whatever is needed to get the job done."

"The diffusion of innovations is the scientific study of cultural change that blends principles of sociology, psychology, anthropology and communication theory," David said. "It has been applied in countless different projects ranging from health to education to computer science, from the most poverty stricken areas of the third world to the most sophisticated forms of high technology marketing. The classic text originated in rural sociology as a study of the adoption of hybrid seed corn in Iowa. The model derived there has been found to be relatively true in every human culture and with regard to every innovation."

"So we know how to cause change?" I asked.

"Absolutely. We know exactly what to do," David stated flatly.

"Then why is the world so screwed up?" Ruth asked.

"Because human beings prefer to implement change in ways that don't work. And systems find ways to pervert the change so that no change actually happens."

"How do they do that?" I asked.

"That's another tangent, which Peter Senge calls the 'Limits to Growth' systems archetype. We'll look at it a little later today."

"Sure."

"There are four paths by which the gospel enters a culture. The four paths create the network of kinship relationships which church growth expert Donald McGavran called 'the bridges of God.' The four paths involve shared relatives, shared interests, shared addresses and the diffusion of innovations. What do the negative statistics tell you is happening?"

"We are not utilizing the four paths?"

"True enough," David said. "And worse, our society is destroying the four paths."

"You need to explain that."

"In the early 1960s sociologists Rodney Stark and John Lofland studied the first conversions to the Unification Church or "Moonie" cult in the United States as a means of identifying why people convert. Conversion only occurred when it followed or coincided with the formation of strong social attachments, typically family ties or close personal friendships. The opposite was also true; if a person maintained strong attachments to a network of non-members, conversion did not occur. Those who joined were often new in town and separated from their family and friends. Therefore, social attachments lie at the heart of conversion, and conversion tends to proceed along social networks. As Laurence R. Iannaccone has said, this principle has been replicated in scores of subsequent studies all over the world. Stark has also identified the same principles at work in the New Testament church in his book *The Rise of Christianity*."

"How does this information affect the four paths?" David asked.

"People join movements when they are disconnected from their previous social networks," I said.

"Yes?" David asked.

"Are they ever disconnected today? In the high tech world, with cell phones and the internet, no one is ever really separated from their past family and friends. So that influence continues."

"True enough," David said. "What else?"

"People join new religious movements to meet human needs, particularly social needs."

"Exactly," David said. "So what does that mean?"

"Previous relationships continue due to high technology, but they are unsatisfying. They may be strong enough to prevent a connection with a new religion, but they are not strong enough to really meet human needs. Therefore the potential convert is trapped in a limbo."

David and the others around the table nodded.

"I think that the weak networks are fine when everything is going alright," I said. "People in crisis are knocking on the door of the church when they have a problem those weak networks can't handle."

"Exactly," David nodded.

"But they aren't there after their problems are solved - they go back to their old networks," Ruth observed.

"Until the next crisis," I muttered.

"So what is happening with the networks between people?" David asked.

"New networks aren't really forming; everyone is hanging on to their old friends in new locations, even when they add new friends."

"And as people get spread thin, what happens to all those many relationships?"

"They are more and more shallow," Ruth said. "To the point of being meaningless."

"What do you observe in the church, John? And you, Ruth? What are the differences between those who move from place to place, and those who stay in place so that multiple generations of families remain in touch locally?"

"The ones who stay in place are very connected to each other. Sometimes I envy that closeness, because we have to move for John's job," Ruth said.

"And they are the least likely to be open to any kind of change. Any pathology that is present is usually unaddressed," I said grimly.

"In any group, the people who will be resistant to change, including remaining in their home towns, will be the pragmatic majority. Likewise, it's the innovators who are most open to moving away and trying a new location. What's the advantage of that according to the Rodney Stark material?"

"If you are meeting someone who lives away from their home network, they are most likely innovators."

"Exactly. Innovators are very comfortable wandering far from their home base."

"Or if they are not innovators or early adopters, they are probably very homesick," Ruth said.

"That's right," I agreed with my wife. "They would be drawn into new relationships because their loneliness would be even more acute."

"That's true, Ruth. You've come up with another insight. Are you sure you are not an innovator?"

"Nope," she said. "Just a pragmatic female in touch with the emotional side of people."

"Middle adopters are very sensitive to how others are feeling," Sam observed. Pam was smiling at Ruth like she was a star pupil who'd just won an award.

"The key issue, we believe, is that modern life is destroying all relationship networks. This is not simply conjecture. Here's a handout on the work of Harvard sociologist, Robert Putnam, based on his book, *Bowling Alone: The Collapse and Revival of American Community*." David set out a handout for Ruth and I to read over.

HEADS: *Robert Putnam's research indicates that American networks of engagement are breaking down and that this loss of "social capital" is the primary cause of many serious social problems.[3] As the church is the primary builder of social networks, the decrease in social capital is both a cause and a result of the decline of church participation in America.[4] Relationships that build community bonds between neighbors are essential to disciple making.*

What are the causes for decline in social capital according to Putnam's research? Factors which probably contribute little to the decline in social capital include divorce, people living together or alone, the decline of the traditional American family, racial issues, big government, the welfare state, two career families and working women.[5] By focusing on these factors, systems successfully avoid change which would result in real improvements in social capital.

Factors which contribute significantly to the decline in social capital include slum clearance which destroys neighborhood relationships, the shift from local businesses replaced by regional giants where people shop as strangers, and the involvement of the power elite in corporate politics rather than community politics. Major factors in the decline include pressures of time and money, especially for two career families (10%), suburbanization, commuting and urban sprawl (10%), television and electronic entertainment (25%), and generational change, where lack of community involvement seems normal (over 50%).[6]

"So this has happened before, in history?" I asked David.

"In the late 1800s, Putnam says. The problem today, however, is our cultural absorption with high tech entertainment. People are engaged in relationships with television characters and know the issues on their favorite show much more intimately than those in their own town. They are plugged in to media entertainment and disconnected from reality."

"How about the electronic games that simulate reality? Where you can create your own family, your own neighborhood, and your own boyfriend?" Pam asked.

Sam snorted. "What about sports that you play by swinging a handheld device at a television screen? Tennis, golf, bowling, baseball, basketball..."

"Or musical instruments that you play electronically while you dance around?" Bill said.

"It used to be very different when I grew up," Cindy said. "The kids would play softball in the streets, all ages together. The older ones showed the younger ones how to play the game. Somebody's mother was always watching out the window and if you didn't behave, your mother got a phone call."

"Children used to learn how to relate to each other in a naturally developing community," David said. "In those same neighborhoods now, all the houses are shut up tight with the people hiding out inside. They're not even in front of the television together; they each have their own television in their own room. No one is learning how to interact with each other."

"If they are even home," Bill said. "The kids aren't at home any more; they are in one athletic league or another. Families rarely even eat together."

"Is it the technology that is doing this?" I asked. "Isn't there something that can be done?"

"We believe that there will be a traditional backlash at some time in the future. That people will realize that life is not more fulfilling with 100 more cable tv channels. We think there will be a movement to do more with other people and do less in front of a virtual screen."

"Be nice if all the computers would just stop working overnight," I said.

"Don't stop there; you need to go all the way back to air conditioning," Pam said.

"Air conditioning?" I asked, bewildered.

"I was talking about this with a church once," Pam said. "And a crusty old retired marine pointed out that this is when, in his childhood, people stopped associating with each other. When they got air conditioning, they hid inside their homes. Back in the 1800s when they overcame this problem, the heat in the summer drove people out of doors to associate with each other."

Cindy shook her head. "I worry about my kids."

"I worry about us," Bill said.

"Think about it," Sam said. "If you are the kind of Christian that believes in hell, what's going to happen when you go to hell and stand in line for a drink of ice water?"

"What do you mean?" I asked.

"Guys in line talk to each other, just like in prison. 'What did you do to get here?' one will ask. 'I killed someone.'"

"I killed a whole family," Pam suggested.

"I raped and pillaged an entire country," Bill suggested.

"I engineered a stock market collapse that made me a billion dollars and put a million people out of work," suggested Cindy.

"I killed my husband," Ruth said, glaring at me in mock indignation.

"And what did you do to get sent to hell?" David asked Sam.

"All I ever did," Sam said with feigned timidity, "was watch television. I paid more attention to my television set than I paid to God."

"Exactly," David said. "On the one hand, we are disconnected from each other and, as was said in the days of Nazi Germany, all that it takes for evil to triumph is for good people to do nothing. On the other hand, all kinds of people are very busy in pursuits that ultimately mean nothing. Nothing at all," he said, shaking his head slowly.

"So the concept of holiness is changing," I suggested.

"Say more," David requested.

"While the old sins are still with us," I said, "and the prisons are full, the reality is that people's lives are very full with activities that are not very sinful by the old definitions and likewise not very virtuous. *I know your works: you are neither cold nor hot. Would that you were cold or hot! So, because you are lukewarm, and neither cold nor hot, I will spew you out of my mouth.*'"

"And the solution then is ..." David said.

Pam read the verse in context. "Rev 3:14 *'And to the angel of the church in Laodicea write: The words of the Amen, the faithful and true witness, the beginning of God's creation. I know your works: you are neither cold nor hot. Would that you were cold or hot! So, because you are lukewarm, and neither cold nor hot, I will spew you out of my mouth. For you say, I am rich, I have prospered, and I need nothing; not knowing that you are wretched, pitiable, poor, blind, and naked. Therefore I counsel you to buy from me gold refined by fire, that you may be rich, and white garments to clothe you and to keep the shame of your nakedness from being seen, and salve to anoint your eyes, that you may see. Those whom I love, I reprove and chasten; so be zealous and repent.*"
She paused for a moment.

"*Rev 3:20 Behold, I stand at the door and knock; if any one hears my voice and opens the door, I will come in to him and eat with him, and he with me.*" She paused again for emphasis.

"*He who conquers, I will grant him to sit with me on my throne, as I myself conquered and sat down with my Father on his throne. He who has an ear, let him hear what the Spirit says to the churches.*"

"I understand what you are pointing out," I told her.

"John, have you ever noticed that this verse is addressed not to the evil people of the world, but to Christians who are clueless as to their true spiritual state?" Pam asked. "Listen to the list: *'wretched, pitiable, poor, blind, and naked...'* Our emphasis on obedience is teaching people to be overcomers, those who conquer ... if nothing else, at least overcoming their own lethargy."

I tapped the handout that David had given me on Putnam's work. "David, we do have volunteers. People turn out all the time for good deeds."

"Putnam didn't say that bowling was declining; his point was that bowling teams are declining. So what's the difference?"

"Bowling is bowling. So other than the bowling itself, what's the difference between a team and a group of friends out bowling?" Pam asked.

"Ugly bowling shirts, for one," Ruth laughed.

"Competition," Bill suggested. "There's more of a challenge with a team."

"And you are more evenly matched with a team," I said. "In a family, parents will be teaching the kids how to bowl. So it's a different purpose."

"A team has a goal - to win," Cindy suggested.

"And what leads to that goal?" David asked.

"Team work," I offered, "which means diminishing problems, strengthening fundamental skills, working together toward a common goal."

"All needed to win," David said. "What else are we missing?"

"One significant difference," I said. "When you are on a team you have a commitment to show up. An obligation, a schedule. If you skip, your team forfeits automatically. Team play teaches commitment."

"So it's not merely relationships that we are talking about, but the presence of a reliable commitment in those relationships? That you can expect something of these people?"

"Yes," I said. "And from that learned trust, you got to know people well enough to borrow a $100 or a car."

"That would be the test," Bill said.

"Communities are disintegrating," David summarized, "because people are no longer willing to invest the time in making and keeping commitments to other people. And because of this, our children are learning that lack of commitment from us."

"That's about the size of it," Bill said.

"And as communities disintegrate, the bridges of God between people go down as well."

"Are you sure?" Ruth asked. "I don't like them, but what about all those people interacting on the internet? Facebook? Myspace?"

"What about them?" David said.

"When you need to borrow $100," Pam asked, "which one of those relationships is strong enough? Who knows you well enough to trust you?"

"I see your point," Ruth said.

"Jesus chose twelve disciples and spent the majority of his time with them for three years to teach them a discipleship system," Sam said. "That's the model we hope to follow. You can't do that on the internet; you need to do it face to face."

"You could do it on the internet if the faith were concepts," Pam said. *"Read this, and if you agree, click here to accept Christ as your savior, click here to print out your virtual church membership certificate."*

"Is Christ a concept?" David asked, looking at each of us in turn. We each shook our heads.

"It's a relationship," Ruth said.

"It's real," Bill said.

"It's about obedience," I said.

"It's about listening to learn how to obey," Cindy said.

"It's about action - serving others," Pam said.

"It's about helping others learn how to follow Jesus," Sam said.

"So this is what we are about," David said.

"Yes, it is," I said, and we all nodded.

David stood up and stretched his arms. "Let's take a break, people." And he walked up the stairs to the outside door.

"Where's he going?" I asked.

188

"Probably going to walk around the block," Bill guessed.

"Does he want company?" I asked.

"Usually not. He does this to think," Bill said and grinned. "It's usually a plus when two pilgrims say something that makes him think."

David called them back to order in about ten minutes. A single sheet of blank paper sat in front of him.

"It's our position," David said, "that the connections between people by which faith moves from one person to another are breaking down in society today. Therefore, any system of disciple making will need at first to build a relationship with the other person sufficient for the gospel to move from a disciple to a non-disciple. Agreed?"

It made crystal clear, perfect sense, I thought, nodding with the others.

"Now let's talk about grace." He drew a horizontal line across the bottom of the page and a heart in the middle.

"What kind of grace is this?" he asked, tapping the heart with the tip of his pen.

"Justifying grace," Ruth answered. David wrote the term under the heart.

"And everything God does before that moment of justifying grace is called?"

"Prevenient grace," I answered. David wrote the term underneath the line to the left of the heart.

"And everything after the moment of justifying grace that helps us grow in faith?"

"Sanctifying grace," Ruth supplied. David wrote the term under the line to the right of the heart and he drew an arrow point at the far end of the line to the right.

"And so, forever and ever, amen," he intoned. "Why is this understanding of grace insufficient for disciple making?"

"Prevenient grace makes disciples," Ruth said. "Sanctifying grace as you've described it results in Christians growing and growing and growing."

"Is that normal?" David asked.

I shrugged. "It's not unheard of, but normally in nature other things become important."

"Like what?"

"For human beings, children. Grandchildren. People. Community. Everything is not about your own individual, personal growth."

"What else?"

"Sanctifying grace and holiness must involve obeying the commands of Jesus Christ. And the command of Jesus Christ is to teach new disciples to observe, and to obey all the commands of Christ."

"And?" David asked gently.

"And that must by definition include the Great Commission."

"And how would you reflect that in this diagram, Ruth?"

She gestured toward the piece of paper; he passed it and the pen around the table to her.

"For a disciple to make disciples, sanctifying grace must curve around and participate as a partner with prevenient grace." She drew an arc from right to left, up over the heart. "When this happens the process becomes a cycle that repeats. A disciple is taught to grow in faith and then make a new disciple, thereby becoming a disciple maker; then the disciple maker teaches the new disciple how to obey until they, likewise, make their own disciples."

"Well said, Ruth. Would you want to add anything, John?"

"She said it well enough. I would add that I like Rick Warren's use of a baseball diamond to illustrate the same purpose."

"What's the difference between the Saddleback baseball diamond and our cycle?" Bill asked.

"In ours, we go around the bases with the other people. Warren doesn't really talk about that. Disciple making, however, is expected of every person. They are very close," David said.

"There are classes for each level in the purpose driven model, so the church provides for people moving from one base to another," Sam said. "Rather than classes, we do the same thing with relationships."

"Relationships are the key to the gospel spreading, so it makes sense to stay with them throughout the process," Pam said.

"You'll build stronger relationships that way," Ruth said. "Strong enough to support the spreading of the gospel."

David took out another piece of blank paper and drew a circle that covered half the sheet. "Time to change the subject to systems. Peter Senge gives us terminology to describe systems. The simplest one is very useful to understand churches and the problem of not making disciples."

"The simplest systems archetype or example Senge offers," David continued, "is called *Limits to Growth*. It describes the reality of what happens when change puts pressure on a system. All of Senge's systems archetypes consist of different combinations of two components, a reinforcing system and a balancing system."

In the center of the large circle David drew a beam balanced on a fulcrum. "The goal of a balancing system is to keep everything functioning in a stable, comfortable, familiar fashion. Happiness is a comfortable stability."

"In order to achieve this stability, balancing systems cycle; they repeat the same process over and over again." David drew a circle around the balancing beam. "Day follows night follows day. Seasons. Everything is a repeating cycle. And when a system gets something right, it locks it in and does it over and over again. That's one of the ways you identify a balancing system."

"It sounds a lot like church," I said.

"What cycles happen in a church, John?" David asked.

"The Christian year. Holidays. The lectionary. Bills come once a month all year."

"The women's bazaar and chicken salad luncheon," Ruth added.

"Yes," I groaned. "Every fall like clockwork."

"So we would be safe if we identified the traditional

church as a balancing system?"

"I think you would be very safe," I said.

David drew a small circle on the left side of the big circle. "This is a reinforcing system. It is an ongoing trend for change; it may also cycle, but it is teleological. It has a purpose which will change the system. The image for a Reinforcing Loop is a snowball rolling downhill increasing in momentum and intensity. Happiness is an emerging trend."

I nodded my understanding.

"The balancing system maintains current homeostasis in order to keep everything running smoothly. It prevents any change that would cause instability. The image for a Balancing Loop is a teeter-totter; happiness is keeping everything in balance."

"This two part system, consisting of a cycling balancing system for maintaining current homeostasis and a linear reinforcing system that brings change, describes a common reality studied by a variety of sociologists, management theorists, historians, psychologists and philosophers. As a common reality studied by many experts, you can find lots of analytical studies and historical realities that utilize it. In our movement, we bring a lot of these together in order to make disciples. I think you've seen this handout before."

The Balancing Loop in Peter Senge's *Limits to Growth* Systems Archetype

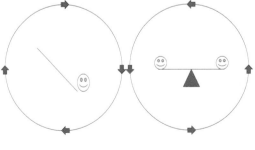

Reinforcing Loop   Balancing Loop

192

Emerging Trend	Smooth Cycles
Brings Change	Preserves Stability
Exciting	Comforting
Conductors	*Resisters*
Leadership	Management
Big Picture	Micro-managers
Vision	Details
Proactive	Reactive
Responds to Potential	Responds to Anxiety
Entrepreneurial	Institutional
Ready to gamble	Risk averse
Visionary Minority-16%	*Pragmatic majority-84%*
Church of Piety (sect)	Church of Power (church)
Antithesis	Thesis and Synthesis
External focus	Inward focus
Mission	Maintenance
Evangelism	Resistance to Growth
Ignores Limits	***Prevents Competency Limits***
Out of control	**Under control**
Pushes the trend	***Thermostat correction***

I nodded. David laid the previous diagram with the smaller and larger circle next to the Limits to Growth handout.

"Normally we refer to this one as the church system or temple system," David said, indicating the big circle. "And the smaller one we call the discipleship system. The discipleship system has two purposes. First, to bring converts from the world into the church." David drew an arrow from the outside through the small circle into the big circle. Then he wrote prevenient where it entered the discipleship system circle and sanctifying where it entered the church system circle. "Second, a purpose which is rarely known or achieved, the discipleship system trains disciple makers to go out into the world and make disciples." He drew another line over the first line and put an arrow point at the far end.

"Does the difference in the size of the circles mean anything? Is it for example, the 80/20 rule?"

"No, the size of the circles is precise. The discipleship

system is 16% and the church system is 84%."

"Don't churches vary?"

"No."

"How can you believe that? Let alone, how can you claim to be so precise when all churches are different?"

"The size of the circles is based on our other scientific study of systems." David lay the handout on the diffusion of innovations down on the other side of his circle diagram. "The discipleship system is a force for change; nothing changes your life as much as the gospel of Jesus Christ as Lord. 2 Corinthians 5:17 *Therefore, if any one is in Christ, he is a new creation; the old has passed away, behold, the new has come.* Therefore, a discipleship system by definition is a visionary minority of 16%, pushing on a pragmatic majority system of 84%. The discipleship system by definition is a spiritual reinforcing process with only 16% of system resources, pushing on a temple system balancing process controlling 84% of the system resources."

I gave a low whistle. "No wonder change is hard."

"The opposition to change is there, but the diffusion of innovations shows you how to handle it. The major point is that Senge's 'Limits to Growth' archetype describes the same structure in reality as the diffusion of innovations adopter framework. The same principles apply and they explain and illuminate each other."

"Surely you are not claiming that all innovators are evangelistic."

"No, but I am claiming that, from the system viewpoint of the church pragmatic majority, all evangelists are either innovators or early adopters. It's not only new ideas that threaten system stability, it's also new people." He drew a rectangular arrow pointer on the paper. "Remember those games from your childhood when you would spin a pointer to determine your next move?"

"Yes," Ruth said.

"Imagine that the diffusion of innovations adopter framework spins on its center like one of those old game pointers, to point in any one of many directions.

Whichever direction you pick, the people will rearrange themselves in the categories of the adopter framework."

"So, youth ministry?"

David nodded. "Will be supported by a visionary minority of 16% and tolerated by a pragmatic majority of 84% - as long as the youth don't create enough anxiety to provoke a thermostat reaction."

"That explains a lot ... about virtually every decision and argument in a church."

"Yes," David said, "every visionary minority is jockeying for its share of resources for its pet projects. All the time."

"I find this a little confusing," Ruth said. "There's some terms that aren't yet defined."

"Let me define them for you," David offered.

"Pushing the trend," Ruth said.

"Innovators and early adopters exercise leadership by attempting to push the balancing system around. This generates resistance and they push harder for the trend," David said. "When they do this, resistance increases until a balancing point is reached that offsets the pressure for change, and thereby restores stability and prevents change. Then the visionary minority push harder and the cycle repeats until they give up."

"Thermostat response," Ruth said.

"The system has a thermostat set for how much instability it will tolerate before clamping down," David said. "If pressure from the visionary minority creates anxiety, the increase in instability will trigger a clamp down not in response to a problem but as a response to the increasing anxiety. When the visionary minority forecast gloom and doom, they mobilize and motivate the forces that resist change."

"Prevents competency limits," Ruth said.

"When the balancing system is overwhelmed, the system falls apart into chaos where there is no stability. Like Iraq after Saddam Hussein's control was destroyed. Like hurricane Katrina overwhelmed the levee system in New Orleans. When the system is overwhelmed and becomes incompetent to control reality, horrific disaster results. Therefore systems will do anything necessary to maintain balance and control at all times," David said.

"Is it as simple as this seems? What if there are two sides to an innovation?" Ruth asked.

David shrugged. "It's a problem with Everett Rogers' research methodology. When you design a research project, you attempt to isolate a single variable and test it. So Rogers' research studied the adoption of hybrid seed corn, an innovation so positive and beneficial that there was no argument possible, thereby perfectly isolating in clear focus what Rogers wanted to study - the rate of adoption. Real life is much more complicated and with multiple variables."

"We believe that Rogers' methodology led to at least one wrong conclusion," Pam said. "He believed that once an innovation was firmly establishing among the early adopters, that full adoption was inevitable. In reality, that's wishful thinking; Geoffrey Moore's work, known as *Crossing the Chasm*, points out the repeated failure of innovations to make it across the chasm between early adopters to middle adopters."

"What is the failure rate?" I asked.

"Traditionally, in diffusion of innovations thinking, the understanding is that 90% of innovations fail to be adopted," Pam answered.

"Once into the middle adopters, a trend does attain critical mass and adoption is inevitable," David said. "Rogers didn't perceive the chasm because he was working with an innovation with no flaws. In the real world, innovations are rarely so perfect."

"What you are saying is that there can be more than one reinforcing process impacting a balancing system."

"Yes," David said, "although we don't usually diagram systems that complicated. Senge has a whole bunch of types with different combinations, but we prefer to focus just on this one."

"So if there can be more than one reinforcing process, can there likewise be more than one discipleship system?"

"Think it through, John, and you tell me."

"As there are an infinite number of positions for a

pointer, my guess would be yes. But how then could you call it a discipleship system?"

"What we believe is that a discipleship system is created by the presence of an active disciple maker. The pointer can point at all sorts of populations or issues; they all involve people. A church can have a reinforcing system which attempts to change the suffering of poor people; if there is a disciple maker making disciples in the midst of that, it functions as a discipleship system."

"If disciples are made, then it is a discipleship system," I said

"By definition," David said.

"No disciples made, no discipleship system? Does that explain the bad news numbers about declining churches?"

"We believe that there is always a discipleship system present, or at least the potential for one. It's also possible for the balancing system to interfere in such a way that disciples aren't made or kept."

"Does that happen much?"

"All the time, because new people, by being new and usually different, change the priorities and the balance of a system. The system reacts to restore balance, and the easiest way to do that is to neutralize the new people. The usual method is enough conflict so that the new people go away OR so that whatever activity that is making disciples is shut down or rendered ineffective."

"Can you tell me what a church would look like with more than one discipleship system?"

David smiled like a child on Christmas morning. "I can. Chapter two in the dissertation, online, describes the world's largest church, the Yoido Full Gospel Church of Seoul, Korea, which has 700,000 members."

"I've heard of it."

"They have 70,000 cell groups, each one functioning as a decentralized discipleship system, attached to the primary church system. Each one makes disciples and makes disciple makers."

"I don't think I'm going to be able to start 70,000 cells or pick up 700,000 members. I'll be lucky to help the

197

church system in my church allow the innovative minority the freedom to make disciples."

"Your people will surprise you. Our methods are based on diffusion of innovations strategies. The evangelism we practice is network based and focused on building relationships so there is usually a good match with these methods and smaller churches. The larger churches, however, have problems adopting them."

"Why?" Ruth asked. "I would think that if they are larger, they would already have a lot of this stuff happening."

"As they grow larger," Pam explained, " they tend to shift from being relationship based to activity based. We believe that people mature more through relationships than through activities; this is why we believe small churches have an advantage. In activity based churches, energy and time are diverted into programs and away from people growing spiritually."

"And we believe that spirituality depends on relationships for growth," Sam said. "Larger churches can mirror the world and be too busy for people to honestly relate to each other. It's a matter between being a participant in a relationship or a spectator at an activity."

"Can you support that biblically?" I asked.

"Sure," Sam said. Everyone in the room but Ruth, David and I pulled out New Testaments and began thumbing through them.

Pam started. *"Matthew 22:36 "Teacher, which is the great commandment in the law? And he said to him, "You shall love the Lord your God with all your heart, and with all your soul, and with all your mind. This is the great and first commandment. And a second is like it, You shall love your neighbor as yourself. On these two commandments depend all the law and the prophets."*

Bill read, *"John 13:34-35 A new commandment I give to you, that you love one another; even as I have loved you, that you also love one another. By this all men will know that you are my disciples, if you have love for one another."*

Cindy read, *"1 Cor 13:1 If I speak in the tongues of*

men and of angels, but have not love, I am a noisy gong
or a clanging cymbal. And if I have prophetic powers,
and understand all mysteries and all knowledge, and if I
have all faith, so as to remove mountains, but have not
love, I am nothing. If I give away all I have, and if I
deliver my body to be burned, but have not love, I gain
nothing."

Sam read, "1 John 4:7-12 Beloved, let us love one
another; for love is of God, and he who loves is born of
God and knows God. He who does not love does not know
God; for God is love. In this the love of God was made
manifest among us, that God sent his only Son into the
world, so that we might live through him. In this is love,
not that we loved God but that he loved us and sent his
Son to be the expiation for our sins. Beloved, if God so
loved us, we also ought to love one another. No man has
ever seen God; if we love one another, God abides in us
and his love is perfected in us.

Pam, Bill and Cindy were looking up other verses as
Sam read his. "Enough, enough," I laughed. "You've
convinced me."

"Certainly, we have," David said calmly. "But systems
resist change. So the best results come when we stop
trying to change the system and let the church system be
what it is and do what it does."

"Now, that makes no sense at all," I objected. "I'm
interested in disciple making for my church. I want to get
them into disciple making, all of them, and be 100%
compliant with the Great Commission."

"If you attempt to do that, John," Sam said gently,
"unfortunately, you will fail and go down in flames the
way most change agents do - presenting your change to
the entire body at once. Don't do that, John. These people
bite."

"Now I know I don't understand," I said.

"John, when you don't understand, it's time to listen,
not object," Ruth said to me. She folded her hands in front
of her and looked right at David. "Stop playing games with
us and tell us what you are going to tell us."

David smiled at Pam. "I told you they were smart,"

199

she said.

"Here's what we want to tell you," David said gently. "Jesus didn't tell you to change the church. Jesus didn't tell you to change the world. Jesus just told you to go and make disciples. When you set that simple goal aside to focus on the church or anything else, you've stopped making disciples. You've stopped being obedient, in other words."

"So just make disciples?"

"Why should anything else be more important? Jesus said 'all authority on heaven and earth has been given unto me.' If he wanted you to change the earth, he would have told you right then. Instead, he told you to make disciples. Go and do that."

"And the focus of our tools is simply to teach you how to do that," Bill said.

"It has to do with system structures," David said. "When you try to change structures, systems step in and prevent you. Just follow what we call the structural principle: *the problem is not to change or replace structure but to utilize existing structures for disciple making.*"

"That's not what my friends tell me."

"Are your friends making disciples?"

"They claim they are."

"And how are they making disciples?"

I ticked their answers off my fingers. "Contemporary worship. Praise bands. Demographically targeted mailings. Sermons that target the needs of the unchurched. Hospitality and a warm welcome. Replacing traditional practices and architecture with what will satisfy the emergent tastes of the unchurched."

"And are these practices making disciples?"

"They say they are."

"I say they are not. How is one recognized as a disciple?"

"By reading God's word."

"I didn't hear that in the list you gave. Perhaps it will become important later in these churches. All the things you mentioned are not only very expensive, they also alter structure in ways that most systems won't allow. Your friends are attempting the build a stainless steel church."

"I guess I can see that."

"We don't care, basically, about all those things. We believe that relationships make disciples, and I'll guarantee you that whenever you find increasing numbers you will find relationship building in one way or another. But we don't care about structure. What we do will allow someone to make disciples in any environment because we are not doing it in or through the church system at all - we are doing it in the discipleship system and letting the church system have the freedom to continue to do whatever it wishes. If we are making disciples, we can let other people choose the hymns and what color to paint the fellowship hall. We don't care."

"I care," I said.

"John does want it his way," Ruth said, smiling.

"It does make a difference to me what color it is," I said.

"And that probably has to do with the part of you who is a professional systems manager in the church system, with graduate degrees to boot. But you can separate that professional ministry from making disciples."

"I'm not sure I follow you," I said.

"I know. I'm not explaining it well," David said. "It has to do with my realizing that my job and disciple making are two different things. I realized a long time ago that I am a bivocational church planter - it's just that my day job is as a local church pastor."

"I understand it, honey, and I'll explain it to you," Ruth said to me, patting me on the arm.

"OK," I said, turning toward her.

"Making disciples is an expression of love, like what you feel for me or for our son, just like making disciples for God is an expression of God's love. It's not a job."

"I still have a job."

"It's not your job to love me, silly," she said. "Even though you better not stop if you know what's good for you."

"You're right, it's not a job to love you."

"Everybody has a job, a ministry, to put their gifts to

work," Pam said. "Everybody also has a family to love. The difference in our approach is that you make disciples with your family rather than on the job; you make disciples in the discipleship system rather than in the church system."

"Sugar packets will explain this, John, better than anything else," Sam said.

"Let's take a break, then, and dive in," David announced.

David took another walk around the block. Ruth seemed very tender toward me, as if I had done something romantic. I didn't have a clue what it was I had done, but I was no fool. I just sat there and held her hand.

CHAPTER NINE: Sugar Packet Theory

"Sugar packets," David announced, laying them down on the table in a straight row.

"Is the order important?" I asked.

"No, not really, but traditionally the crackers go first. It's just a sequence of five stages which represent the development of spiritual maturity."

"I've heard about this," I said "I read something once."

"You know all about this," David said, "but you probably haven't read much about it because it is too simple. The only author who's had much to say similar to what we teach is Greg Ogden, in his book, *Transforming Discipleship: Making Disciples A Few At A Time*. We call it developmental spirituality, which could be described as having five basic stages correlating to human development: *newborns, children, adolescents, parents* and *grandparents*." As he said each word David pointed to the packets in order, beginning with the crackers. "The goal of developmental spirituality is to fulfill each stage properly and move the individual onward to full developmental spiritual maturity. Problems occur when a person becomes stuck at one stage - arrested development - or is forced prematurely to the next stage, which is codependency. Churches can become imbalanced such that the majority of ministry is focused on meeting needs at one stage rather than ensuring a steady flow of persons through all of the stages."

"How long does it take for a discipleship system to bring a convert to full spiritual maturity?" I asked.

"Cell churches believe this goal can be achieved in one year," David said. "The three year ministry of Jesus described in the Gospels produced several generations of disciples. We believe that grace works on God's timing, so people mature - unless they are hindered - and grow at the pace God desires."

"If God desires it, how can human beings hinder it?" Ruth asked.

"In pediatrics it's called 'failure to thrive' - deprived of the nurture needed, the infant just stops growing. We believe that the church system deprives spiritual newborns of the consistent emotional and spiritual nurture of relationships that they need to be able to grow up spiritually." He looked at the others. "You ready, guys?" he asked the others in the room. Out came the New Testaments.

"The first stage of spiritual growth is newborn." David pointed to the crackers. "We could say infancy, but people don't like being called infants even if it is true. Who wants this one?"

"I do," Pam said. "*2 Corinthians 5:17 Therefore, if any one is in Christ, he is a new creation; the old has passed away, behold, the new has come.*"

Bill read, "*1 Peter 1:23 You have been born anew, not of perishable seed but of imperishable, through the living and abiding word of God; for 'All flesh is like grass and all its glory like the flower of grass. The grass withers, and the flower falls, but the word of the Lord abides for ever.' That word is the good news which was preached to you. So put away all malice and all guile and insincerity and envy and all slander. Like newborn babes, long for the pure spiritual milk, that by it you may grow up to salvation; for you have tasted the kindness of the Lord.*"

Cindy read, "*John 3:3 Jesus answered him, 'Truly, truly, I say to you, unless one is born anew, he cannot see the kingdom of God.' Nicodemus said to him, 'How can a man be born when he is old? Can he enter a second time into his mother's womb and be born?' Jesus answered, 'Truly, truly, I say to you, unless one is born of water and the Spirit, he cannot enter the kingdom of God. That which is born of the flesh is flesh, and that which is born of the Spirit is spirit.'*"

"Newborns are pretty much like babies. Do you remember that stage?" David asked.

Ruth and I looked at each other. "Yes, we do," we said in unison.

"Remember how good it was when your son would sleep through the night? Could feed himself? No longer needed diapers?"

"Yes, I do," I said.

"I remember it fondly now; I sort of miss the days when he was a baby," Ruth said. "But I know that it was awful as well and I've never been so tired in my life."

"You love your newborns but they wear you out," Sam said.

"What would it have been like if you had quints?" Pam asked.

"Arggh!" Ruth said.

"Exactly," Pam smiled. "How about a hundred babies, all crying at the same time?"

"No, thank you," I said fervently.

"Sure about that?" Pam asked me with a wink. Suddenly I remembered the parable about the church being a spiritual orphanage where the pastor cared for dozens of crying babies.

"The next stage is that of a child," David said. "Children are curious. They explore their world and ask a million questions. They play and express their joy."

Bill read, "John 8:31-32 *Jesus then said to the Jews who had believed in him, 'If you continue in my word, you are truly my disciples, and you will know the truth, and the truth will make you free.'*"

"Children, in other words, are disciples," David said. "A disciple by definition is interested in learning. Therefore we find spiritual children where people are learning, in Bible studies or Sunday School. Children, in other words, self select for these activities."

"So, John," David says to me, "here's your first challenging concept. If the children hang out in Sunday School, where do the newborns gather?"

"In worship," I said. "I got that a long time ago. Seventeen percent of worship attenders are in a class or Bible study. That's leaves 83% in the worship service at the Newborn level."

"So you don't want to impress me with how mature your people are?"

"No, I love my people and I see the newborn characteristics in them."

"So, one place we can turn to make disciples is among

religious people we find in the worship service. That has become the method of the church system."

"That can be explained, I hope," I said.

David drew out a fresh sheet of paper and drew the large circle again. "This is the church system, complete with everything that traditional churches have. Worship services in a temple with a professional, highly trained high priest. Staff put on programs and committees organize activities. Money is collected."

"Don't forget to have plenty of parking," I pointed out.

"Definitely." He made a mark at the bottom of the circle. "Church systems are enamored with the front door and getting people into worship through the front door, which faces the parking lot. Everything you mentioned that your friends were doing earlier is aimed at getting people into the front door of the church. Strangers walk through that door and are warmly welcomed by other strangers; they enjoy the friendly atmosphere and then leave as strangers. If these strangers attend worship often enough, then it is believed that the magical mystery moment will occur when they become disciples. And what is wrong with that belief, John?"

"I don't know. What is wrong, David?"

"It's not working. It's unchallenged, a sacred cow. If it was working, then all those worship attenders would be in Sunday School within a year ... but they're not, even in the most committed, enthusiastic, emergent churches. Instead we have these giant holding tanks for immature Christians assembled for enjoyable worship. And the immature Christians just sit there, not growing. They love it. The drop off for anything more serious than worship is at least two thirds. And eventually, you get the same division - about 17% move into a weekly experience of studying God's word."

"It's pretty darn close to the diffusion percentages of 16% and 84%," Ruth said.

"It is," David nodded. "And that is some success - 17% - but it's a very poor system for making disciples if 83% of Christians remain at the infantile level of spiritual

206

maturity. No sane person could really call that successful."

"Or worth imitating," I said.

"And you have the problem of the back door," David said, making a mark at the top of the circle. "People wander into the church system, wander around for a while, and then wander back out into the world. If you don't cater to their every need, they drop out sooner. Running a spiritual daycare where 83% of participants are in the nursery means that the few mature people you have are exhausted with taking care of them. With such large crowds there is little hope of really keeping an eye on each person."

"Of course," Sam said drily, "if you kept an eye on each person, then you'd be developing relationships and you'd have something else entirely."

David drew the smaller circle on the side of the church system. "The discipleship system represents the side door to the church. The one, like in your home, that is not used by visitors, company or guests, but the door used by family. Newcomers enter side by side with people who belong; no one comes in as a stranger because everyone enters with someone with them."

"Partnership," I said.

"Exactly," David said. "You can form partnerships in the nursery, but it's much more efficient for people to start out in partnerships. That's why you have to go out into the world to make disciples - to form those partnerships out there."

"I see that," I said.

"If you form the partnerships in the world," David said, "the church system doesn't have to change to accommodate new people."

"Are you saying that the new people lose their preferences?"

"No, just that the relationship formed in a partnership more than makes up for any conflict in their preferences."

"Who writes about this? I know you have a source."

"The basic one in the cell church literature is Bill Beckham, *The Second Reformation: Reshaping The Church*

207

For The Twenty-First Century. He calls these immature Christians 'Eddies.'"

"Why in the world would he do that?" I asked.

"It's a story. I think I have a handout on it in the file." He pulled out a piece of paper and handed it to me to read.

The Discipleship System and Beckham's "Eddies"

William Beckham, growing up in the American south, likes to quote a Henry G. Bosch story about a customer noticing the absence of a slow moving store clerk named Eddie: "Where's Eddie? Is he sick?"

"Nope," came the reply. "He ain't workin' here no more."

"Do you have anyone in mind for the vacancy?" inquired the customer.

"Nope! Eddie didn't leave no vacancy!"

There are quite a few "Eddies" in most churches today. They leave, and no one even notices. Why? First, because there is no real sense of the Body of Christ in which members are involved in a functioning manner. Second, many, by their own decision, have chosen to sit on the church bench on the sidelines of the action.[7]

Beckham points out that the percentage of "Eddies" in most churches is upwards of 80%. They participate in worship and little else. They are passive consumers of pastoral care, unable to care for themselves spiritually, and demanding that the entire church revolve around caring for their dependency needs. This burns out those who are willing to serve and the church turns away from mission and evangelism to maintenance - the maintenance of spiritual infants. The following long quote by Beckham is the clearest definition I know of what is wrong with the church today:

Eddie's contract with the traditional church is to be pampered, to receive ministry and to be entertained. In exchange, he will be counted in the numbers and will give an offering from time to time to support the system. Consumer Christians represent 80% of church members who are supported and ministered to by the other 20% who produce.

This means that Eddie is anything but a neutral factor in the ministry of the church. In fact, he probably represents its most serious debilitating factor. Eddie is a major consumer in the church itself, requiring many producing Christians to care for his needs. Consumer Christians neutralize the productivity of the 20% of mature members who expend most of their time and energy ministering to Eddie, Mrs. Eddie and all their Little Eddies. . . .

When all the Eddies sit down on church pews, you can almost hear the sucking sound as they draw ministry to themselves. How many producing Christians would you estimate are required to maintain the kind of program that will attract Eddie and keep him happy in the traditional church? Whatever the number, it is high maintenance and low return on the time, effort and money, because Eddie seldom contributes in a positive way to either the edification of the church or the evangelism of the world.

Eddie may leave if he finds another church he feels meets more of his needs. Eddie will gravitate toward the strongest ministry pull and the most guaranteed benefits. Eddie can always find spiritual sounding reasons to justify his migration to greener pastures. "We are concerned for the spiritual welfare of our family. This new church has such a wonderful program for our children." Or, "Their style of worship is so exciting and moving. We want to worship God like that." Or, "I am fed by the wonderful peaching of that pastor. He is such a spiritual man of God." Who can question Eddie's motives when he gives such spiritual sounding reasons?

When Eddie leaves, he and his type "leave no vacancy" in the real ministry or work of the church. They just leave an empty spot on a pew on Sunday morning, a little less change in the offering place and one less member to have to pamper and please. Church leaders then must go out looking for another Eddie or two to replace the ones lost. What is going on here?

Churches of all sizes are held hostage by consumer Eddies who are the prime target audience for most twentieth century churches. Indeed, some of the most popular church growth strategies of the past several decades are built around consumer Christians in one way or another. Clever marketing schemes try to attract and hold the Eddies floating around in a self-centered society.

Why has the church agreed to allow its most immature members to dictate the ministry focus of the church? Why does the church tolerate manipulation - practically blackmail - from those members who contribute the least to the work of the church?

Eddie has his hook into the one-winged church because his presence is the measure of success in one-winged church circles. . . . And Eddie will not come if we do not minister to him and give him what he wants.

209

The traditional system needs Eddies to fill a pew, to be counted in the numbers on Sunday, to financially support the construction of new buildings and the addition of new staff "ministers." All of these hooks are necessary to attract more consumer Eddies, who can fill more pews, which creates a need for new and better buildings to attract more Eddies, which means bigger buildings and on and on the cycle goes. Eddie is the driving force behind the "noses and nickels" game of the traditional church.[8]

The task of the discipleship system is to cause spiritual infants to grow up through stages of maturity to become spiritual parents and grandparents. When developmental needs for nurture and safety are met, spiritual infants begin to developmentally mature. When cells function as nuclear families and cell leaders function as spiritual parents, this nurture is delivered and spiritual infants grow up.

David stretched his arms to relieve tension. "Basically, the baby Christians that refuse to grow up begin to harden in their immature state. They demand to be taken care of and are often able to reorganize the church into an entity that is designed to keep them happy and comfortable. Does that sound familiar?"

"It sounds like how you described the balancing system. And the pragmatic majority."

"And so it becomes normal for people to enter via the front door and receive ministry from the church without ever really growing up or giving anything back. These people are consumers - consumers of pastoral care. They are identified by their hungry cries and complaints. Their motto is this: *Pastor, I'm just not being fed. So feed me!*"

"I know plenty of those people," I admitted.

"After they have their bottle and are burped and rocked a bit, they can actually be quite pleasant once their needs are met," Ruth said.

"Ah, good. You see the cute side of newborns still. Normally, those of us who expect more find ourselves getting angry at them because they won't grow up."

"I can see that," I admitted.

"Which leads to another tradition," David said smiling. At these words the others around the table leaped at the crackers, smashing them with their fists. "If you let your frustrations go, all you will have are smashed crackers."

The others were all grinning like fools. "When I saw them do that, I almost fell out of my chair," Cindy laughed.

Ruth smiled bravely, but I could tell that her chair had almost toppled over backwards.

David arranged the packet of smashed crackers and the pink sweetener packet that stood for spiritual children in a vertical column. "So we have a rule in our movement: *you can be frustrated, but don't smash the crackers!* Now we want to ask you to name some specific people that fit into these categories and describe them. No need to use last names."

Ruth and I each came up with the names of three spiritual newborns and three spiritual children. We identified how they were connected in the church system and whether they were positive or negative in their influence.

"I'm thinking through the people who cause conflict in my church. By definition, they should be infants, but they are not at that level."

"That's impossible," David said, gesturing at Pam who had her New Testament ready to read.

"1 Corinthians 1:10-12 *I appeal to you, brethren, by the name of our Lord Jesus Christ, that all of you agree and that there be no dissensions among you, but that you be united in the same mind and the same judgment. For it has been reported to me by Chloe's people that there is quarreling among you, my brethren. What I mean is that each one of you says, 'I belong to Paul,' or 'I belong to Apollos,' or 'I belong to Cephas,' or 'I belong to Christ.'"* Pam turned a few pages and continued. "*1 Corinthians 3:1-4 But I, brethren, could not address you as spiritual men, but as men of the flesh, as babes in Christ. I fed you with milk, not solid food; for you were not ready for it; and even yet you are not ready, for you are still of the flesh. For while there is jealousy and strife among you, are you not of the flesh, and behaving like ordinary men. For when one says, 'I belong to Paul,' and another, 'I*

211

belong to Apollos,' are you not merely men?"

"Conflict is always caused by spiritual immaturity," David said. "Paul goes beyond that ... to divide up into groups where one is right and others are wrong is flesh. It is carnal. It is the primary sign of immature spirituality."

"They have to be more than infants," I protested. "Why, one was the chairman of the board at the church!"

"Don't confuse position within the church system with spiritual maturity. Let's look at the definitions we are developing and see how they apply. Give us a name for this individual - doesn't have to be his real name."

"Let's call him Eddie then."

"OK. Did Eddie attend worship?"

"Yes, he was the head usher."

"Was his influence positive or negative at worship?"

"Positive, I guess. He greeted people. He saw to it that details were taking care of, which I greatly appreciated."

"So worship was his primary focus. Was he involved in Sunday School or a Bible study that you know of?"

"Not at that time, not that I know of."

"Then he was not a disciple. Not a bad person, but not a disciple. A worker, but not a disciple. There's a difference."

"Is that judging?" I asked.

David shrugged. "Judging? Or diagnosis? Either one is fair, I guess. If you are the church soul doctor, sometimes you have to make a diagnosis." David paused. "Jesus suggests judging leaders by their fruits, good or bad. Consistently, was this man's influence for good or bad?"

"Good, as far as he was concerned."

"Was potential lost? Did he hold the church back?"

I had to think for a moment. "Nothing new certainly happened while he was in charge."

"So there was no innovation. Did he support you?"

"To my face, yes. Behind my back, not always. Of course, he was being pushed around by other people. Triangulated."

"But he was less than honest with you?"

"I'd have to say yes."

212

"Was he a tither?" Sam asked.

"I don't know. That church didn't want me to know what people were giving."

"John Maxwell has some wonderful material on leaders and financial giving," Sam said. "Some of his experience is that leaders like you describe frequently do not tithe."

"He did make the comment once that he and his wife gave their time rather than money."

Sam nodded wisely. "It sounds like he fits the pattern of an Eddie put in charge."

"How do you come to that conclusion?" I asked.

"Let's count down the items," Sam said. "First, he's not involved in study, so he's not a disciple by definition. He doesn't teach either, which is a part of being a disciple. He works in the church, but gathers to himself power and influence. Occasionally he whispers behind the back of his pastor. But fundamentally, if he's not a disciple, he can't be a disciple maker. And since he doesn't tithe, Jesus is not the Lord of his life."

"Whoa!" I said. "Where do you get that conclusion?"

"From Jesus," Pam said gently. "*Matthew 6:21: For where your treasure is, there will your heart be also.* If his money is not surrendered, his spiritual priorities are not what they should be."

"Are you saying he should not be a leader in the church?" I asked. David said nothing, but Sam, Pam, Bill and Cindy all made the sign of the "L" on their foreheads.

"Remember, John, in our movement this style of leader is actually a loser," Pam said gently. "We are focused on following and submitting to God's will, not gaining power and influencing others to do what we want. And one of the clearest indications of our focus is what we do with our money."

"Sociologically," Sam said, "that may be changing. I think the 'Lord of your life' thing relates to giving God the priority over any scarce resource. And in the USA in the 21st century, the scarce resource, more and more, is time rather than money. When we consider where our money goes and where our time goes, either indicate what is in control and has the priority in our life."

"Would you agree?" David asked me.

"I guess I have to agree. That is what Jesus said with regard to money, and a *One Minute Minister* is very conscious of submitting our time, minute by minute, to the will of God. It would have been good if the Bible said more about time management."

"But it does," Pam said. "There's some confusion in the gospels because of the desire of leaders to accuse Jesus, but the gospels are very clear about time management."

"You've lost me," I said.

"A person who does not tithe robs God, according to Malachi 3. But the tithe of time involves a commandment: Remember the Sabbath day and keep it holy."

"And it's more than a tithe of ten percent; the Sabbath day is a seventh or 14.3%."

"I see what you mean. But Jesus always relaxed the Sabbath laws rather than enforcing them."

"True, but the way the traditions of the elders came to enforce the Sabbath took that time away from the will of God, so the Sabbath became legalistic rather than freeing up time for obeying God."

"And for rest and relationships," Pam said.

"What do you mean by that, Pam?" Ruth asked.

"Before the tabernacle was built in the wilderness and worship on the Sabbath began, there was one basic principle: on the Sabbath day you go in the tent with your family and don't come out or we will kill you. The original Sabbath day took away every means by which people ignored or avoided, used or abused others in their families."

"It would be very difficult to hide feelings in that sort of Sabbath," Cindy said. "People would be forced by inactivity to talk with each other, to pray, to think things through before acting or making decisions."

"We're not here to challenge you, John, or to criticize," Sam said. "But Jesus is Lord involves Christ being Lord over your time and your money. How are you doing with that?"

214

I looked at Ruth for her agreement to discuss that in this place; she nodded.

"We've been working toward tithing our income. Right now, it's very close to ten percent of our net income. Someday I'd like it to be ten percent of the gross and even more."

"The tithe is your definition of the tithe," Sam said. "Some people argue with some justification that every penny belongs to God, so one should make decisions on the result of prayer rather than just designating ten percent."

Pam chuckled. "In our experience, while people say that they pray about how much God wants them to give, the amount of their final decision is usually based on their level of spiritual maturity. The more spiritually mature people are, the more they give."

"If you are ever in a church that allows you to know the amounts of member giving," David said, "it will always surprise you who is generous - and who is not."

"How do you reconcile this?" I asked David. "Tithe - is it on gross or net?"

"It's still your decision, John. And the tithe does not automatically go to the church treasurer; there are all sorts of charities and mission projects which are worthy of support. It's a decision through prayer that is between you and God."

"We do use tithing as an indicator of maturity, however," Pam said. "We talk about it among newborns and children, but don't demand it."

"It's a prerequisite for going farther?" I asked.

"Not a prerequisite; more like we simply begin to talk about it clearly and distinctly," Pam said. "People who want to accept their spiritual responsibilities are ready to grow; people who don't want to accept their spiritual responsibilities don't really want to grow up, and so they will avoid discussion on the topic."

"What about the Sabbath day?" Ruth asked.

"What about it, Ruth? What do you say?"

She looked at me. "I wish John would spend more time at home and more time with me and little John."

"I do, too," I admitted.

"I don't say anything about it because I don't want to nag. And I know the demands of the church people have to have a priority."

Sam shrugged. "John does have a job to do, but he also has a lot of power and discretion. If he's not using that power wisely, perhaps we can encourage him to do better."

"One of my goal questions is about spending more time with my son," I confessed.

"Perhaps the other could be about learning how God wants you to keep a Sabbath," Sam suggested. "As you keep praying about this you can work it out with Bill as a part of your JUMP group experience. That's what it's for, after all, your personal growth."

David took a blank piece of paper out of the folder and put in on the table. He took his pen and drew a cross that pretty much filled the page. He placed the smashed package of crackers in the lower right hand quadrant of the cross and the pink sweetener package in the upper right quadrant.

"This horizontal line is the line of discipleship; when you cross it, you are committing yourself to participating in learning. If your position is above the line you are a disciple; if you have not yet crossed that line, you are not a disciple. Jesus Christ called us to make disciples."

"If you call people over the line a disciple, what do you call people below the line?" I asked.

"That's a good question; we are so focused on people becoming disciples, I don't think we really have a name for it, do we?" He looked around the table for suggestions.

"Believers," Bill suggested.

"Worship attenders," Cindy said firmly. "All the people, almost all the people Jesus preached to attended worship in the temple; they weren't disciples."

"I've heard the analogy that a person isn't a Christian just because they go into church any more than you become a car when you go into your garage," Sam said.

"I like that saying," Pam said. "I think you could call them Christians. Although some really aren't. Many have

216

Jesus as their savior; they just haven't done much of anything with that relationship."

"Are they going to heaven?" Ruth asked.

"We don't know the answer to that," Pam said. "We think so, but we know that is God's decision."

"So you don't believe you have to be a disciple to go to heaven?"

"Being a disciple is not about going to heaven; it's about pleasing God. And like a little baby, parents love it when the baby grows up and learns how to walk. That's what all parents want. But they still love the baby while it is a baby. Babies go to heaven, but parents want them to grow up. Christians go to heaven, but God wants them to become disciples."

"And very few are becoming disciples," Sam said, "at least, by our biblical definition. I think I like the term 'not a disciple yet' as my choice."

"Pre-disciple?" Ruth suggested. We all laughed.

"I suppose you could say 'child of God' with the understanding that it is an infant child."

"When our system works," Pam said, "people who convert skip the infancy stage and enter the church system as disciples. It saves a lot of work, time and trouble."

"Now that sounds interesting," I said.

"Think about it," Pam said. "When the institutional church invites people in the front door then it's like they are epoxy glued to the pews. You can't pry them loose and you can't get them involved in anything else other than worship."

"Maybe fellowship," Bill said. "Because it's fun. Playtime."

Pam shook her head. "That's a part of the worship system; visiting with one another. It's how they sort of build their relationships."

"How do you bring people into the church at the child level?" I asked. I wanted to know the answer.

"When people come in through the discipleship system, they are already in a weekly learning group. They are already disciples because they stay in the discipleship system and aren't moved into the church until they are

217

beyond that level."

"You mean a JUMP group?"

"No, we call them *circles of grace*. Small groups. But basically we watch over them apart from the church system and within the discipleship system until they are ready for a JUMP group."

"So they are not introduced into the church system until they are disciples?"

"While each person has the freedom to do as they wish, it's something we picked up from the world's largest church; people there start out in the weekly cell meeting. If that's where they start then it is inevitable that they will eventually attend worship."

"Of course, if we make disciples out of worship, they are already in the temple system. It's better though, we think, if we nurture people spiritually in a small group until they are at the child level."

"So this is how the world's largest church does it?" I asked.

David tapped the diagram of a discipleship system. "They have 70,000 of these faith communities. The goal is for each one to make two disciples a year; they don't meet that goal as only 20,000 are converted each year."

"That's significant," I said.

"It's only two people a year per group," David reminded me. "That's not so hard for people working together. And these people first have contact with the church through their neighbors in the cell group. They do not encounter the church first through attending the worship system."

"Not at all?" I asked.

"The services are broadcast on television and the Internet, but they are far from seeker sensitive or seeker friendly. Even though it seats 12,000, people have had to wait in lines for over an hour for a seat in the sanctuary because of the crowding. So their connection with the church is with the relationships in the small groups of the discipleship system rather than the church system centered on the worship service. They enter the church through the side door, not the front door."

218

"The numbers are rather astonishing," I said.

"It's our contention," David said, "that you could close the front door, which is the concept that people are invited to worship and then afterward become disciples. And with a functional discipleship system, there would be more than enough people coming into the side door."

"The church system evangelizes through the front door, John, through invitation, hospitality, worship and activities that they believe meet the needs of irreligious persons," Sam said. "There's no objection on our part to that. But we believe that the more effective way to make disciples is through the relationships created in small groups through a discipleship system - what we call the side door."

"Let's take another break," David suggested.

"This vertical line is the dividing line," David began when we had reassembled, pointing at the cross he had drawn on the paper. "The horizontal line is the line of discipleship. The vertical line is the line of Lordship, of obedience to God. This is also highly supported in scripture."

The others had their New Testaments out. Pam read *"Matthew 7:21: Not every one who says to me, 'Lord, Lord,' shall enter the kingdom of heaven, but he who does the will of my Father who is in heaven. On that day many will say to me, 'Lord, Lord, did we not prophesy in your name, and cast out demons in your name, and do many mighty works in your name?' And then will I declare to them, 'I never knew you; depart from me, you evildoers.' "Every one then who hears these words of mine and does them will be like a wise man who built his house upon the rock; and the rain fell, and the floods came, and the winds blew and beat upon that house, but it did not fall, because it had been founded on the rock. And every one who hears these words of mine and does not do them will be like a foolish man who built his house upon the sand; and the rain fell, and the floods came, and the winds blew and beat against that house, and it fell; and great was the fall of it."*

219

Bill read, "Luke says it simpler: *Luke 6:46 Why do you call me 'Lord, Lord,' and not do what I tell you?*"

Cindy read, "*Matthew 28:18-21: And Jesus came and said to them, "All authority in heaven and on earth has been given to me. Go therefore and make disciples of all nations, baptizing them in the name of the Father and of the Son and of the Holy Spirit, teaching them to observe all that I have commanded you; and lo, I am with you always, to the close of the age.*"

"The key understanding when one crosses over the vertical line is a commitment to Jesus Christ as Lord," David said. "To make a commitment to obey, not just the letter of the law, but the heart of it."

Pam started. "*Matthew 22:36: 'Teacher, which is the great commandment in the law?' And he said to him, 'You shall love the Lord your God with all your heart, and with all your soul, and with all your mind. This is the great and first commandment. And a second is like it, You shall love your neighbor as yourself. On these two commandments depend all the law and the prophets.'*"

Bill read, "*John 13:34-35: A new commandment I give to you, that you love one another; even as I have loved you, that you also love one another. By this all men will know that you are my disciples, if you have love for one another.*"

Cindy read, "*John 3:35: the Father loves the Son, and has given all things into his hand. He who believes in the Son has eternal life; he who does not obey the Son shall not see life, but the wrath of God rests upon him.*

Sam read, "*John 12:49: For I have not spoken on my own authority; the Father who sent me has himself given me commandment what to say and what to speak. And I know that his commandment is eternal life. What I say, therefore, I say as the Father has bidden me.*"

Pam read, "*John 14:12: Truly, truly, I say to you, he who believes in me will also do the works that I do; and greater works than these will he do, because I go to the Father. Whatever you ask in my name, I will do it, that the Father may be glorified in the Son; if you ask anything in my name, I will do it. If you love me, you will keep my commandments.*"

Bill read, "*John 14:21: He who has my commandments and keeps them, he it is who loves me; and he who loves me will be loved by my Father, and I will love him and manifest myself to him.*"

Cindy read, "*John 15:8: By this my Father is glorified, that you bear much fruit, and so prove to be my disciples. As the Father has loved me, so have I loved you; abide in my love. If you keep my commandments, you will abide in my love, just as I have kept my Father's commandments and abide in his love. These things I have spoken to you, that my joy may be in you, and that your joy may be full. This is my commandment, that you love one another as I have loved you.*"

Sam read, "*John 15:14: You are my friends if you do what I command you. No longer do I call you servants, for the servant does not know what his master is doing; but I have called you friends, for all that I have heard from my Father I have made known to you. You did not choose me, but I chose you and appointed you that you should go and bear fruit and that your fruit should abide; so that whatever you ask the Father in my name, he may give it to you. This I command you, to love one another.*"

Pam read, "*1 John 2:3: And by this we may be sure that we know him, if we keep his commandments. He who says 'I know him' but disobeys his commandments is a liar, and the truth is not in him; but whoever keeps his word, in him truly love for God is perfected. By this we may be sure that we are in him: he who says he abides in him ought to walk in the same way in which he walked.*"

Bill read, "*1 John 4:19: We love, because he first loved us. If any one says, 'I love God,' and hates his brother, he is a liar; for he who does not love his brother whom he has seen, cannot love God whom he has not seen. And this commandment we have from him, that he who loves God should love his brother also.*"

Cindy read, "*1 John 5:1: Every one who believes that Jesus is the Christ is a child of God, and every one who loves the parent loves the child. By this we know that we* love the children of God, when we love God and obey his commandments. For this is the love of God, that we keep his commandments. And his commandments are not burdensome. For whatever is born of God overcomes the world; and this is the victory that overcomes the world, our faith."

"The symbol that Jesus uses for that commitment to obedience is the commitment to carry one's own cross just as he carried his," David said. "These verses identify what we mean by the concept *Jesus is Lord.*"

Sam read, "*Matthew 16:24-26 Then Jesus told his disciples, "If any man would come after me, let him deny himself and take up his cross and follow me. For whoever would save his life will lose it, and whoever loses his life for my sake will find it. For what will it profit a man, if he gains the whole world and forfeits his life? Or what shall a man give in return for his life?"*

Pam read, "*Matthew 10:34-39: Do not think that I have come to bring peace on earth; I have not come to bring peace, but a sword. For I have come to set a man against his father, and a daughter against her mother, and a daughter-in-law against her mother-in-law; and a man's foes will be those of his own household. He who loves father or mother more than me is not worthy of me; and he who loves son or daughter more than me is not worthy of me; and he who does not take his cross and follow me is not worthy of me. He who finds his life will lose it, and he who loses his life for my sake will find it.*"

Bill read, "*Philippians 2:1-14: So if there is any encouragement in Christ, any incentive of love, any participation in the Spirit, any affection and sympathy, complete my joy by being of the same mind, having the same love, being in full accord and of one mind. Do nothing from selfishness or conceit, but in humility count others better than yourselves. Let each of you look not only to his own interests, but also to the interests of others. Have this mind among yourselves, which is yours in Christ Jesus, who, though he was in the form of God, did not count equality with God a thing to be grasped, but emptied himself, taking the form of a*

222

servant, being born in the likeness of men. And being found in human form he humbled himself and became obedient unto death, even death on a cross. Therefore God has highly exalted him and bestowed on him the name which is above every name, that at the name of Jesus every knee should bow, in heaven and on earth and under the earth, and every tongue confess that Jesus Christ is Lord, to the glory of God the Father. Therefore, my beloved, as you have always obeyed, so now, not only as in my presence but much more in my absence, work out your own salvation with fear and trembling; for God is at work in you, both to will and to work for his good pleasure. Do all things without grumbling or questioning... And it gets progressively more unreal from there," Bill said, laughing.

Cindy read, *"Matthew 20:25-28: But Jesus called them to him and said, "You know that the rulers of the Gentiles lord it over them, and their great men exercise authority over them. It shall not be so among you; but whoever would be great among you must be your servant, and whoever would be first among you must be your slave; even as the Son of man came not to be served but to serve, and to give his life as a ransom for many."*

Sam read, *"Matthew 23:8-12: But you are not to be called rabbi, for you have one teacher, and you are all brethren. And call no man your father on earth, for you have one Father, who is in heaven. Neither be called masters, for you have one master, the Christ. He who is greatest among you shall be your servant; whoever exalts himself will be humbled, and whoever humbles himself will be exalted."*

Pam read, *"Matthew 25:14-30: For it will be as when a man going on a journey called his servants and entrusted to them his property; to one he gave five talents, to another two, to another one, to each according to his ability. Then he went away. He who had received the five talents went at once and traded with them; and he made five talents more. So also, he who had the two talents made two talents more. But he who had received the one talent went and dug in the ground and hid his master's money. Now after a long time the master of those servants came and settled accounts with them. And he who had received the five talents came forward, bringing five talents more, saying, 'Master, you delivered to me five talents; here I have made five talents more.' His master said to him, 'Well done, good and faithful servant; you have been faithful over a little, I will set you over much; enter into the joy of your master.' And he also who had the two talents came forward, saying, 'Master, you delivered to me two talents; here I have made two talents more.' His master said to him, 'Well done, good and faithful servant; you have been faithful over a little, I will set you over much; enter into the joy of your master.' He also who had received the one talent came forward, saying, 'Master, I knew you to be a hard man, reaping where you did not sow, and gathering where you did not winnow; so I was afraid, and I went and hid your talent in the ground. Here you have what is yours.' But his master answered him, 'You wicked and slothful servant! You knew that I reap where I have not sowed, and gather where I have not winnowed? Then you ought to have invested my money with the bankers, and at my coming I should have received what was my own with interest. So take the talent from him, and give it to him who has the ten talents. For to every one who has will more be given, and he will have abundance; but from him who has not, even what he has will be taken away. And cast the worthless servant into the outer darkness; there men will weep and gnash their teeth.'"*

"Do some people protest that this is not fair?" I asked.

Pam shrugged. "It says, *to each according to his ability*, so the one with the least ability still had an opportunity, and an opportunity that was within his capabilities, however limited."

"This parable is a primary scripture for the servant level," David said. "Whatever you have comes with a responsibility to use it wisely for the Master; some have less responsibility, some have more, but all are held responsible."

Bill read, *"Luke 16:10-15: '"He who is faithful in a*

very little is faithful also in much; and he who is dishonest in a very little is dishonest also in much. If then you have not been faithful in the unrighteous mammon, who will entrust to you the true riches? And if you have not been faithful in that which is another's, who will give you that which is your own? No servant can serve two masters; for either he will hate the one and love the other, or he will be devoted to the one and despise the other. You cannot serve God and mammon.' The Pharisees, who were lovers of money, heard all this, and they scoffed at him. But he said to them, 'You are those who justify yourselves before men, but God knows your hearts; for what is exalted among men is an abomination in the sight of God.'"

Cindy read, *"Luke 17:7-10: Will any one of you, who has a servant plowing or keeping sheep, say to him when he has come in from the field, 'Come at once and sit down at table'? Will he not rather say to him, 'Prepare supper for me, and gird yourself and serve me, till I eat and drink; and afterward you shall eat and drink'? Does he thank the servant because he did what was commanded? So you also, when you have done all that is commanded you, say, 'We are unworthy servants; we have only done what was our duty.'"*

Sam read, *"John 12:24-26: Truly, truly, I say to you, unless a grain of wheat falls into the earth and dies, it remains alone; but if it dies, it bears much fruit. He who loves his life loses it, and he who hates his life in this world will keep it for eternal life. If any one serves me, he must follow me; and where I am, there shall my servant be also; if any one serves me, the Father will honor him."*

Pam read, *"John 13:12-17: When he had washed their feet, and taken his garments, and resumed his place, he said to them, "Do you know what I have done to you? You call me Teacher and Lord; and you are right, for so I am. If I then, your Lord and Teacher, have washed your feet, you also ought to wash one another's feet. For I have given you an example, that you also should do as I have done to you. Truly, truly, I say to you, a servant is not greater than his master; nor is he who is sent greater than he who sent him. If you know these things, blessed are you if you do them."*

"We believe that when a person makes a commitment of this strength to Jesus Christ as Lord, their life begins to be changed by that commitment. They are tested by it and strengthened through that testing. They are no longer children; they are ready for more. They enter a period of spiritual adolescence."

Sam read, *"Hebrews 12:5-11: And have you forgotten the exhortation which addresses you as sons? -- "My son, do not regard lightly the discipline of the Lord, nor lose courage when you are punished by him. For the Lord disciplines him whom he loves, and chastises every son whom he receives." It is for discipline that you have to endure. God is treating you as sons; for what son is there whom his father does not discipline? If you are left without discipline, in which all have participated, then you are illegitimate children and not sons. Besides this, we have had earthly fathers to discipline us and we respected them. Shall we not much more be subject to the Father of spirits and live? For they disciplined us for a short time at their pleasure, but he disciplines us for our good, that we may share his holiness. For the moment all discipline seems painful rather than pleasant; later it yields the peaceful fruit of righteousness to those who have been trained by it."*

"What we are describing here," David reminded us, "is a process of spiritual maturity. It is a linear process that should move smoothly from one stage to another. The first two stages are characterized by nurture; the last two stages are characterized by challenge and hardship. It's hard to be a teenager and it's hard to be a parent."

"I can accept that," I said. Ruth nodded her agreement.

"At the newborn stage, the primary need is nurture and is best met by personal relationships rather than programs or events. When infants feel safe, they want to explore their environments and involvement expands from worship to include fellowship as the spiritual infant develops caring relationships." David touched the packet

226

of smashed crackers. "If the right sort of nurture is not present, the infant can harden into an 'Eddie' who demands that the church revolve around meeting his or her needs. This narcissism and complaint is the source of most church conflict and absorbs the energy of the church that should be invested in disciple making."

David pointed to the pink sugar packet. "Curiosity develops and the newborn crosses the line of discipleship and becomes a disciple. Disciples are found in opportunities for learning, such as Sunday School, Bible study or prayer meeting. They love the sermon whereas infants only tolerate it. They read books and devotional materials. Like children, they ask thousands of questions and pursue the answers. The church loses its way when it gives answers to the questions of the past rather than hear the questions of the present."

"That's because of the vast amount of change in our culture, right?"

"No, John, cultures don't change." He pulled out the diffusion of innovations handout from the pile on the table and set it on top. "Systems don't change. The concept that the church is shrinking because it is not in step with current reality is based on a false assumption."

"And what is that?"

"The false assumption is that church involvement is based on attracting non-Christians in through the front door by being hip. An 'emergent church' is fundamentally an oxymoron - a 'hip institution.' This misunderstanding develops because the innovators ask their questions the loudest, and they drown out the questions of the pragmatic majority. The basic pragmatic questions haven't changed much - how do I find happiness, overcome poverty, find meaningful work, make a lifelong marital commitment, raise happy children and enjoy love, joy and peace in my life? Because of cultural change, the church's answers to those questions will be different, slightly, but the questions aren't that different. The same human needs dominate the human race in every century because we remain essentially human."

I looked at Ruth; she nodded.

227

"What's lost in the large group attempting to answer cultural questions with a 'hip' worship service is that such a service must anticipate the questions that people would ask; the service is a scripted presentation, so you have to guess the questions the culture will ask in advance. A conversation in a small group, however, can immediately answer the exact question a person asks reflecting their exact situation in current reality. Therefore, the conversation is much more effective as a means of communicating the gospel."

"And services that address innovator questions primarily attract innovators," Pam said. "In fact, they swarm to anything new."

"And just as rapidly exit when they hear of something else new and interesting at another church," Bill said.

I thought for a minute. "If I hear what you are saying about the diffusion of innovations applied to evangelism, then beginning with the innovators should eventually draw in the rest of the framework."

"True in principle," David said. "In practice, innovators change so rapidly that a church that attempts to aim at them finds them a moving target. Second, a church that attempts to keep current with the constantly shifting needs of innovators will change so fast that it will not be able to attract and hold the pragmatic majority. It may successfully evangelize the 16% that are the visionary minority, but miss the 84% that are in the pragmatic majority."

"But aren't those the people that are already in the traditional church?" I asked.

"No, John. That's another basic misunderstanding," Pam said. "The diffusion of innovations adopter framework is universal. If you line up 100 innovators, the framework will still apply, just shifted to a more innovative center point. Among those hundred innovators, there will still be a visionary minority and a pragmatic majority. Each adopter category remains full."

"So what happens when an innovator moves from my church to one of the highly innovative emergent churches?"

Sam held up one finger. "First, the emergent church becomes slightly less innovative as your innovator joins their pragmatic majority. Your member is not an innovator in this new context; more often they are a late adopter or even a laggard that slows down the momentum of the emergent church. You'll frequently find a developing conflict within emergent churches of people attempting to bring them back to more traditional, familiar forms."

I nodded.

Sam held up a second finger. "The 100% that is your church will still have 2.5% innovators, 13.5% early adopters, and so on. The framework doesn't change. But the whole focus of your church will shift slightly to the right of the framework and become more pragmatic."

"This might be more helpful, John, for you to see the diffusion framework as fitting every aspect of a culture, groups as well as individuals. Out of all churches, 2.5% are innovator churches and 16% of churches are laggard churches. But within those churches people are not uniform; they keep their individuality and express the categories of the adopter framework."

"My church is definitely in the pragmatic majority," I said.

"And there lies a hidden and unappreciated strength for evangelism," David said.

"You've lost me. How can my old fashioned church have the advantage over innovator churches in a rapidly changing culture?"

"John, according to the diffusion of innovations, we do not have a rapidly changing culture. What we do have are rapidly changing innovators who, as always, get lots of attention. What sort of news story is it to report that Old First Church downtown is the same today as it was yesterday? So news programs always draw attention to the innovators."

"This sounds a bit like Richard Nixon's reference in the early seventies to the silent majority," Ruth said.

"That's a good example," David said. "What is so often misunderstood when we look at the diffusion of innovations adopter framework is this. We assume that our church, the church of the pragmatic majority, perfectly meets the needs of all people just like us."

"When obviously it does not," Sam pointed out.

"Therefore, the assumption is that the decline in church members is due to the innovator segment of the society growing as people leave a church that is no longer in step with society," Pam said.

"Which is not correct because the percentage of innovators and early adopters remains constant," Sam said.

"You are right, I've heard this a thousand times. What then are we missing?"

"According to census bureau research by Presser and Stinson, the percentage of the population in church worship on a given Sunday is 27%."

"I can see that in urban areas where so many of the unchurched congregate," I said.

"No, John, these figures are universal. There is some data to indicate that rural Americans are more unchurched than urban Americans. The assumption that is made is patently false - again, the reason given that unchurched people are unchurched is because they are somehow not like us, that they are made up of other ethnic cultures or socioeconomic backgrounds."

"It's a convenient face saving excuse," Sam said, "for the failure to make disciples. How can a non-Spanish speaking church be faulted for being unable to reach a Spanish speaking unchurched culture?"

"The primary motivation in most bureaucratic systems is to excuse their ineffectiveness in one way or another," Bill pointed out.

"So what is this hidden strength that my traditional church has?" I asked.

"The principle is that the diffusion of innovations adopter framework applies universally to all gatherings of people," David said.

"Therefore, you need to apply it also to lost people as a cultural segment," Pam said.

"And what does that mean?" I asked.

"Simply," Bill said, "it means that 16% of unchurched people are attracted to innovative churches doing all the flashy bells and whistles in their attempt to draw in the unchurched."

David smiled. "And the remaining 84% of the unchurched are from the pragmatic majority; they have no problem with traditional worship, small churches, traditional architecture, orthodox theology and all the other aspects of a traditional church."

"So they are more likely to be drawn to my type of church?" I asked.

"No," David said, "because that assumes that people attend a church that fits their prejudices. We believe that, once saved, they are equally attracted to any kind of church, because the gospel of Jesus Christ as Savior and Lord will totally change their lives - including their preferences. And once they have that changed life, they will attend the church - whatever that church is - of the friends that helped them find Christ."

"We are told that the unchurched will never accept the ways of the traditional church," I said.

Pam shrugged. "That's what they say." She opened her New Testament. "Listen to what Jesus says: *Luke 5:37-38 And no one puts new wine into old wineskins; if he does, the new wine will burst the skins and it will be spilled, and the skins will be destroyed. But new wine must be put into fresh wineskins.* You agree with that?"

"Of course," I said. "That's the verse they always quote about the need for change."

"Then hear this," Pam said. "*Luke 5:39 And no one after drinking old wine desires new; for he says, 'The old is good.'* You agree with what Jesus says there?"

I nodded slowly.

"The King James translates it as 'the old is better' - not just as good, better," Bill said.

David let that sink in for a minute before continuing. "What's missing in the whole institutional attraction methodology is that institutions don't make disciples, according to the Great Commission. People are not drawn to church, they are brought to church. It's disciples who make disciples, people who make disciples. Not services of worship, revivals, altar calls, sermons - no matter how good! - or any of the other tricks we use to gather a crowd. What makes disciples of the unchurched are existing disciples going out into the world, making partnership relationships with the unchurched and God pouring grace into the lives of the unchurched through their relational connection to an active, practicing disciple." David smiled. "Not that disciples can't be made institutionally. With God, all things are possible. It's just that this is comparatively rare when there is no relationship present to act as a conduit for grace."

"So this is the reason for the slogan that the first step in disciple making is to be one?"

"Yes, but for two reasons. First, we believe that a convert needs an example of a genuine disciple in order to become one. Second, unless a convert becomes a disciple, they can never become a disciple maker. All they can do is perform the task assigned to them by the evangelistic institution: invite their friends and relatives to worship services. Once those family and friend connections are exhausted, the institutional approach is out of energy."

"And that's another problem," Bill said. "Pushing converts into pushing their relatives around to get them immediately into church often harms those relationships and hinders the flow of grace from God into the lives of the unchurched connected to the new disciple."

"People don't like to be manipulated, John," Cindy said. "And a lot of the institutional methods are based on manipulation because no honest relationship has truly formed."

"The other principle is that if you are not with the other sheep, you are lost," Bill said. "By our definition, lost does not mean theologically lost, it just means not with the other sheep. Some of those lost sheep are lost sheep of the house of Israel. They are sheep, not goats, they are children of God and they will go to heaven. We don't attempt to judge that status in a person's life. We just notice whether people are present or not with the other sheep."

"And this statistic corrects another excuse of the church," David said. "If the definition of unchurched is merely not with the others in church on any given Sunday, what is the percentage of unchurched in any given community?"

"The percentage you named is 73%," I said.

"When you translate that to actual numbers," Pam said, "the numbers are kind of exciting."

"In a county seat town I once lived in," David said, "the ministerial association tested this out in 1999. There were approximately 24,000 people in town. By contacting all the churches in town, even the small ones - there were over 55 - and adding the worship attendance figures together for the month of October, they determined that the average attendance in worship during a Sunday in October was 6000 people for the whole community. The purpose of their study was to realize the impact of the church on the community."

"The impact of that study for me as a disciple maker," Pam said, "is my excitement at the realization that there were over 16,000 unchurched people in that town that day. That I could stand in line at the Walmart in that town or any town, and 3 out of 4 persons in line with me were unchurched."

"Or three out of four persons in almost any secular grouping of people," David said.

"But some of those people already have a church," I protested. "They are already members of a Baptist, Catholic, Presbyterian or some other church in the community."

"For us as disciple makers," Pam said, "the fact that they can say which church they are avoiding on Sunday makes no difference to us. If they are not with the other sheep, they are lost sheep and available for disciple making."

"So we are talking about sheep rustling now? Taking members from other churches?"

"No, John, that's not what we mean. If a person is not attending church, we perceive that they are not really part of that church even if they have their membership there. Research into activating inactive members shows that they are resistant to returning to the church that they are avoiding. That they are much more likely to return to a different church through conversion than ever return to the church that they decided to avoid when they chose to be lost."

"Some people who are lost know the way home," Bill said. "They just don't want to go there."

"For us as disciple makers," Pam said, "what we are interested in is not church membership or the lack of it. What we are commanded to do is to go and make disciples. Furthermore, while we are interested in people with no church background whatsoever, it is very clear that the evangelistic, disciple making ministry of Jesus was clearly focused on the lost sheep of the house of Israel. There are many reasons for this, but for our adoption of Jesus' methods for disciple making, we believe that it is important not to ignore people who at one time had a stronger connection to a local church than they do today. Jesus didn't ignore them, and we shouldn't either."

"It may be a part of my conditioning, but I don't like the idea of taking members from other churches. I'd rather reach out to the unchurched who have no church connection."

"Paul felt the same," Daid said. "*Romans 15:20, thus making it my ambition to preach the gospel, not where Christ has already been named, lest I build on another man's foundation, but as it is written, 'They shall see who have never been told of him, and they shall understand who have never heard of him.'* And Paul, as the apostle to the Gentile world, certainly does apply Jesus' system to reaching out to those people," David said. "But there's something else you are missing, John."

"And what is that?"

"The Rodney Stark research," David said.

"That converts have no other strong relationships?"

"Exactly. If they have lost a connection to their former faith network, then when they activate their faith as disciples, they will join the faith network of their new friends. If they still have their old friends, when they activate their faith they will return to their old faith network and begin attending their old church."

"Which means all that work to make a disciple is wasted," I said.

"Only if your only goal is to make a disciple that will join your church," David said mildly. "Jesus commanded us to go and make disciples. We were not commanded to go and make only members for our own church. We don't care in the slightest if Baptists who become disciples return to the Baptist church or Catholics who become disciples return to the Catholic church."

"Although we do keep in touch with them," Sam said.

"What's the point of that if they go back to the Catholic or Baptist church?"

"First of all," Pam said, "these people are either spiritual infants or spiritual children who have just been born again. If you facilitate that born again experience, to us you are their spiritual parents. You wouldn't abandon your own child on the doorsteps of a church, would you?"

"Of course not," I said.

"Then why would you abandon these spiritual children on the doorsteps of the church they used to attend?"

"So it would be a bit like a Baptist family adopting a Catholic child - they would see that the Catholic child goes to Catholic church and fully participates."

"Exactly," Pam said, "and they would fully love that child as a part of their family even if the child did not participate in their church."

"I wonder over time which will be more effective," I said.

"Rodney Stark's research implies that the stronger relationship will pull the individual into the faith of the other. Therefore, a Catholic raised by loving Baptists will have a predisposition to Baptist ways even if they remain in the Catholic church because of the power of relationships."

"And if they ever become dissatisfied with the

Catholic Church, they would be predisposed to be a part of a Baptist church?" I asked.

"Yes. The church of the people who nurture them spiritually, whatever the denomination, will be their second choice," Pam said. "If something happens to their first choice, they move to their second choice."

"That could have a large numeric impact," I said.

"If you bless people," David said, "many of those people will return to the source of their blessing. What's more important is that they follow Christ, and if Christ seems to lead them back to the church of their childhood, it would be wrong for us to interfere."

"This doesn't mean that their return won't have problems," Bill pointed out.

"What do you mean by that?" I asked. "Most churches would welcome them back; they love a lost sheep who comes home on their own power. It's a vindication of their old ways for a stray to come back."

"But that stray has been affected by the time they spent being lost," Bill pointed out, tapping the diffusion of innovations adopter framework. "When they return, what sort of Baptist or Catholic are they?"

"Do you mean which position do they take in the adopter framework?" I asked.

"Yes."

"They are coming back inside from the outside. Their connections are stronger with the world outside their home church and they are out of touch with the world inside their home church," I thought out loud. "Therefore they would have to be innovators."

"Exactly," David said. "And what does the church system do to innovators? Particularly innovators who come home announcing that they found Christ, not in the home church, but out in the wilderness?"

"They will be ostracized and rejected," I said, wondering in amazement.

"Possibly," Pam said. "Or they will connect with early adopters who will trumpet their story even louder try to push the home church to change ... and this segment of the home church will be rejected and ostracized."

236

"Or they may succeed," David said, "in drawing a following and finding a way to integrate their experience of becoming a disciple in their new home church."

"And so your disciple making methods move into another church context," I said.

"Yes," Pam said happily. "Either way, Christ is glorified and disciples are following Him. That's why our movement for disciple making is ecumenical. We will either get these good people back, or we will send them out as missionaries to make disciples in their former home church. Both fulfill the Great Commission."

"Doesn't this destabilize another church?" I asked. "Does that do harm?"

"Churches are always being challenged by change," David observed. "The pragmatic majority of 84% who make up the balancing system of a local church are not really threatened by a lost person returning to their church as a disciple and eventually a disciple maker. Instability might occur if disciple making catches on, but we don't have a problem with that because that instability will resolve quickly, either with rejection or full adoption. The balancing system is much stronger than we realize and very capable of preserving stability. Our request is simply that the new synthesis allow disciple making to occur."

"It will not resolve without complaining, however," Bill said. "But the laggards are always complaining."

"And there's one other principle that hasn't been said," Pam pointed out. "We teach disciple making in a methodology that is informed and based on the diffusion of innovations. Knowing what works for diffusion and practicing those methods should allow for as smooth a transition of people into discipleship as possible. Trying to change a system with knowledge is more effective than pushing ahead in ignorance."

"So what is the first step in that change?" I asked.

"Disciples," David said, tapping the child segment of his chart, "must become servants. They must cross the vertical line of Lordship obedience and serve others as Christ did.

They began to pull out their New Testaments and Pam began to read. *"John 13:1 Now before the feast of the Passover, when Jesus knew that his hour had come to depart out of this world to the Father, having loved his own who were in the world, he loved them to the end. And during supper, when the devil had already put it into the heart of Judas Iscariot, Simon's son, to betray him, Jesus, knowing that the Father had given all things into his hands, and that he had come from God and was going to God, rose from supper, laid aside his garments, and girded himself with a towel. Then he poured water into a basin, and began to wash the disciples' feet, and to wipe them with the towel with which he was girded.*

He came to Simon Peter; and Peter said to him, "Lord, do you wash my feet?" Jesus answered him, "What I am doing you do not know now, but afterward you will understand." Peter said to him, "You shall never wash my feet." Jesus answered him, "If I do not wash you, you have no part in me." Simon Peter said to him, "Lord, not my feet only but also my hands and my head!" Jesus said to him, "He who has bathed does not need to wash, except for his feet, but he is clean all over; and you are clean, but not every one of you." For he knew who was to betray him; that was why he said, "You are not all clean."

When he had washed their feet, and taken his garments, and resumed his place, he said to them, "Do you know what I have done to you? You call me Teacher and Lord; and you are right, for so I am. If I then, your Lord and Teacher, have washed your feet, you also ought to wash one another's feet. For I have given you an example, that you also should do as I have done to you. Truly, truly, I say to you, a servant is not greater than his master; nor is he who is sent greater than he who sent him. If you know these things, blessed are you if you do them."

"If you know these things, blessed are you if you do them," I repeated.

"Yes," Bill said, "that's one of those commands you are supposed to teach your disciples to wash feet."

"This sort of church would be one that my denomination would call missional."

"Missional? How do they define that?" David asked.

"Missional. On a mission from God. Servants, committed, ready for the challenge."

"Oh, that." David smiled. "Well, people who are at this level are certainly committed. They are also intense, melodramatic and risk taking, which is one reason we call them spiritual teenagers."

"I don't think teenagers is what they mean by missional. In fact, I think they'd be offended."

"I understand. I'll bet they use the term in a context of talking about churches that are focused on maintenance, right?"

"Right."

"A maintenance focused church is probably one that is focused on survival - doing what is needed to survive and function. It is focused on its own welfare and taking care of itself. It is focused on people on the inside of the church."

"That's exactly what they say."

"And the missional church is focused on taking care of others. It's focus is on people outside the church, the poor, the hungry, and the oppressed. I'll be they quote the passage Jesus quoted at Nazareth in Luke 4. You know the one, Pam?"

"Yes, I do," Pam said, turning to it in her New Testament. "*Luke 4:18 "The Spirit of the Lord is upon me, because he has anointed me to preach good news to the poor. He has sent me to proclaim release to the captives and recovering of sight to the blind, to set at liberty those who are oppressed, to proclaim the acceptable year of the Lord."*"

"That's the one," I said.

"This is a very lovely sounding trap. It sounds good and it's trapped a lot of religious people. What's the problem with being 100% maintenance?"

"Well, it's selfish, for one. And it's not very Christlike; it avoids the cross or any sort of sacrifice for others."

"Well said. Now what's the opposite problem, the one

of being 100% missional?"

"Totally focused on others?"

"Yes."

"Well, it would drain the church of resources. I guess it would be a form of institutional suicide."

"Have you known institutions to advocate institutional suicide?" David asked.

I laughed. "Quite the opposite. But I have known institutions that continually called for others to sacrifice themselves for the benefit of that institution. And sometimes to the point of death. What is the name for that?"

"I suppose it would be some sort of parasite," Bill suggested.

"I agree," David said. "Institutions will frequently call for the sacrifice of others. But do they sacrifice themselves?"

"Not in my experience," I said.

"Balancing systems exist for the preservation of the institution. That's their nature. So when one part of an institution over the years calls for another part to make a sacrifice, what does that mean?"

"One institution is consuming another?"

"Probably. *Cui bono* - who benefits? From the missional church? The poor?"

"Yes," I said.

"At what cost?"

"Well if the little church doesn't maintain itself, then it will go down the drain."

"But it will look good while it does," Pam said.

"It will. The problem here is one of balance," David said. "A bureaucratic denomination is calling for its units to not maintain themselves but instead sacrifice - send more money to headquarters. Why not instead slash the headquarters budget?"

"Why not?"

"It's a matter of balance, John. And that's the trap. Missional vs. maintenance. Where do we find Jesus teaching about the same sort of balance?"

"I don't know."

"John, you've heard it a thousand times. About six times today so far. Where does Jesus teach about a balance?

I thought for a moment. "Of course. Love your neighbor as yourself."

"And that's the balance between missional and maintenance. Neighbor and self."

"I don't hear that kind of balance in the call to be missional," I said.

"Only if it is misleading. As if the local church was so selfish as to be totally concerned with itself, or if the denominational headquarters was so selfish as to call for its suicide in order to minister to the poor."

"Balance is healthy. One or the other to an extreme is unhealthy."

"Of course, for two entities to take up two extremes keeps them in balance."

"I think the local church can resent the implication that they don't care for the poor and oppressed," I said. "And they often feel that the denominational headquarters doesn't care about them or their survival."

"Do you think that sometimes they might be right?"

"Sometimes. But you said this was a trap. What's the trap?"

"In all this focus on whether we should take care of ourselves or take care of the poor, what's being neglected?"

"The primary commandment - to love God with all our heart soul, mind and strength."

"Does God want the local church to ignore the poor?"

"No."

"Does God want the local church to empty its bank accounts and sell the building so that it can feed the poor somewhere else?"

"No. At least I don't think so."

"So, John, what do you think God wants?"

"I think God wants the church to love God with all their heart soul mind and strength."

"Can an institution do that, John? Or can only the individuals within the institution do that?"

241

"Umm."

"You see, John, part of the problem is that we are always speaking of the church as if it was an individual with a single mind, single purpose or single mission. The church is hundreds, thousands, millions of individuals all a part of something so amazing they can't even understand it."

I nodded.

"The problem, John, is what we call an institutional world view. The church is an institution, or at least the church system is. And we can believe that the church is a corporation instead of a cooperation, but that doesn't change what it is. The problem is not whether the corporation, the institution, is missional. The real question is whether or not the individuals in the corporation are missional. How many of them are missional, John?"

"Not very many."

"Not very many are even disciples, John, so how can they be missional? Self care is what the infancy stage is all about - if they can't grow out of that, how can we get to missional?"

"What does the church system do then?" I asked. "It is a corporation and it has corporate objectives."

"And it is welcome to them," David said. "In our philosophy, John, we don't really pay much attention to the church system, to the institution. It's just not very relevant to what we are doing, which is making disciples." David looked from face to face around the table.

"If we love God with all our heart mind and soul," Sam said, "then we are going to want to obey the God we love. That's what it means to be missional, which is to obey God. And God gives the church - us - a great variety of tasks because each one of us is different. But each one of us is designed to work according to the way we are made, and when we all do what we are supposed to do, it all perfectly fits together."

"Jesus explained it in John 2," David said. "That he intended to replace the institution of the temple with his body. Paul explained that the meaning of the term *body of*

Christ was the human network of the church."

"In AD 70," Pam said, "the Jewish people revolted and the Roman government - another balancing system - destroyed the temple and the civil religion of the nation of Israel. For the next 300 years the church consisted of the body of Christ. When the Roman emperor Constantine turned to Christianity to function as a unifying force within the declining Roman empire, he made Christianity the new balancing system. Christianity became a civil religion again. And what was their first task?"

"What would you want me to say?" I was a little frazzled. "I suppose that's when they started rebuilding temples."

"Exactly," Pam said. "All the energy began to flow into rebuilding the temple. Worship in a temple may be an innate human need. But scripturally, the church is and has always been the human network created by the discipleship system."

"So the institutional church is the temple system; it coexists with the human network we call the body of Christ and our movement likes to call a discipleship system," David said. "We make disciples; that's what obedience means to us. The institution can have its goals, programs and events; we don't interfere with any of those things, we just make disciples and we make disciples into disciple makers."

"So you ignore the institutional church," I said.

"Not really," I said. "We just let it be what it is. It's a container for the grace of God."

"I have a huge shell on my table at home, John, you must have seen it," Bill said.

"I have, Bill. It's huge."

"Something used to live in that shell. When it died, the shell became home to something else that lived in it. That's the institutional church, the temple. It's a beautiful shell that's empty; the discipleship system is the thing that lives in it. The shell provides the disciples with shelter and protection."

"So it is symbiotic?"

"Yes. But the life is not in the shell itself. It's within

243

the shell, just like we are operating within the church."

"John Wesley did the same thing."

"We think so."

"They did persecute him."

"We hope that, with the information we have from the diffusion of innovations and from the Limits to Growth systems archetype, that we will be able to achieve a symbiotic relationship."

"They persecuted them in the book of Acts as well."

Pam shrugged. "We live in a more civilized world today. Persecution is more likely to be disapproval or church conflict rather than dipping Christians in oil, putting them up on poles and using them for human torches."

"They did that?" I asked.

"Emperor Nero's picnic," Pam said.

"We can see the diffusion of innovations operating in the New Testament. Persecution revved up and died down, and you can see the Christian church of Acts coexisting with the Jewish temple relatively well until one thing happened."

"And what was that?" I asked.

Pam opened her New Testament and read, "*Acts 6:7: And the word of God increased; and the number of the disciples multiplied greatly in Jerusalem, and a great many of the priests were obedient to the faith.*"

"So your theory is that persecution arose when the Christians started to meddle with the worship in the temple?"

"When you attempt to change the worship forms in the temple," Pam said, "you bring change to the whole system at once. That raises up the violence in the laggards and they attack."

Sam pointed again to the diffusion framework handout. "Part of the reason the diffusion of innovations works is that the change moves from category to category in the adopter framework; by the time it gets to the laggards, it's not news and it's not as threatening."

"The violence in Acts toward the Christians - it's all laggard behavior," Pam said.

"Do you have some modern examples?"

David produced an envelope. "This is a good one to act out," he said. "Each of you take a slip of paper from the envelope. Whoever gets the one marked pastor, swap with John."

We passed the envelope around. There were seven of us and Pam got two pieces of paper because there were eight.

"This is a demonstration of the adopter framework. John is the pastor and he has the Pastor's question. We're all amateur actors here and it will be more fun if you ham it up. John, would you begin by reading your question, the Pastor's question?"

"There's a light bulb burnt out in the sanctuary - can you help?" I asked.

"And now for the Innovator's answer," David said.

Pam read, "*Innovator: If you'll just be patient, my nuclear fusion bulb will be at the prototype stage real soon now. Never needs changing and uses no electricity.*"

David gestured to me. "There's a light bulb burnt out in the sanctuary - can you help?" I asked.

"And now for the Early Adopter's answer," David said.

Sam read, "*Early Adopter: Has anyone analyzed whether it's in our best interests to spend the extra money on those long lasting bulbs?*"

David said, "These two are the innovative minority, the reinforcing trend, the 16% of a culture that desires change. Beyond here is the chasm in action." He nodded to me.

"There's a light bulb burnt out in the sanctuary - can you help?" I asked.

"And now for the Middle Adopter's answer," David said.

Ruth said, "That's me. *Middle Adopter: Sure. (Gets ladder, puts new bulb in.)* Is that it?"

"Middle adopters are extremely practical," David said. "They get things done, but they don't usually do something new to get them done. What's worked in the past is fine with them. They are the leading edge of the

245

pragmatic majority. And now for the Late Adopter's answer," David said.

"There's a light bulb burnt out in the sanctuary - can you help?" I asked.

Bill read, "*Late Adopter: Are you sure we need a new bulb? There's nothing wrong with the old bulb. Give it a chance. My mother gave that bulb to the church as a memorial to my grandfather; see the plaque next to the fixture? Have you tried praying for healing for the bulb? Where is your faith?*"

"And we have a comment on late adopters to read. Who has that?"

"I do," Sam said. "*Understanding Late Adopters: Many of the people who attend religious services in our society are not interested in theology, want nothing too exotic and dislike the idea of change. They find the established rituals provide them with a link with tradition and give them a sense of security. They do not expect brilliant ideas from the sermon and are disturbed by changes in the liturgy. In rather the same way, many of the pagans of the late antiquity loved to worship the ancestral gods, as generations had done before them. The old rituals gave them a sense of identity, celebrated local traditions and seemed an assurance that things would continue as they were.*"[9]

"This comment describes a sociological situation true in the Jewish temple, in the temple of Artemis of the Ephesians in Acts 19 and in our modern temples. People have lost touch with the spiritual reason to be there - they have no real relationship with God. So what do they have left that they treasure and are in touch with?"

"The customs of the temple," I answered.

"This is why change is so threatening to the late adopters; the *way-it-has-always-been* is all that they have."

"And these are the Eddies you were talking about earlier."

"The nice ones," David said. "The people who were invited to worship and found it comforting but who never learned more about their faith or ever became committed

246

to it beyond letting it meet their needs." David shrugged. "All they know is what they like, and they like what is familiar. They are still with us and fill up every temple. They don't pull their weight, but at 34% they have a great influence on the middle adopters, who primarily want to keep everything running smoothly. But the violent Eddies are the laggards. If you threaten the late adopters, you get anxiety. If you threaten the laggards, you get trouble. John, would you please ask the question again?"

"There's a light bulb burnt out in the sanctuary - can you help?" I asked.

"And now for the Laggard's answer," David said.

Cindy read with exaggerated scorn: *"Laggard: After a while, the truly faithful really begin to sense God at work in the dark. Perhaps God prefers the dark. When God wants a new bulb, He will change it Himself. Stop interfering with the will of the Lord with your devilish desire to change everything!"*

"And lest you think we are exaggerating, we have two examples from modern life. You'll find a lot of laggard commentary on the internet..."

"Isn't that a contradiction?" I asked. "Aren't laggards against innovation?"

"That's the problem with Roger's research conclusions and why Moore's adaptation is more helpful. Laggards arise to oppose a change contrary to their heart issues. They don't oppose all change, but they do oppose the change brought in this version of the framework. So they can be adept at the internet and other forms of technology. You will find a lot of laggard poison expressed on the Internet. And perhaps it is better for the church that it is released there rather than upon people. Lest you think we are exaggerating, though, we have a couple of examples of real testimonies by laggards. Who has laggard testimony number one?"

"I do," Pam said. *"Laggard Testimony #1: I began to have grave concerns about the changes brought into my church by my pastor after he attended a pastors conference sponsored by Rick Warren's Saddleback Church. Eventually, my wife and I were forced to leave* that church (amicably) after private meetings with our pastor and a couple of deacons. In our church, Rick Warren started a slippery slope that included a softened and shortened sermon, dropping the name "baptist" from the church name, putting the hymnals in the church attic, selling the organ, needing earplugs to attend praise and worship time, watching an unicyclist parade through the sanctuary, participating in a live, interactive congregational marketing survey during church service time and starting a building program when neither attendance nor the budget supported doing so. Sound familiar? If not, these seeker-sensitive things will soon be coming to your church if Rick Warren has his say. . . . This movement has hijacked evangelical Christianity over the past decade or so and has now displaced countless bible-believing Christians from their churches."

"And number two?" David asked.

"I think you have it," Pam pointed to the larger piece of paper in front of him.

"I think you're right," David smiled. "I love this one. It is just so perfect." He stood to read it with ceremony. "*Laggard Testimony #2: I took a break from writing for a couple of months to further research the 'seeker-sensitive,' 'church-growth' movement; that tumorous plague that has become to the Christian community what AIDS is to the homosexual community. Those who have been infected always deny it publicly believing in their hearts they are righteous and extraordinary rather than depraved, dying and delusional . . .*

You'll know that your church is becoming 'seeker-sensitive' when the worship service begins to resemble an Amway convention run by pod people in polo shirts whose savior looks more like Bill Clinton with sunglasses and a saxophone than the Son of God hanging from a lonely cross for the sins of the world."

I shook my head. "How do we deal with this conflict? This all brings back a lot of painful memories for me."

"And for me as well," Ruth said.

"That's because, in conflict, the minister is usually

abused. And the family of the minister feels the effects of the abuse, either directly or indirectly."

"So how do we achieve this massive change - shifting the church toward disciple making - without creating the massive conflict?"

"You've just indicated the cause of the conflict, David. Avoid that, and you will achieve your goal."

"What did I say," I asked Ruth. She was a much better listener than I was.

"Changing the whole church, I think," she said. "They've said several times that change must move from category to category through the framework. I think what they means is that the laggards don't even know about the change until it's adopted by the late adopters."

"You are exactly right," David said.

"Isn't that a little devious?" I asked.

"Why?" David asked.

"Don't you need consensus for change? Or a vote?"

"Why?"

"It just seems natural. Normal."

"Normal in a system means that change won't happen," Pam observed. "You don't want to or need to follow those rules."

"So how do we do this, David?" I asked.

"Our goal is to make disciples and raise up disciple makers. Our goal is not to change the system, because that would cause the system to turn against us and stop us, with violence if necessary. We want to work within the system to achieve our goals, but we don't need the system's active involvement to achieve them. All we need from them is a willingness to coexist and enough freedom in the system for some individuality to exist." David smiled. "Most systems allow differentiation; they allow all kinds of special interest groups. What they don't allow is one special interest group to force its ways on the rest of the system."

"How does this work itself out in a practical way?" I asked.

"It's very simple. You make your change voluntary. You really only want to work with the people who want to work with you anyway. Second, you do your work in a small group, not in the large group, i.e. not in worship."

"Doesn't discipleship effect worship? How can you read all that scripture and not want to shift the purposes of worship to fit with it?" I asked.

David shrugged. "We just believe in following the New Testament, John. Jesus taught in the temple, in a corner of the temple court which would correspond to one of the world's largest fellowship halls. He talked with the people who came to him. Some came with hostility and with questions to trap him, certainly, but generally he did not attempt to force all those in attendance to listen to him."

David took a drink of his water. "There is no record in the New Testament of Jesus ever having a role in the worship of the temple, John. And how could he? Worship was the responsibility of the tribe of Levi and he was of the tribe of Judah. Nor did the disciples in the book of Acts have any involvement or control over the temple worship services, or the means to influence them. At least not until a number of the priests converted - and then you had persecution that drove them out, the very minute the temple liturgy was threatened with change."

"So Jesus taught those who would listen to him," I said.

"And did not bother - often - those who would not listen to him."

"So we advocate no change to the system," David said. "We attend worship in the temple just as the disciples did; we are, after all, orthodox Christians just like the others in attendance. We give into the offering, and compared to the Eddies, we are generous givers. When they need laborers for tasks in the temple, they find us to be hard and willing workers; the only exception is that we won't allow ourselves to be put in charge of programs because we save our energy for disciple making."

"Sometimes we will teach Sunday School classes or short term Bible studies," Sam said. "But we don't generally serve in the temple bureaucracy. And as we are not perceived to be attempting to gather any political power in the temple, those with political power leave us be to make disciples. And that's all we want anyway. So a symbiotic partnership can develop."

"Disciple making takes place in the discipleship system," David said, touching the small circle on the side of the larger church system circle. "It takes place in a small group made up of volunteers. No one is excluded; it's just that there is no attempt to include everyone."

"Aren't the Sunday School classes and other Bible study type programs a part of the discipleship system?" I asked.

"The church system does have a sort of discipleship system. They organize the invitation of lost people into the worship service. They organize classes and Bible studies for learning for those who attend worship to move into. You could say that they are the discipleship system that exist within the church system. And with lots of effort, these can be effective. They are the way the church system does discipleship. And we don't interfere with the church system. We just do it our way as well. And we do it over here, on the side, as a reinforcing trend operating within a small group."

"How do you keep the laggards from learning what you are doing?"

"Innovators and early adopters are very aware of everything happening in the system; they are very curious about change and new discoveries. As these are the people we want to enlist in the change we propose, 'Jesus is Lord,' we are glad when they spend the energy to attend our small group 'event' and draw them in when we can. The pragmatic majority, however, is busy operating the machinery of the temple. They are not curious unless there seems to be a threat. We don't mind being perceived as odd or eccentric. What would happen if you offered a new Bible study in your church, mentioning it quietly as an opportunity and not promoting it?"

"I'd have a few people - very few - show up," I answered.

"Only the people who are interested," David said. "Only the people who are ready for a change. And for a

251

diffusion of innovations change process, that's all you want there. You don't want to broadcast change; you want to stimulate conversations about change only among those who are ready for it. Broadcast information goes to everyone including those who are not ready for it, such as the laggards. Conversations slowly spread new information across the adopter framework."

"So a series of sermons on making disciples is out of the question," I said.

"If you want to stir up conflict which will prevent disciple making, preach about it in worship," David said with finality.

"What do I preach on, then?"

"John, what you preach about is a matter between you and God where you are obedient. If your sermons are expressions of whatever book you are reading now or whatever has you excited, your sermons are more about you than they are designed to help your people. Would you agree?"

I tried not to feel defensive. "That's not what I do now. But disciple making is not only important, it is what the Bible teaches. Shouldn't I be preaching it?"

"Yes," Pam said, "but why not preach it like Jesus did? To those who are interested. Go off into the country, like Jesus did, and preach it to those who will walk 5, 10, 15 miles with you into the wilderness to hear what you have to say."

I couldn't help laughing. "I wouldn't have anyone to preach to then!"

"So be it," said Pam. "The spiritual needs of newborns revolved around safety, security and belonging needs. They grow up when they are nurtured according to their needs and the opportunity you have to provide for those needs is in worship, as that is the only way most of them participate in the church."

"Each level of spirituality, each sugar packet, has different needs," David said. "And it's wise to meet those needs in an environment appropriate for them."

"Conflict arises," Sam said, "when you feed people information that they are not ready to hear. It's like forcing solid food on an infant before they are ready. All it does is create pain and vomiting; they can't absorb it."

"Nor is it appropriate to teach the mechanics of intercourse in sex education to second graders. It's not an issue for them. Information needs to be shared at the proper time. God's time."

"So I guess what you are saying is that I can't teach my people about discipleship," I said.

"No," Pam said, "what we are saying is that not all of your people are the same. The idea that everyone in an institution is the same is a basic concept of institutionalism. Allow your people their differentiation and diversity."

"There is no one right answer for all the people," Sam said. "Nor is there one management style that works in every situation. Hersey and Blanchard pioneered that concept back in the 1960s in *Management of Organizational Behavior*. It's important to deliver the appropriate leadership style that is needed. When you make disciples, you deliver the appropriate disciple making style that is needed by the person in each of the levels."

"This is interesting," I said. "Take me through the levels and explain this."

"OK," David said. He laid his pen on the chart with the tip pointing to the section for spiritual infants. "What level is this?"

"Spiritual infants."

"What nurture do infants need?" David asked.

I heard Ruth snort at my side. "Ruth could give a better answer than I could," I said.

"Then let her. Ruth, what are the needs of an infant?"

"Warmth, comfort, love, reassurance when they are afraid, food when they are hungry. Basically, nurture."

"Would this also apply to spiritual infants?" David asked.

"I believe so," Ruth said.

"We believe that a relationship bond forms between an infant and a parent. We try to provide the same sort of nurturing bond between a spiritual parent and a spiritual

253

infant. The tool we use for that is called the Prayer Tool, which Pam will be explaining to you as a part of *descending grace*. When you are ready, John." David looked at Cindy.

"Ruth is halfway along," Cindy volunteered. "She'll finish *descending grace* later this week."

"I'm falling behind," I said, smiling at my wife.

"You ask ten times as many questions," Ruth informed me. "It takes time to answer them."

"The prayer tools helps form a partnership or spiritual parental bond that meets the deepest needs of spiritual newborns. Existing as they do within a spiritual orphanage," David said.

"A spiritual orphanage?" I asked. "I don't really like that term. Is that what a church is to you?"

"John, what else would you call an institution that typically attempts to care for babies, 83% of which never leave the infant stage? Given the challenges you have as an administrator of this orphanage, most pastors are doing a commendable job attempting to cope with the problem."

"Spiritual children need spiritual parents," Sam said. "Through the prayer tool we arrange for spiritual adoptions to take place, which only eases the burden on a minister to provide pastoral care."

"So this quadrant, over the line of discipleship from the servant quadrant, is the domain of the spiritual parent." David wrote the term in the square with a flourish.

"Did Jesus use this terminology?" I asked.

"No, but Paul did." David gestured at Pam; the open New Testaments appeared again.

Pam read, "*2 Timothy 2:1-2: You then, my son, be strong in the grace that is in Christ Jesus, and what you have heard from me before many witnesses entrust to faithful men who will be able to teach others also.*"

"You'll note, John, that what we have here are four generations. Paul explicitly identifies Timothy as his spiritual son and encourages him to share the gospel with those who will be good parents to their own spiritual children. We call this generational disciple making -

generation by generation."

Bill read, *"Galatians 4:19: My little children, with whom I am again in travail until Christ be formed in you!"*

Cindy read, *"1 John 2:12-14: I am writing to you, little children, because your sins are forgiven for his sake. I am writing to you, fathers, because you know him who is from the beginning. I am writing to you, young men, because you have overcome the evil one. I write to you, children, because you know the Father. I write to you, fathers, because you know him who is from the beginning. I write to you, young men, because you are strong, and the word of God abides in you, and you have overcome the evil one."*

"Children, young men, fathers?" I asked.

"Children are disciples," David said. "Young men are spiritual teenagers or servants. Fathers are parents and grandparents."

"What about infants?" I asked.

"Infants are unable to form the concepts which John discusses with the children; they can't talk yet and don't understand ideas."

Sam read, *"1 Cor 4:14-17: I do not write this to make you ashamed, but to admonish you as my beloved children. For though you have countless guides in Christ, you do not have many fathers. For I became your father in Christ Jesus through the gospel. I urge you, then, be imitators of me. Therefore I sent to you Timothy, my beloved and faithful child in the Lord, to remind you of my ways in Christ, as I teach them everywhere in every church."*

Pam read, *"Phil 2:22: But Timothy's worth you know, how as a son with a father he has served with me in the gospel."*

Bill read, *"1 Th 2:7-12 But we were gentle among you, like a nurse taking care of her children. So, being affectionately desirous of you, we were ready to share with you not only the gospel of God but also our own selves, because you had become very dear to us. For you remember our labor and toil, brethren; we worked night* and day, that we might not burden any of you, while we preached to you the gospel of God. You are witnesses, and God also, how holy and righteous and blameless was our behavior to you believers; for you know how, like a father with his children, we exhorted each one of you and encouraged you and charged you to lead a life worthy of God, who calls you into his own kingdom and glory."

Cindy read, "Philemon 1:10 I appeal to you for my child, Onesimus, whose father I have become in my imprisonment."

"Paul and John use the terms of fathers and sons, of parents and children," David said.

"What term did Jesus use?" I asked.

Bill said, "The term is laborers. Matthew 9:36 When he saw the crowds, he had compassion for them, because they were harassed and helpless, like sheep without a shepherd. Then he said to his disciples, "The harvest is plentiful, but the laborers are few pray therefore the Lord of the harvest to send out laborers into his harvest. And he called to him his twelve disciples and gave them authority over unclean spirits, to cast them out, and to heal every disease and every infirmity."

Cindy read, "John 4:34 Jesus said to them, "My food is to do the will of him who sent me, and to accomplish his work. Do you not say, 'There are yet four months, then comes the harvest'? I tell you, lift up your eyes, and see how the fields are already white for harvest. He who reaps receives wages, and gathers fruit for eternal life, so that sower and reaper may rejoice together. For here the saying holds true, 'One sows and another reaps.' I sent you to reap that for which you did not labor; others have labored, and you have entered into their labor."

"All around us, John, there are people who are white with the harvest," David said. "They are ripe and ready for adoption. If they are not picked, they can rot in the fields. The implication is there: God will not allow fruit to mature until there are laborers ready to pick it. That's why we have so much spiritual immaturity in the church. There is a lack - Jesus said this explicitly - a lack in the number of people ready and trained to participate in the harvest." David wrote 'harvest laborers' in the square under the words 'spiritual parents.' "When people take up the challenge of the harvest of souls, they cross the discipleship line again and change from disciples into disciple makers." He then wrote 'disciple makers' in the square. "And in our movement they use the prayer tool for this purpose."

"Disciples are best made in a small group which functions like a spiritual family," Pam said. "We offer four types of small groups. One is the most basic form of caring - intentionally having conversations with people and praying for them. Sort of an unorganized small group."

"We call these 'conversations of grace' and organize them through the Prayer Tool," Pam said.

"Then there is the JUMP group - a small group of two or three or four. It is normally for people who are at the child stage and ready to grow in faith."

"When would you not use it at a stage other than the child stage?"

"Sometimes a spiritual infant is highly motivated, usually by a personal problem they need to solve. The JUMP group provides a lot of personal, direct support in a time of crisis and pulls them right through the problem into maturity."

"We've also found," Sam said drily, "the people with a high level of theological education want to skip the relationship building stages and jump right into a JUMP group."

"I can imagine that this is so," I said."They are task oriented and don't want to waste time on building relationships, right?" I heard Ruth repressing a giggle next to me.

"Sometimes they just want to use their big theological vocabulary," Ruth said, giving way to the laughter.

"Guilty, guilty, guilty," I said.

"When people are ready for a JUMP group, we invite them into a JUMP group. It doesn't matter why they are ready."

David made a circle on either side of the line of discipleship. "We also provide two other kinds of small

257

groups that we call circles of grace. One is on the spiritual infant side and basically provides small group fellowship."

Pam smiled. "We find that spiritual infants like to get together with other people their own age and play. So we let them play."

"Like going to the playground in the park?" I said.

"With a group of parents of small children, sometimes it's exactly that. Or a trip to the zoo, a picnic, or a barbecue at someone's house. God works through the conversations of grace that happen at these informal fellowship gatherings."

"What happens if you are task oriented and skip the conversations?"

"Relationships don't form that allow the spiritual infant the sense of security that allows curiosity to develop. Being task oriented about spirituality immediately undercuts God working through relationships to bring people over the line of discipleship."

"You don't have to haul out the New Testaments," I said. "I clearly remember how important it is to love one another."

"It's forgotten as a priority in most churches," David said. "And we believe that it is the most significant reason why there is so little maturity from infant to child level. Spiritual people deny time and energy to relationship building fellowship in order to invest it in spiritual growth classes - only to find little interest in classes among newborns until after the caring relationships are built."

"There's an old saying," Sam said. "No one cares how much you know until they know how much you care."

"The circle of grace on the other side is a relationship building small group with topics that meet the needs of people moving from one level to the other in the early stages - infancy, childhood."

"What needs are those?" I asked.

"Usually it takes a while for interest in Bible study to develop, and we have the JUMP group for that. When infants begin exploring their world, their curiosity usually leads them either into getting their questions answered or into seeking solutions for their problems. In our day this

258

can be finding a new job, improving a marriage, raising kids, all the things in normal life that people talk about in conversation. But because it is learning that satisfies curiosity, it's on the child side of the line."

"Because curiosity is the sign of the developing child," I said.

"One way to destroy curiosity," Pam said, "is to force the child to learn what the child is not interested in. But if we allow children to explore where they wish, they love learning. So we monitor spiritual children, and arrange for circles of grace on any topic that interests them. When their interest turns to Bible study, we invite them to participate in a JUMP group." She shrugged. "Sometimes the JUMP group only addresses the first question - what they are reading and what they are going to do about it. They can stay on the first question for months, but eventually they are drawn into the whole structure of *ascending grace*."

"Growing up is fun," Cindy said. "All kids want to be 'big' like the big kids. Unless you make it a cheerless chore to grow up."

"What are the spiritual needs of teenagers?" I asked.

"They no longer fit in the nursery levels," David said. "They are restless and independent. The JUMP group allows them to explore their individuality. And we have another process, the Quest process, that helps with the adolescent rite of passage from child to parent level."

"Will we be doing that?" I asked Bill.

"It's an option," Bill said. "It's up to you. The main goal of Quest is for a person to identify their spiritual gifts and develop a small group ministry to utilize them. Usually pastors already have that need met in place and don't need to do a Quest to fulfill that purpose."

"What about the other events?" Ruth asked. "The Gathering? And Solomon's Porch?"

"Circles are for relationships," David said. "These two events also build relationships, but around specific tasks. The Gathering is a monthly event which is for everyone who is involved in a circle of grace or a JUMP group. It gives them a chance to see everyone else and keep those relationships fresh."

"We also use it to model the next steps in the discipleship process and reward achievement," Sam said.

"That's the purpose of the testimonies!" I exclaimed. "I'll bet those people were on a Quest."

"They were," Bill said, smiling. "And people moving up through the stages of their 4x12."

"Solomon's Porch focuses on the skills of spiritual mentoring," David said. "It's for people who have someone in their JUMP group they are looking after."

"What happens at the Porch meeting?" Ruth asked.

"It's not a secret. Often they just talk in small groups around tables about what they are doing with their pilgrims. Sometimes there are presentations on the questions or other aspects of disciple making. A lot of planning in support of Quests also goes on at Porch; a good Quest involves the whole community in helping the pilgrim."

"And a pilgrim eventually crosses the line of discipleship again and becomes a spiritual parent. It's built into the Quest, I assume."

"Right. They begin to relate to people and develop their own pilgrim relationships."

"I'm a bit confused about when parenthood starts."

"We watch over people with the prayer tool and nurture them until they are ready for a JUMP group. Even though a JUMP group is for spiritual children who are far from newborns, that's when we consider a 'birth' to happen that creates a spiritual parent because the role of partnership is clarified."

"And what happens to your spiritual parent when you become a spiritual parent?"

"They become a spiritual grandparent, of course," David said and wrote the term in the spiritual parent square.

"And what do spiritual grandparents do?" I asked.

"Like regular grandparents, they help the parents with the grandchildren. As in real life, most new parents need that assistance. Some parents are so together they don't need much help, but most parents need grandparents."

David set down his pen and they all looked at Ruth and I

"Is that all?" I asked.

"That's the whole discipleship system," David said.

"When do I start on *descending grace*?" I asked.

"How about Monday morning?" Pam offered.

"Let me guess. 7 am again, right?"

"If you're ready, John."

"I'm ready," I sighed.

"And you have lots of questions, I'll bet," Pam said.

"You do know him," Ruth said.

"I don't have any questions; today answered them all. Thank you, David."

David nodded to me and smiled.

"But I'm sure I'll have several hundred by Monday," I said looking at Pam.

"Bring it on, bring it on," Pam said, laughing. "Questions don't scare me."

And with that, we cleaned up the room and all went home. Tomorrow morning I would enter the school of descending grace.

END NOTES

1.James Allan Francis, *The Real Jesus and Other Sermons* (Philadelphia, PA: Judson Press, 1926), 123-124. Text used is quoted from San Joaquin Valley Information Service, *'One Solitary Life' Authorship,* under http://www.sjvls.org/bens/bf007sl.htm (accessed June 15, 2007).

2.Everett M. Rogers, *Diffusion of Innovations,* 4th ed. (New York: Free Press, 1995), 1. See Seminar Two on the resources page at www.disciplewalk.com.

3.Robert D. Putnam, *Bowling Alone: The Collapse and Revival of American Community* (New York: Simon and Schuster, 2000). Putnam's work is online at The Saguaro Seminar, *Civic Engagement in America,* http://www.bowlingalone.com/ (accessed June 15, 2007).

4.Putnam, *Bowling Alone,* 65-79, 391-392, 408-410.

5.Putnam, *Bowling Alone,* 277-283, 201-203.

6.Putnam, *Bowling Alone,* 283-284. Social capital is more than community voluntarism where strangers temporarily join together for a task. Bowling teams over time develop covenant bonds of mutual obligation that would allow one to borrow $100 or a car for the weekend. Cf. Nancy T. Ammerman, "Organized Religion in a Voluntaristic Society, " *Sociology of Religion* 58, no. 3, 1997, 203-215, under http://hirr.hartsem.edu/bookshelf/ammerman_article2.html (accessed May 16, 2007). Peter Drucker points out that people historically come to cities for the freedom of anonymity over the obligations of community; Peter F. Drucker, *Managing in the Next Society* (New York: St. Martin's Press, 2002), 225-232.

7.Bill Beckham, *The Second Reformation,* 41. *My apologies to anyone named Eddie!*

8.Bill Beckham, *The Second Reformation*, 44-46. Family systems theory suggests that churched Eddies also triangulate in order to control their access to the nurture they need; their desire to control the source of nurture for their dependency is the covert source of most church conflict.

9.Karen Armstrong, *A History of God: The 4,000-Year Quest of Judaism, Christianity and Islam* (New York: Knopf, 1993), quoted in Herbert Benson with Marg Stark, *Timeless Healing: The Power and Biology of Belief* (New York: Simon & Schuster, 1996), 179.